INDIGENOUS TOURISM MOVEMENTS

Edited by Alexis C. Bunten and Nelson H.H. Graburn

Critical studies of Indigenous culture and identity often conceive of cultural tourism as a mechanism by which members of dominant societies consume and appropriate the cultures of subaltern groups who are forced, through necessity, to participate in an industry that capitalizes on difference. However, cultural tourism is frequently marketed as an economic panacea for communities whose traditional ways of life have been compromised by the dominant societies with whom they are associated.

Indigenous societies are responding to these opportunities – or threats, depending on perspective – in innovative ways that set them apart from their non-Indigenous predecessors and competitors. Most Indigenous-owned tourism venues are relatively young, and have been made possible through the growth of communications technology, the rapid expansion of domestic and international travel industries, and government policies intended to rectify multigenerational trauma resulting from past colonial engagements, assimilation, genocide, and slavery.

Using "movement" as a metaphor, this collection of essays uses tourism as a critical lens to explore the shifting identity politics of indigeneity in relation to heritage, global policy, and development. Through an examination of a range of contemporary case studies based in North America, South America, Asia, Africa, and Australia, the volume offers critical insights into the rapidly growing Indigenous tourism phenomenon.

ALEXIS C. BUNTEN manages the Indigeneity Program for the Bioneers Collective Heritage Institute based in San Francisco, California.

NELSON H.H. GRABURN is a professor emeritus in the Department of Anthropology at University of California, Berkeley.

Indigenous Tourism Movements

EDITED BY ALEXIS C. BUNTEN
AND NELSON H.H. GRABURN

UNIVERSITY OF TORONTO PRESS
Toronto Buffalo London

ISBN 978-1-4426-5019-0 (cloth)   ISBN 978-1-4426-2829-8 (paper)

Library and Archives Canada Cataloguing in Publication

Indigenous tourism movements / edited by Alexis C. Bunten and Nelson H.H. Graburn.

Includes bibliographical references and index.
ISBN 978-1-4426-5019-0 (cloth). – ISBN 978-1-4426-2829-8 (paper)

1. Heritage tourism – Case studies.   2. Indigenous peoples – Case studies.
I. Bunten, Alexis C., editor   II. Graburn, Nelson H.H., editor

G156.5.H47I53 2018   338.4'79104089   C2017-906402-9

University of Toronto Press acknowledges the financial assistance to its publishing program of the Canada Council for the Arts and the Ontario Arts Council, an agency of the Government of Ontario.

Canada Council Conseil des Arts
for the Arts du Canada

ONTARIO ARTS COUNCIL
CONSEIL DES ARTS DE L'ONTARIO
an Ontario government agency
un organisme du gouvernement de l'Ontario

Funded by the   Financé par le
Government   gouvernement
of Canada   du Canada

Canadä

Contents

List of Figures   vii

Preface   ix

Acknowledgments   xv

Notes on Contributors   xvii

1 Current Themes in Indigenous Tourism   1
  ALEXIS CELESTE BUNTEN AND NELSON H.H. GRABURN

Part One: Identity Movements

2 Deriding Demand: A Case Study of Indigenous
  Imaginaries at an Australian Aboriginal Tourism
  Cultural Park   31
  ALEXIS CELESTE BUNTEN

3 The Maasai as Paradoxical Icons of Tourism
  (Im)mobility   56
  NOEL B. SALAZAR

4 The Alchemy of Tourism: From Stereotype and
  Marginalizing Discourse to Real in the Space of
  Tourist Performance   73
  KAREN STOCKER

Part Two: Political Movements

5 Indigenous Tourism as a Transformative Process:
The Case of the Emberá in Panama   99
DIMITRIOS THEODOSSOPOULOS

6 San Cultural Tourism: Mobilizing Indigenous Agency
in Botswana   117
RACHEL F. GIRAUDO

7 The Commodification of Authenticity: Performing and
Displaying Dogon Material Identity   140
LAURENCE DOUNY

Part Three: Knowledge Movements

8 Streams of Tourists: Navigating the Tourist Tides in
Late-Nineteenth-Century Southeast Alaska   165
KATHRYN BUNN-MARCUSE

9 Experiments in Inuit Tourism: The Eastern Canadian Arctic   198
NELSON H.H. GRABURN

10 Beyond Neoliberalism and Nature: Territoriality, Relational
Ontologies, and Hybridity in a Tourism Initiative in Alto
Bío Bío, Chile   222
MARCELA PALOMINO-SCHALSCHA

Epilogue: Indigeneity, Researchers, and Tourism   242
NELSON H.H. GRABURN

Index   259

Figures

2.1 Creation story in the Bulurru Storywaters Theater   32

3.1 Map of Tanzania showing the Arusha region, where most Maasai live   58

4.1 Sculpted jaguar, by Mario Garita   78

4.2 Sculptor Mario Garita's representations of indigeneity of the Americas   79

4.3 Sculptor Mario Garita's representation of a South American shaman figure   80

6.1 Map of Botswana showing where many San communities live   119

6.2 San women and a man demonstrate melon-tossing game   129

7.1 "Tourism has a human face" – poster promoting tourism in Mali   147

7.2 Crafts on sale in a shop belonging to village chief   150

7.3 Hand-made "mass-produced" *Hogon* crowns and pendant pieces   154

7.4 Artisans artificially age pendants by burying them in soil   156

7.5 Mask representing the *Hogon* and worn at his funeral   157

8.1 Pacific Coast Steamship Company timetable cover, 1906, showing Kasaan village   173

8.2 Silver bracelet attributed to Billy Wilson   175

8.3 Postcard of Raven totem pole, Wrangell   177

8.4 Model of Wrangell Raven pole, made by Frederick Alexcee (Tsimshian)   178

8.5 Model paddle, marked "Fort Wrangell" and decorated with a design of Howkan Eagle and a whale   180

8.6   Tsimshian basketry purse (Metlakatla?) with "ALASKA"
        in red false embroidery   181
8.7   Made-for-sale dagger with copper bear pommel   182
8.8   Tsimshian basket decorated with strawberries   185
8.9   Silver bracelet, possibly a mountain avens flower   187
9.1   Map of the eastern Canadian Arctic   199

Preface

ALEXIS CELESTE BUNTEN

This book has been nearly a decade in the making. Nelson H.H. Graburn and I first discussed the preliminary concept for it in 2007, when I began a postdoctoral fellowship at University of California, Berkeley under his mentorship. I hoped to explore whether some of the critical ideas put forth in my 2006 dissertation, a case study of a tribally owned tourism business in Alaska, applied to other Indigenous tourism contexts.[1] My strategy was twofold: to conduct comparative research into the critical issues that Maori tourism entrepreneurs faced in Aotearoa/New Zealand, and to facilitate productive conversations with other scholars studying Indigenous tourism worldwide.

At the time, only one work truly explored the critical issues raised within the topic of Indigenous tourism, Chris Ryan and Michelle Aiken's edited volume *Indigenous Tourism: The Commodification and Management of Culture* (2005). Perhaps it is unsurprising that its editors hailed from New Zealand, where organized Indigenous tourism had been in existence for over a century and played an important role in domestic tourism. Unlike this volume, Ryan and Aiken's volume focused more on the development and sustainability of Indigenous tourism as a market commodity. It offered more of a "business school" perspective on Indigenous tourism, rather than the critical, social-science perspective presented in this volume. In addition, several essays and chapters found in broader anthologies of tourism explored the social aspects of Indigenous tourism, but this scholarship was piecemeal, rendering it difficult to assemble concepts pertinent to Indigenous tourism into a cohesive narrative or frame of reference. And while these volumes explored the groundbreaking intellectual territory of Indigenous tourism, none were edited by an Indigenous person, and they contained little to no contributions by Indigenous authors, who might offer insights informed by Indigenous worldviews and approaches to research.

Although Nelson has been exploring critical issues in Indigenous tourism since long before his seminal 1976 publication of *Ethnic and Tourist Arts*, the politics and representation of Indigenous tourism from the experience of Indigenous hosts have until recently been surprisingly absent from the scholarly record. Scholars interested in the topic tended to be isolated from each other and siloed within departments that did not offer adequate resources to examine these issues. Well-established structures of inequality prevented Indigenous voices from entering scholarly productions as anything other than an "informant" or at best collaborator. My 2006 dissertation was the first of its kind to explore issues of cultural commoditization via tourism written by a Native host who chose to put herself on display.[2] Even at the time, however, I knew that many others were looking into similar issues in other parts of the world.

Although I cannot represent Indigenous peoples per se, I am Alaska Native, and grew up socialized into Indigenous ways of experiencing tourism in both Hawaii and Alaska, where I spent a good deal of, respectively, my childhood and adult life. Nelson and I attempted to incorporate as many Indigenous perspectives as possible leading up to the publication of this volume. Between 2007 and 2013, we organized several events that explored Indigenous tourism from thematic and pragmatic perspectives, starting with a major three-day symposium, "Indigenous Tourism Movements," at UC Berkeley, that brought together most of the contributors to this volume for the first time. From this initial event, Nelson and I (2009) co-edited a special edition of the *London Journal of Sport and Creative Activities* on the topic "Current Themes in Indigenous Tourism," which became the nexus for this volume. We continued to refine our ideas through a series of events and panels in the United States, France, United Kingdom, and New Zealand that brought together Indigenous and non-Indigenous scholars from around the world.[3] Simultaneously, I collaborated with practitioners on the ground, to bring together leaders in indigenous tourism from the United States and New Zealand through workshops at the American Indian Alaska Native Tourism Association annual conference, and tribally sponsored events. I continued to refine my own ideas through feedback to presentations to peers at Indigenous-centric scholarly events.⁴

While the majority of chapters in this volume have been adapted from the original 2009 University of California Berkeley Tourism Studies Working Group Symposium, we also invited other work presented at these other events. During the production period, a handful of Indigenous scholars in North America, New Zealand, and Australia agreed to revise and submit five additional chapters. During the editing process, this volume's group of contributors experienced retirements, academic job offers, multiple monographs, tenure, and a handful of children. Not surprisingly, some of the original contributors pulled out, and others were pulled in. As a result, this volume is missing two critical dimensions that Nelson and I strongly feel should be present in the "next generation" of Indigenous tourism research: the inclusion of more Indigenous voices, and greater representation of "Asian indigeneity."⁵

Barring more Indigenous voices, and a critical lens on tourism in Asia (which we address in the introduction), this volume addresses a wide range of theoretical concepts made visible through the lens of Indigenous tourism, in which we locate the critical intersections between politics, commerce, identity, and social change made possible through Indigenous tourism in many different contexts and settings, past and present. In the future, we hope to see our colleagues expand upon the ideas presented in this book through different ontological worldviews, especially via the perspectives of under-represented peoples, as well as through case studies from more places – in Asia, Oceania, Central and South America, and beyond. We'd like to see future work in this area question current definitions of indigeneity, examine who can define it, and further explore ways that this label affects representation, identity, and economic possibilities.

NOTES

1 My dissertation has since been revised and published by University of Nebraska Press under the title *"So, How Long Have You Been Native?": Life as an Alaska Native Tour Guide* (2015).

2 I owe a great debt to similar articles preceding and influencing my dissertation, namely Dierdre Evans-Pritchard's (1989) '"How 'They' See 'Us': Native American Images of Tourists," which explored Indigenous perspectives but was written by a non-Native, and Carol Chiago Lujan's

(1993) "A Sociological View of Tourism in an American Indian Community: Maintaining Cultural Integrity at Taos Pueblo."
3 These events were organized in partnership with Institute de Recherche et d'Etudes Supérieures du Tourisme; Equipe Interdisciplainaire de Recherche et d'Etudes Supérieurs du Tourisme; Center of Museums, Heritage and Material Culture, University College London; and via the Annual Meeting for the Association of Social Anthropologists of the UK and Commonwealth, the Association of Social Anthropologists of Aotearoa/ New Zealand, the Australian Anthropological Society, and the American Anthropological Association, among other events.
4 These included the annual Native American Indigenous Studies Association events and meetings; the Annual Symposium of Native American Graduate Student Research and Scholarship at the University of Washington; the Amah Mudson Speaker Series in collaboration with the American Indian Resource Center at University of California Santa Cruz; the Manu Ao seminar via the Manu Ao Inter-University Maori Academy for Academic and Professional Advancement; and the Advanced Management of Maori Resources seminar at the School of Business, Victoria University, Wellington.
5 Given that China has fifty-five minority nationalities and the world's largest domestic tourism market, ethnic tourism in that country may be the most important venue for such research (Graburn 2015).

REFERENCES

Bunten, Alexis C. 2015. *"So, How Long Have You Been Native?": Life as an Alaska Native Tour Guide*. Lincoln: University of Nebraska Press.
Bunten, Alexis C., and Nelson H.H. Graburn. 2009. "Introduction: Current Themes in Indigenous Tourism." *London Journal of Tourism, Sport and Creative Industries* 2: 2–11.
Evans-Pritchard, Dierdre. 1989. "How 'They' See 'Us': Native American Images of Tourists." *Annals of Tourism Research* 16 (1): 89–05. http://dx.doi.org/10.1016/0160-7383(89)90032-7.
Graburn, Nelson, ed. 1976. *Ethnic and Tourist Arts: Cultural Expressions from the Fourth World*. Berkeley: University of California Press.
Graburn, Nelson. 2015. "Ethnic Tourism in Rural China: Cultural or Economic Development." In *Ethnic and Minority Communities as Tourist Attractions*, edited by Anya Diekmann and Melanie Smith. Bristol: Multilingual Matters.

Lujan, Carol Chiago. 1993. "A Sociological View of Tourism in an American Indian Community: Maintaining Cultural Integrity at Taos Pueblo." *American Indian Culture and Research Journal* 17 (3): 101–20. http://dx.doi.org/10.17953/aicr.17.3.522uq22n6888l101.

Ryan, Chris, and Michelle Aiken. 2005. *Indigenous Tourism: The Commodification and Management of Culture*. Amsterdam: Elsevier.

Acknowledgments

We are deeply grateful to the founders and members of the Berkeley Tourism Studies Working Group; to Douglas Hildebrand, whose patience and commitment greatly assisted in the publication of this volume; to Jenny Chio, who helped organize so many of the events leading up to this collection and assisted early in the editing process; to Maria Gravari-Barbas, who made possible the intellectual space to explore the ideas presented in this book through a series of symposia supported by the Institut de Recherche et d'Études Supérieures du Tourisme at University of Paris I Panthéon-Sorbonne; to Laurence Douny for organizing an important opportunity to share early versions of our papers and exchange ideas at the Center of Museums, Heritage and Material Culture, University College London; and to Kathy Graburn and Siamak Naficy, who supported our seemingly endless "book-making" hours. Finally, we want to acknowledge that without the support of many departmental funding streams at University of California Berkeley, especially the Canadian Studies Program, the US National Science Foundation, and the Ford Foundation, as well as the space to exchange ideas made possible by the American Anthropological Association, the Association of Social Anthropologists of the UK and Commonwealth, the Association of Social Anthropologists of Aotearoa/New Zealand, and the Australian Anthropological Society, this volume would not have been possible.

Notes on Contributors

Kathryn Bunn-Marcuse is director of the Bill Holm Center for the Study of Northwest Native Art at the Burke Museum and curator of Northwest Coast Art department, where she manages the Native artist grant program and publication series with University of Washington Press. She is also an assistant professor in the art history department, where she teaches Indigenous North American art at the University of Washington. Her publications focus on the indigenization of Euro-American imagery, nineteenth-century Northwest Coast jewellery and other body adornment, and the filmic history of the Kwakwaka'wakw. She curated *Here & Now: Native Artists Inspired,* which showcased new Northwest Coast artworks that were inspired by historical pieces in the Burke Museum's collection.

Alexis Celeste Bunten is project manager for the Bioneers Indigeneity Program. Dr Bunten has collaborated with governments, corporations, communities, and NGOs to promote cultural perpetuation, heritage, and economic development. She has written widely on self-commodification, workplace organization, and cross-cultural forms of capitalism, with publications in *American Indian Quarterly* and *American Ethnologist.* Her book *"So, How Long Have You Been Native?": Life as an Alaska Native Tour Guide* (2015) explores critical issues surrounding cultural Indigenous tourism.

Laurence Douny is an associated researcher at the Laboratoire d'Anthropologie des Mondes Contemporains at the Free University of Brussels, and honorary research fellow at the Department of Anthropology at University College London. She has conducted extensive field research in West Africa, where she focused on material culture, technology, environmental anthropology, and recently on the social and historical formation of Indigenous heritage landscapes in the framework of the trans-Atlantic slave trade. Her latest books are *Living in a Landscape of Scarcity: Materiality and Cosmology in West Africa* (2014) and (as co-author) *Wrapping and Unwrapping Material Culture: Archaeological and Anthropological Perspectives* (2014).

Rachel F. Giraudo is an associate professor of anthropology at California State University, Northridge. Her research interests include indigeneity and identity politics in southern Africa, cultural heritage, tourism, and development. She is currently working on a book manuscript, "The Heritage Curse: Culture as a State Commodity," examining how the appropriation of culture through heritage tourism initiatives in southern Africa affects relationships of ethnic minorities and Indigenous peoples with the state. Her writings have appeared in the *International Journal of Heritage Studies*, *World Heritage Sites and Tourism: Global and Local Relations*, and *Routledge Handbook of Global Citizenship Studies*. Rachel's latest project examines cannabis tourism within the political context of cannabis legalization in the United States.

Nelson H.H. Graburn earned his BA at Cambridge (1958), MA at McGill (1960), and PhD at Chicago (1963). He has taught at UC Berkeley since 1964 and held visiting positions in Canada, France, the United Kingdom, Japan, Brazil, and China. Dr Graburn has researched kinship, art, and identity in twenty-two Canadian Inuit communities (1959–2010) and domestic tourism, multiculturalism, and heritage in Japan (since 1974) and China (since 1991). His books include *Ethnic and Tourist Arts* (1976); *Japanese Domestic Tourism* (1983); *The Anthropology of Tourism* (1983); *Tourism Social Sciences* (1991); *Multiculturalism in the New Japan* (2008); 旅游人类学论文集 (*Anthropology in the Age of Tourism*) (2009); *Tourism and Glocalization: Perspectives in East Asian Studies* (2010); *Tourism Imaginaries: Anthropological Approaches* (2014); and *Tourism Imaginaries at the Disciplinary Crossroads: Places, Practices, Media* (2016).

Marcela Palomino-Schalscha is a lecturer at Victoria University of Wellington with research interests that lie at the intersection of development studies, human geography, and political ecology, with special emphasis on Indigenous issues. She theorizes the politics of scale and place, diverse and solidarity economies, decolonization, and tourism and development in Latin America. One aim of her work has been to explore how Indigenous ontologies and knowledge (multiple and mixed) are hybridizing modern and Western knowledge and ways of being, posing important theoretical and practical implications for development, economic, and environmental thinking and cross-cultural relations, with consequences that affect all people.

Noel B. Salazar is a research professor in anthropology at the University of Leuven, Belgium. He is co-editor of *Tourism Imaginaries* (2014) and the *Anthropology of Tourism Book Series* (Lexington) and author of *Envisioning Eden* (2010) and numerous peer-reviewed articles and book chapters on tourism. Salazar sits on the editorial boards of, among others, *Annals of Tourism Research, Journal of Sustainable Tourism, Journal of Heritage Tourism,* and *International Journal of Tourism Anthropology*. In addition, he is on UNESCO's and UNWTO's official roster of consultants and is an expert member of the ICOMOS International Cultural Tourism Committee and the UNESCO-UNITWIN Network "Culture, Tourism and Development."

Karen Stocker is an associate professor in the Division of Anthropology at California State University, Fullerton. She is the author of *Historias Matambugueñas* (1995), *"I Won't Stay Indian, I'll Keep Studying": Race, Place, and Discrimination in a Costa Rican High School* (2005), and *Tourism and Cultural Change in Costa Rica: Pitfalls and Possibilities* (2013), as well as various articles and chapters in edited volumes. Her research interests have included varied facets of Costa Rican culture, such as gender, indigeneity, Chorotega narrative practices, schooling, and tourism.

Dimitrios Theodossopoulos is professor of social anthropology at the University of Kent. He is currently conducting research in both Greece and Panama, focusing on processes of resistance, exoticization, indigeneity, authenticity, and the politics of cultural representation and protest. He is the author of *Troubles with Turtles* (2003) and *Exoticisation Undressed* (2016) and editor of *When Greeks Think about Turks* (2006), *United in Discontent* (2010), *Great Expectations* (2011), *De-pathologising Resistance* (2015), and *Against Exoticism* (2017).

1 Current Themes in Indigenous Tourism

ALEXIS CELESTE BUNTEN AND
NELSON H.H. GRABURN

Indigenous peoples have been involved with tourism since they first hosted visitors via exploratory and early colonial encounters.[1] Recently, Indigenous-owned and -operated tourism has been expanding, made possible through industry-wide trends, policies designed to boost economies through tourism, and reclamation of Indigenous resources. The past few decades have witnessed unprecedented recognition of Indigenous peoples' rights, most notably in the 2007 United Nations Declaration on the Rights of Indigenous Peoples. Since the historic passing of this living document, Indigenous peoples from around the world have witnessed formal recognition of their existence, the return of ancestral lands, apologies for past injustices, the termination of unwanted development, and financial support and reparations set aside for economic improvement.[2] Despite this progress, many Indigenous peoples remain disenfranchised members of the global body politic; their lands continue to be excised, life ways outlawed, health threatened, and the access to improve these conditions stymied.

Indigenous tourism arose from within this dichotomous framework of opportunity and exclusion that permits Indigenous peoples to continue to be objectified by outsiders. While a growing body of literature addresses the Indigenous tourism industry, such scholarship tends to emphasize a development framework of case studies to improve best practices (Butler and Hinch 2007; Carr, Ruhanen, and Whitford 2016; Hinch and Butler 1996; Ryan and Aicken 2005; Ryan and Huyton 2002; Solfield 1993; Zeppel 2006). Although this "business" approach to scholarship is valuable for those who wish to enter the tourism market or improve upon existing offerings, it tends to avoid larger issues of politics, identity and representation and ignore reasons for development that go beyond the economic. Among the limited studies on this topic within the social sciences, Indigenous tourism is framed as the consumption and/or appropriation of peoples often forced by necessity to participate in an industry that capitalizes on difference (Comaroff and Comaroff 2009; Greenwood 1989; Root 1996), obfuscating an Indigenous perspective or decolonizing framework. In a marked departure from such previous work, this volume considers tourism venues as crucial sites where discursive consciousness arises from cross-cultural interaction mediated by consumer demand. *Indigenous Tourism Movements* explores Indigenous cultural tourism drawing from the metaphor of "movement" in several ways. First is the idea of physical movement through time and space, the *literal movements* of hosts and guests as they encounter each other through the intercultural borderzone made possible by tourism. Second, this work locates the identity and politics embedded in Indigenous *social movements* inherent in touristic activities. Finally, it evokes the *intellectual movement* of cultural knowledge through time and space.

The chapters presented in this volume explore the major areas of critical interest within this growing body of research, illustrating the complex and multifaceted articulations of "indigeneity" made possible by limitless movement and transfer of ideas, capital, technology, objects, and bodies that characterize the current era of late capitalism. Contributing authors approach these issues from a variety of interdisciplinary lenses, including anthropology, tourism studies, Indigenous studies, art history, and geography. The tourism sites featured in this volume span a variety of business models and places, from the negotiation of pan-Indigenous representation at a community-owned cultural centre in a Costa Rican village to an Australian Aboriginal theme park.[3] The communities represented share features that define them as "Indigenous." Themes particular to the contemporary experience of indigeneity thus reoccur throughout the volume, with those features of indigeneity commodified through the touristic encounter highlighted.

Defining Indigeneity

Indigenous tourism negotiates within the discourse of difference. Typically, this takes the form of staging the world as a museum in which Indigenous cultures are experienced in a uniform, sanitized, synchronic design regardless of location, ethnicity, and history.[4] By touring the sites of this global "museum," tourists can ultimately affirm and reinforce what they think they already know about the world presented in a predictable format (Bruner 2005). Bunten (2010) describes this phenomenon as a "cultural tourism formula" that has presented Indigenous peoples with a basic model to begin to take control of their representation, albeit one designed to appeal to tourists' desires and the capitalist commercial system that underpins all tourism enterprises.[5]

Despite pervasive structural constraints that can invigorate unproductive stereotypes and showcase disparities between hosts and guests, tourism has increasingly come to connote the transmutation of alterity from a liability to an asset (Graburn 2015). In addition to providing jobs and contributing to local economies, tourism can enable workers to reinforce connections to ancestral homelands, cultures, and identities. As the primary setting for interpersonal dialogue between Indigenous and non-Indigenous peoples, tourism is instrumental in shaping the dominant global society's viewpoints about critical issues that Indigenous peoples face. Thought of in this way, Indigenous tourism can be viewed as a powerful tool for building understanding.

Visitors come to understand what it means to be Indigenous as they make personal connections with their hosts. Although hosts are familiar with what it means to be "Indigenous" and regularly describe it as part of their labour, most of the existing literature on Indigenous tourism avoids addressing the concept of indigeneity. In contrast, several of the authors in this volume argue that Indigenous identity is neither static nor unproblematic. Graburn, in *Ethnic and Tourist Arts* (1976), an early consideration of Indigenous contributions to the tourism market, employs the notion of the "Fourth World" to refer to peoples occupying lands that had been overrun by the modern techno-bureaucratic nations of the First, Second, and Third Worlds.[6] The commonly used concept "Indigenous" indicates "Native" people differentiated from "Others" in a specific place. However, all of the terms applied to the Indigenous "hosts" discussed in this volume ("Aboriginal," "autochthonous," "Native," "First Nations," "minorities," "ethnic groups," "tribal," "Fourth World," and so on) are artefacts of the colonial encounter (Carniero da Cunha and de Almeda 2000).

A designation of "indigeneity" is easier in most of the settler-dominant ex-colonies where racial separations are distinct and *mestizaje* is not the majority practice for marriage or alliance. In the latter case, anthropologists may be fairly vague about the cultural status, even the cultural identity, of Indigenous tourist hosts and craftspeople.

For instance, in much of Latin America, one may not know in detail how "traditional" or even "Indo" the makers of Teotihuacan ceramics and Peruvian pyro-engravings were (Graburn 1976). One might say these makers of tourist arts, rather than being identifiable as culturally colonized people with a separately named culture, could be considered peasants, or *mestizos* of mixed Indigenous and settler ancestry, or just rural members of the dominant national culture – even though some of their ancestors were undoubtedly the original inhabitants with deep roots in the land and nature (cf. chapter 4). In this case, they may be said to perform folk culture and to make folk arts, "folk" being a well-known category with a long European history referring to the productions of the usually rural, illiterate lower classes of a stratified agrarian society (see Redfield 1956).

The UN has taken a central role in defining Indigenous identity in the contemporary world. The term "Indigenous," appearing in treaties and conventions after the post–World War II establishment of the UN, has come to stand in for the vulnerabilities that these groups of people face vis-à-vis dominant powers within a decolonized world (Brownlie 1992). Recent efforts to raise awareness and cultivate networks to address these issues include the UN's Working Group on Indigenous Populations, begun in 1982; the Indigenous Peoples' Decades (1995–2004, 2005–2015); a Permanent Forum on Indigenous Issues, founded in 2002; and, in 2007, the UN Declaration on the Rights of Indigenous Peoples. As the concept has taken root internationally, the term "Indigenous" has come to indicate a commonality or global identity among Indigenous peoples as

> those which, having a historical continuity with pre-invasion and precolonial societies that developed on their territories, consider themselves distinct from other sectors of the societies now prevailing in those territories, or parts of them. They form at present non-dominant sectors of society and are determined to preserve, develop and transmit to future generations their ancestral territories, and their ethnic identity, as the basis of their continued existence as peoples, in accordance with their own cultural patterns, social institutions and legal systems. (Martinez-Cobo 1986, 5)

While this description includes most of the people deemed "Indigenous" today, it cannot fully express the de-territorialized aspects of indigeneity, the cosmopolitanism of migrant communities, and the complexities of intercultural indigeneity formed through assimilation and intermarriage. A more political definition of "indigeneity" bases it on criterial and relational attributes (Merlan 2009, 303–6). These criteria concern what kinds of people, historical continuity with respect to territorial claims pre-dating invasion or colonization, a continued self-definition as a distinct people, and a determination to transmit ancestral territories and ethnic identity to future generations. Relational attributes include the imposition of state policies governing those deemed to belong to a different category of people within national boundaries; and a "Fourth World" of imbalanced power produced through conquest, colonization, and exclusionary treatment within nation states.

The influence of outside political entities has sometimes forced the legal recognition of Indigenous status and tipped the balance in favour of formerly submerged local groups. For instance, although Japan signed the UN treaty of Indigenous rights in 1997, they refused to recognize Ainu rights at that time.[7] In July 2005, Japan's Shiretoko National Park in Hokkaido was named Japan's third UNESCO World Heritage site. Although the Japanese government effaced Indigenous Ainu participation in initial appeals, the World Conservation Union ultimately named the Ainu as co-stewards of Shiretoko's national heritage. In June 2008, the Japanese government finally recognized the Ainu as the Indigenous peoples of Japan, but continues to equivocate on whether Ainu should be granted land and resource rights as Indigenous peoples, and avoids discussion of Ainu self-determination. Although rights reclamation work has been articulated primarily through the United Nations system, ecotourism projects in Shiretoko enable Ainu to "perform indigeneity" at home by reclaiming land-based practices to establish a legal precedent for nature-Ainu relationships (Cotterill 2011).

The chapters in this volume further the idea that Indigenous identity is dependent upon contact with non-Indigenous peoples to validate its meaning within the larger context of identity politics. Perhaps this is no more fraught than in the realm of human rights, where recognition and acknowledgment of one or more of the aforementioned relational criteria determine Indigenous "existence." To this end, Stocker's contribution to this volume (chapter 4) provocatively asks: Who legitimizes culture? Identity? Locals? Government ministries? While locals and nationals are quick to assert who is Indigenous depending on the stakes involved and the claims associated with such status, the UN's answer to this dilemma is not to address it at all.

Though the UN has proposed working sets of criteria for Indigenous identity, it has yet to formally adopt a definition of "Indigenous" beyond a vague notion of self-designation. According to a UNESCO report, Indigenous peoples make up "370 million individuals or 5% of humanity, representing over 5,000 languages and cultures in more than 70 countries all over the world,"[8] yet exactly who or what legitimizes such identity is fraught with contention. Self-designation perhaps provides some kind of internal confidence in one's identity, but outside acknowledgment determines Indigenous groups' legitimacy on the global stage. Legal recognition can provide opportunities for certain protections and rights, including policies designed to facilitate access to local economies. Indeed, many nations would be wise to foster Indigenous inclusion in the economy, as a weak Indigenous business sector can threaten social and political stability on multiple levels. Hailey's 1992 warning could easily describe conditions in many contemporary states: "It has been a salutary lesson of the last few years to observe the repercussions of the political violence that can arise because the indigenes are fearful that their economic future and traditional rights are being undermined by what they see as outsiders" (1992, 4).

Policy that determines any special or differential rights associated with Indigenous identity can help or hinder Indigenous participation in tourism. Although state management of Indigenous populations varies from policies of genocide to assimilation and protectionism (and in some instances oscillates between them), several nation states have begun to market their Indigenous peoples to promote international tourism.[9] Prior to the most recent widespread state support of Indigenous tourism, the 1990s witnessed an international turn to multiculturalism (Kymlicka 2007) and the World Bank adoption of "Ethno-Development." While efforts to address Indigenous economic development are certainly a starting point, they do not heal the legacies of discrimination, relocation, enslavement, and exclusion from participation in democratic processes whose ongoing effects hamper the ability of many contemporary Indigenous groups to share equal opportunities with other groups (See Bartholomew and Levi 2003).

Among the nation states that acknowledge their Indigenous populations, the rights that accompany this political recognition vary from nation to nation. In Anglo-settler colonial nation states, for example, indigeneity is often tied to groups' struggles to regain or maintain sovereignty and self-determination. These governments (and many others) tend to recognize Indigenous communities' rights based on assumptions of conquest (*terra nullius*, for example), treaty, case law, and the unstable policies that accompany it. In the United States, where the concept of tribal sovereignty predates the Constitution, federally recognized Indian tribes are afforded an unequal form of sovereignty defined as "domestic, dependent nations," but this status is always under threat. Other nations flatly refuse to recognize any special rights or recognitions for their Indigenous populations (DeLugan 2012, Lewallen 2008).

Two outstanding considerations for Indigenous tourism emerge from this discussion. First, any examination of Indigenous tourism must consider the ways that governing bodies promote or deny hosts' Indigenous status and accord them differential rights, if any. It is important to note, however, that while state-determined criteria are significant from a human rights standpoint, the tourism industry is not concerned with such matters when it comes to identifying who is and is not considered Indigenous. Second, attention must be directed to the "criteria" that determine indigeneity, which, for legal purposes, are always determined by dominant forces.[10]

The theory of intersectionality offers a useful way of thinking about how people within the same racial categorization can experience oppression differentially based on other vectors of social identity formation. Just as Indigenous identity is difficult to tease apart from class identity, intersectionality considers how a racialized identity cuts across other forms of domination that create categories for identifying and relating to others, such as patriarchy, racism, and heterosexism. For example, the "tourist gaze" Bunten discusses in chapter 2 almost always locates Indigenous hosts within gendered meta-narratives of progress, with Indigenous peoples located in the feminized realm of the "natural" and guests associated with urbanization and the maleness of "modernity." Similarly, Salazar (chapter 3) describes how the Maasai are imagined in terms of the male warrior, with Maasai women occupying the domestic sphere of the home. On the other hand, the minority *minzu* subjects of ethnic tourism in China are "feminized" and the role of women is highlighted, except in the cases of the Tibetans and Uighur (Graburn 2015). These touristic discourses reproduce ideas of what it means to be Indigenous vis-à-vis the Western ideologies of gendered identity, reproducing structures of power at different levels – Western (or Chinese) patriarchy over Indigenous peoples, and Indigenous men's domination over women. Indigenous hosts must also fulfil notions of "indigeneity" constructed in the media and commercialized through the tourism industry (Adams 1984).

Through tourism, many of the communities represented in this volume are taking an active role to redefine their identities in relation to visitors, the state, and international bodies that seek to control their lives to varying degrees through assigned categories of indigeneity. Interestingly, state and supranational forces that impact Indigenous tourism tend not to take into account the wishes and assertions of the peoples themselves, nor do they focus on the nature of the difference between the local, minority peoples and the surrounding, majority cultures, the very *thing* that tourism commoditizes.

Nationalism, Totemism, and Indirect Tourism

Indigenous peoples have long constituted an important part of the identity of the colonies and nations in which they have become encapsulated by conquest and colonization. This kind of relationship resembles totemism,[11] which has been said to involve a mystical bond (Durkheim 1915) between a human group that has chosen to represent itself by identification with a distinctive Other from the order of "nature," thereby being "good to think" (Levi-Strauss 1963, 77, 89). This is particularly true of the colonies and ex-colonies spawned by Europe and scattered around the world. These colonies or nations have always had the problem of establishing an identity separate from that of the "mother country" (e.g., England, France, Spain) and the even more difficult problem of separating themselves from other, often adjacent, "daughter countries" (e.g., Canada vs. the United States, Australia vs. New Zealand, Mayotte vs. Réunion, Algeria vs. Tunisia, Costa Rica vs. Guatemala, Peru vs. Bolivia). The sources of the concept of "distinction" usually lie in the realms of "nature," such as fauna, flora, and landscape, and often include the Indigenous peoples of the colonized territory and history. For instance, the identity of the nation of Mexico is inseparably bound up with the Indigenous peoples and civilizations conquered and subjugated, splendidly presented for domestic and foreign tourist consumption in the Museo Nacional Antropologia (Graburn 1970). This "totemic" use of Native identity has continued until today, especially in the form of mascots of sports teams and universities. And like other forms of representation based on appropriation, Indigenous peoples alternatively resist and embrace it in touristic display (see chapter 4, where the Stocker discusses the reappropriation of Indigenous imagery for community-based tourism).

The venues for displaying these distinctions include postage stamps, national textbooks, and museums (DeLugan 2012). At the international level, symbols of distinction are essential for display (and sale) in tourist destinations and world fairs. For instance, at the Great Exhibition of 1851 in London, the Canadian Hall was dominated by a moose head, a large Algonkian birchbark canoe, and a large railway steam locomotive – assuring the audience that Canada was more than taiga, tundra, and prairie. At the 1967 World Fair in Montreal, both Canada and the United States displayed totem poles representing Northwest Coast Indians, confusing many European visitors. Demonstrating *plus ca change, plus c'est la même chose*, the Canadian pavilion at the 1986 World Fair in Vancouver was dominated by a huge Northwest Coast war canoe and the famous Canadarm,[12] another tribute to high-tech modernity.

In discussing tourist arts proffered to visitors in the Peruvian part of the Amazon rain forest, Aspelin (1977) used the term "indirect tourism" to describe the availability of crafts made by the Indigenous Mamainde people. The Mamainde were never visible to the tourists; they lived hours or days away by canoe, and their crafts were bought by *mestizo* or non-Indigenous middlemen to be traded to outsiders in small towns on the main rivers. This same relationship to Indigenous peoples via arts, crafts, dolls, or clothing "standing for" both the people themselves and the region or country being visited is still found all over the world. Visitors to Toronto purchase Canadian Inuit scuptures, as visitors to Los Angeles buy Southwest Native American pottery. Ainu wooden bears stand for the Ainu and Hokkaido prefecture, where foreigners buy them as mementos of the country of Japan. Indirect tourism on a global scale is found in UNESCO gift stores, where nearly every nation is represented by its minorities or folkloric peoples of the near past (Scotsmen in kilts for Great Britain, minority nationalities for China, "Hill people" for Vietnam, "tribals" for India, and so on). But indirect tourism always falls short by the common measure of authenticity, which MacCannell (1976) assures us is the fundamental desire of alienated modern (Western) tourists.

In her examination of early ethnic tourism in Alaska, Lee (1999) shows that there was a hierarchy of perceived authenticity in the experiences of Victorian-era visitors arriving by steamer. At the lowest end would be the purchase of Native-made baskets, masks, and the like from one of the mainstreet souvenir emporia. These would be much less meaningful to the traveller than purchasing Native souvenirs directly from an Indigenous peddler, and the Native Alaskans knew this, settling themselves dockside during the tourist season with bundles of souvenirs made by distant family and friends.[13] A distinct step up would be to purchase directly from the Indigenous artist, and many hawkers indeed claimed to be the creators of their wares, knowing this was a common tourist desire (see Bunn-Marcuse, chapter 8; Graburn, chapter 9). At the most "authentic" end of the continuum was the possibility of seeing the object made or used in a traditional ceremony and purchasing it directly from the maker or traditional owner. Thus, personal closeness to the Indigenous artist was the *sine qua non* of the "sacred journey" (Graburn 1977) taken by early Alaskan tourists. In her studies of Karen Hill tribe tourism in Thailand, Conran (2006) emphasizes that intimacy and closeness with the Indigenous peoples is most highly prized (e.g., the clothes worn, music and dances performed, and souvenirs offered); that is, experiential authenticity (usually judged by intense bodily and emotional states) is more important than objective or constructive authenticity. The case studies in this volume focus only on direct tourism interactions, that is, Indigenous encounters.

Identity Movements

Part 1 of this volume, chapters 2–4, starts with the assumption that the cross-cultural encounters made possible through Indigenous tourism do not take place on value-neutral ground. Instead of engaging in Sisyphean debates over authenticity, appropriation, and the invention of culture, the contributors to this volume consider the representations taking place in the touristic encounter as highly multifaceted refractions of postmodernity in which history, politics, media, commerce, and culture are laden with entangled possibilities (Clifford 2007, 209). The conditions of cultural tourism reproduce tropes of indigeneity while opening pathways for emergent and creative expressions of identity to spread into the global consciousness. They produce a conceptual space of contact laden with ideological baggage that impels potential visitors to seek out the Indigenous Other. In turn, Indigenous tourism operators profit from outside acknowledgment of their special status. Within this paradigm, hosts mark their difference according to hegemonic discourses of Indigeniety widely circulated through popular media and advertising.

Indigenous-owned tourism tends to reproduce popular forms of cultural display, while simultaneously deconstructing it (Bunten 2008; Harkin 2003). Bunten (chapter 2) introduces the imaginary of the "Indigenous Other" through a case study of the Tjakupai Aboriginal Cultural Park, Australia's most successful cultural tourist attraction and the industry's largest employer of Aboriginal people. Through a series of mediated presentations and activities, Tjapukai workers demonstrate iconic aspects of their culture that speak to imaginaries for the Indigenous Other as "close to nature," "magical," and "living relics." Aboriginal hosts present themselves in loincloths and decorated with body paint; they play the didgeridoo, throw boomerangs, prepare bush foods, and "inhabit" replicas of pre-contact spaces. While this particular imaginary draws visitors to the tourism site, it can also trap Indigenous hosts into representing themselves in ways that do not resonate with the complexity of their contemporary lives.

The mandatory performance of the Other in the tourism context is a critical activity, which reflects the double consciousness implicit within the representation of identity. Tourism workers' performances are in dialogue with tourist imaginaries, but they also reflect their own imaginaries about heritage, colonization, work, and the tourists themselves. A cursory visit might leave the impression that Tjakupai and places like it are simply in the business of reproducing Western fantasies of the Other, but a closer look reveals there is a lot more going on. A careful examination of tour content reveals how Aboriginal hosts see themselves in time and place relative to settler society. As at Indigenous tourism venues elsewhere (see Bunten 2008), Tjakupai workers are engaged in varied levels of covert acts of resistance, that range from looping a documentary about the ongoing effects of colonization, to clarifying that didgeridoos are not part of the regional repertoire (while performers on site play the instrument), explaining how the incredible diversity of Aboriginal peoples defies stereotyping, and performing a song whose lyrics assert Aboriginal custody of Australia. In this way, Tjakupai workers turn the imaginary for the Indigenous Other on its head. Visitors feel varying degrees of satisfaction that their desire for the Indigenous Other has been met – from displeasure at the staged "authenticity" of the encounter to an unselfconscious sense of connection to their hosts – whilst the hosts use the tourism space to impart their worldviews.

Indigenous hosts navigate complex, entangled tourist imaginaries, including their own hopes of what they will gain from the workplace. Salazar (chapter 3) discusses the ways that the Maasai reconcile playing to colonial imagery with their own aspirations for socio-economic and technological mobility. Tourists come to Tanzania hoping to witness a young male warrior alone on the Serengeti or a woman, bare breasts covered with colourful beads, sitting cross-legged next to a hut. The Maasai comply with these desires in part out of economic necessity, but also because many of their traditional cultural activities are now against the law. Without access to their prior way of life, many Maasai want to be a part of the modern cash economy, but they can only do so by projecting themselves as frozen in the past, as part of the touristic *mis en scène*. In a cosmopolitan twist of fate fuelled by the Indigenous imaginary, Maasai hosts are transformed from subalterns – neither allowed to live outside the cash economy nor fully able to participate in it – to ambassadors for the global Indigenous movement's resistance to Western consumerism.

Paradoxically, the very features of the Indigenous imaginary that feed tourist desires for the Other are often the same ones that are hidden or even lost through historical processes of domination. Self-identifying as Indigenous has only recently had positive ramifications in terms of measurable self-determination and the economic benefits that can result from engaging in tourism. For the Chorotega of Northwest Costa Rica and many other Indigenous survivors like them, masking traditional practices and assimilating to the dominant society has in the past served as a survival strategy. Stocker (chapter 4) discusses a Chorotega community currently engaged in reconstructing the material and performative aspects of their culture via tourism as a pathway to development. Having lost many of the very aspects of their pre-contact culture that might normally satisfy the tourist gaze, community members draw from multiple sources, including both local and "outsourced" representations (such as the Mayan Jaguar or Plains Indian face paint), to mark their Indigenousness. While one perspective suggests that the Chorotega are victims of internal colonization, appropriating any iconography that can be easily marketed, Stocker argues that these images actually strengthen the Chorotega people's sense of solidarity in relation to and with other Indigenous groups

Political Movements

In each of the examples presented in this volume, tourism has opened up new venues for representation to outsiders by creating avenues for social movements to take root and grow. Because Indigenous tourism depends upon visitors' desires to consume an acknowledged Other, it shapes and is shaped by discourses of indigeneity. This set of conditions has elicited well-known debate on explore whether tourism, through commodification, destroys that which it seeks to preserve.[14] Several of the cases presented in Part 2 of this volume offer a marked departure from this approach: instead of focusing on imposed definitions of "what makes whom Indigenous," chapters 5–7 probe the systems and agents that legitimize Indigenous identity and the political and economic rights afforded by outside recognition. The authors acknowledge that Indigenous enterprise is nested within diachronic relations of power between Indigenous groups and those that dictate the structures and networks in which tourism operates. Multiple and overlapping spheres of influence – from communities to international bodies – manipulate opportunities tied to Indigenous identity to serve congruent and conflicting interests. Within this context, Indigenous tourism professionals marshal social and cultural capital to control their representation.

Foremost, Indigenous peoples' power over their futures depends on their abilities to perpetuate their cultural identities despite inconsistent policy and shifting social attitudes. In his discussion of Indigenous tourism in Panama (chapter 5), Theodossopoulos shows that tourism has the potential to mobilize identities to various audiences for different political ends, rendering engagement in tourism as itself a kind of social movement. The author tells the story of a small group of Emberá who settled in forested areas along the river Chagres, where they were able to live off game, fish, and lumber without government intervention until the 1985 establishment of the Chagres National Park that imposed restrictions on hunting and cultivation. This disruption of their semi-subsistence economy drove many Emberá to leave their home to compete for unskilled paid employment in nearby Latino cities, until a national development initiative permitted them to make an income through eco- and cultural tourism while remaining on parkland. Rather than forcing them to become further marginalized ethnoattractions, this policy empowered the Emberá to build coalitions through an economic enterprise that justified their continued habitation in the park. Over time, the Emberá have come to view themselves as cultural ambassadors who possess the power to teach outsiders (at national and international scales) to recognize their values and rights as Indigenous people.

Theodossopoulos argues that tourism provides Indigenous groups new avenues to "reach out to the world" in search of supportive connections, shifting tourism from an economic endeavour to a political one with the potential to transform the discourses and policies of the dominant society. Similarly, Giraudo (chapter 6) suggests that now that Botswana is eager to promote tourism as part of an effort to diversify the nation's overall GDP, the industry may set off a chain reaction that compels the government to extend Indigenous-based rights to the nation's Khoisan-speaking peoples under pressure from non-Indigenous tour operators, non-governmental organizations, and visitors themselves. Despite their international reputation as the first peoples of Africa, due to popular media that regularly depicts them as "ancient" hunter-gatherers (and possessing the "oldest" DNA of all humankind), the San people are unrecognized as Indigenous by the Tswana majority government. Ironically, Botswana's policy insists that *all* of its citizens are "Indigenous," thereby allowing unselfconscious, forced assimilation of San groups to the more recently arrived Tswana-controlled system.

Despite Botswana's multicultural-liberal legislation, its treatment of the San resembles acts of cultural genocide directed at Indigenous peoples elsewhere, such as residential schooling and removal from ancestral homelands. In spite of state efforts to assimilate or expunge San peoples' distintiveness, there is an increasing international demand for ethnic and eco-tourism featuring Khoisan-speaking peoples. Tourism, because it is a main venue through which the San can reach out to tell their story to the world, provides San hosts and their allies an opportunity to shift Botswana's national policy from a false discourse of equality to a system that accords differential rights to the San based on their status as "the" Indigenous peoples of Botswana.

Giraudo's chapter demonstrates how tourism could pave the way for policy that begins to recognize Indigenous peoples' customary rights within a multi-ethnic nation state. The Malian government actively encourages the nation's multiple ethnic groups to engage in touristic activities that showcase their diverse cultures and ongoing relationship with the land. Unlike Botswana, which assaults indigineity as part of a broader goal of presenting its citizens as part of a modern, "multicultural" state, Mali encourages its peoples to showcase their identities in terms of a pre-(Western)-contact past. However, even this more nativist attitude towards internal ethnic groups can make it difficult for Indigenous peoples to determine their lives. Mali's supportive stance towards the Dogon people aligns with UNESCO's goals in designating that people's ancestral home as a World Heritage Site due to its remarkable landscape, linked to the Dogon religious system and architecture. This status resulted in a management plan designed to conserve the area, help preserve the Dogon way of life, and provide economic development, in part via tourism. As these national and international bodies stepped in to preserve Dogon culture, the Dogon themselves became increasingly defensive of their cultural patrimony. Douny (chapter 7) describes how the Dogon adapt and transform local material culture to suit touristic desires while veiling "private" cultural values, thereby protecting them from damage resulting from commodification and outside political influence. This type of "covert resistance" in the tourism setting (Bunten 2008) permits locals to participate in dominant commercial structures while reproducing internal cultural values. Although hosts are often happy to showcase superficial markers of "culture," they must balance the desire for the economic benefits of participation in tourism with the potential loss of internal morals and values. This case highlights hosts' creative responses to the tourism industry's unyielding propensity to devour and transform local cultures, demonstrating a range of strategies one community adopted to harness the past in order to control their future.

Knowledge Movements

Culture is not static, despite colonizing frameworks that mandate ongoing knowledge and practice of "tradition" in connection to place, in order to legitimize Indigenous status and rights.

The movement of cultural knowledge is therefore vital to the social and intellectual lifeblood of what it means to be Indigenous today. Section 3 of this volume, chapters 8–10, explores the shifting nature of Indigenous traditional knowledge, as well as the knowledge necessary to engage in a successful tourism business on their own terms. "Knowledge movement" in this context refers to the practical know-how needed to run a tourism business, a sense of what tourists want to understand, and how to manipulate touristic desire. It also speaks to the academic pursuit of learning what aspects of the touristic enterprise might be studied to understand larger processes in place within an industry that profits from difference. Scholarship in this area is now able to reconstruct the knowledge that Indigenous entrepreneurs had in the past, and can look with a long lens at how tourism practices have changed over time with a view towards future modes of knowledge transmission.

One of the major roadblocks to Indigenous tourism development is lack of business knowledge. Having been isolated from the global economy until recently, Indigenous leaders often face a steep learning curve when it comes to the practical steps necessary to develop tourism, such as cross-cultural communication, applying for business loans, developing partnerships, satisfying government codes and regulations, marketing their products, establishing client bases, and growing their businesses. Although Indigenous groups are frequently eligible for government subsidies and other types of development initiatives, many view this aid with scepticism; they feel that in order to use it, they must follow specific models that limit profitability and chip away at self-determination.

Although structural and context-dependent variables such as legal recognition and the ability to develop alternately enable and threaten their entrepreneurship, Indigenous peoples continue to engage in tourism, taking advantage of outsiders' perennial desires to encounter them. Written documents evidence visitors' shifting attitudes towards Indigenous hosts, as well as the ways in which political and economic conditions have changed for them over time. Deconstructing these records can reveal the impacts individuals have had in dismantling dominant ideologies supporting exploitative and destructive structures of power. Oftentimes, the collective action necessary to mobilize this change was initiated through the tourism encounter.

Bunn-Marcuse (chapter 8) provides a glimpse into the early relationships between Northwest Coast artists and collectors through a cross-examination of historical documents regarding artworks made in turn-of-the-century Southeast Alaska. Tourism advertising of the time positioned Alaska Natives as "savages" in the process of assimilating to the American way of life. This attitude was part of larger hegemonic ideologies that justified the US federal policy of appropriating Indigenous peoples' resources while forcing them onto the lowest social rungs of the dominant society by cutting off traditional economies. Within this paradigm, Indigenous arts and handicrafts were simultaneously considered artefacts of a dying race and evidence of a pathway to civilization that "taught" Natives how to engage in the cash economy. While the tourist literature implied that "ignorant" Northwest Coast peoples were easily tricked by non-Indigenous middlemen into selling off their material culture, Bunn-Marcuse demonstrates that the reality was much more complex, granting a certain agency back to Northwest Coast artists. The author argues that Northwest Coast entrepreneurs developed a sophisticated understanding of colonial demands and touristic expectations, while maintaining local kinship obligations necessary for cultural survival. The tourism economy of the Victorian era created a liminal space for Indigenous incorporation into the cash economy that relied upon core cultural values that would later be translated into future economic and political activities outside the tourism arena.

While many accounts of Indigenous tourism tend to discuss Indigenous peoples versus their non-Indigenous clients through the language of power and resistance, Graburn's (chapter 9) case study of Canadian Inuit tourism serves as a reminder that relationships and categories are much more fluid than reconstructions of the past imply. Chronicles of enterprise in very remote areas or outside the reach of official development rarely make it to the "official" record. However, Graburn's remarkable lens on Nunavut tourism spans his fifty-year career as an anthropologist, exploring themes of tourism, arts, and economic development in northern Canada and beyond. Graburn describes Inuit engagement in tourism, until the 1999 establishment of the territory of Nunavut granted Indigenous control over Inuit land and resources, as both sporadic and the result of partnerships between Inuit and non-Inuit producers, each bringing a different set of cultural capital to the enterprise. Unlike most case studies of Indigenous tourism, this chapter compares many different touristic ventures within a single cultural region over time, as innovative Inuit and their partners experimented with several different products and adventures, some of which succeeded and others failed. Graburn's examination paints tourism as a co-production between Inuit and non-Inuit living side by side, in contrast to backward-looking narratives of egoistic settlers who oblige local Natives to perform for visitors.[15]

These "experiments" in tourism depend on kinship and affect across cultural and power divides, demonstrating how Inuit and non-Inuit partnered to develop attractions and activities compatible with cross-cultural means of production. Inheritors of these efforts and current development personnel often attribute current successes to individual-level, present-day efforts, whereas Graburn reminds us that credit should be shared with those long gone as well as the unborn. This chapter ends with a snapshot of the present-day population as they use the lessons passed down to them to decide how tourism fits into their contemporary lives, if at all. Graburn points to our shared humanity, reminding us that hosts and guests alike can't always anticipate the directions that tourism will take. The analyses presented in chapters 8 and 9 replace erasures in current narratives about Indigenous tourism with new understandings of the ways that the past informs the contemporary Indigenous experience.

Palomino-Schalsa's contribution (chapter 10) also decentres dominant discourses that locate Indigenous peoples in positions of alterity by exploring the ontological underpinnings of hosts' motivations and actions. The author presents Trekaleyin, a Pewenche tourism organization in Alto Bio Bio, Chile, whose operations educate visitors about hosts' physical and spiritual connections to their ancestral homelands. In the face of contradictory multicultural policy and the criminalization of Mapuche social protest, the Pewenche have embarked on creative means, via tourism, to resist neoliberal disenfranchisement from their ancestral territories. Trekaleyin guides visitors to more than just experiences of exotic people and places; Pewenche hosts invite their guests to share in a worldview in which the dead are still present, where places maintain ongoing connections to people, rituals involve the dialogue of humans and non-humans, and dreams transmit knowledge and strength. The tourism encounter consists of trekking across Pewenche territory, where hosts illuminate the relationship of these beliefs to current conflicts over land use that impinge on their right to exist as Mapuche people. By sharing this experience, Trekaleyin's hosts and guests articulate the possibility of overturning the displacement of Indigenous voices in future debates over land tenure and environmental issues. Trekaleyin's story, like that of all the tourism operations discussed in this volume, highlights the transformative potential of the human connections made possible through late capitalism, demonstrating that these encounters are more than just educational, amusing, or thought provoking. They cultivate the moments where Indigenous pasts and futures can be imagined in the present.

Indigenous Futures

This volume expands the limited existing scholarly engagement with Indigenous tourism by exploring the industry's critical links to tradition, heritage, human rights, policy, arts, and activism. Likewise, the authors represented in this volume see tourism as much more than a means of diversifying economies and providing jobs. They raise a range of important questions about the commoditization of indigeneity. Is tourism another form of internal colonization slowly chipping away at Indigenous identity the more that hosts exploit themselves in service of the global capitalist system? Or is Indigenous tourism more like a cleverly disguised means to denaturalize dominant ideologies of conquest and power as hosts shift outside perceptions one visitor at a time? Could Indigenous participation in an industry that markets difference restructure the economic systems established to maintain the inequality that defines hosts in relation to guests? By exploring these and other questions, the authors in this volume demonstrate that tourism, often overlooked in scholarly investigations into Indigenous matters, shapes Indigenous futures in ways far beyond the economic.

Academics, government officials, and NGO personnel charged with playing some role in understanding how Indigenous tourism works often spin their wheels in development rhetoric. Either they concentrate on helping communities to create tourism (often without robust consultation) or they critique it for impacting prior lifeways. Instead, they should be paying attention to the important role this industry has to play in shifting the contexts that have led Indigenous peoples to engage in tourism at all. It is often assumed in the development world that tourism is simply about bringing revenue to cash-poor Indigenous communities, but hosts' motives are far more complex. As the case studies in this volume attest, tourism development links economic incentive to many other kinds of goals. While some Indigenous tourism enterprises appear ideologically ambitious, like Trekeylin's efforts to shift visitors' understanding of the human relationship to nature, others participate in ad hoc tourism simply to live according to a precolonial lifeway, as with the Batek living within the boundary of a national park. Some hosts use tourism as a means to simply stay put under the threat of potential removal and legislative non-existence, like the Khoisan-speaking peoples of Botswana. Most hope to improve their material conditions, like the Maasai, who use tourism dollars to more fully participate in modern Kenyan society. And in an ironic twist of fate, others, like the Chorotega of Northwest Costa Rica, use tourism to rediscover themselves in the aftermath of cultural genocide.

Indigenous tourism adopts different contexts in which the main economic transaction – "culture" for money – takes place. Settings presented in the chapters below vary from a thoroughly modern Australian Aboriginal multimedia venue, to a purpose-built thatch Embera village on the banks of the Chagres River, to the Northwest Coast Indian women who simply knock on tourists' cabin windows hoping to sell their wares. Despite the differing motives and forms that Indigenous tourism takes, all Indigenous hosts use tourism as a means to gain or maintain some degree of self-determination. As such, most see tourism as an opportunity to build public support for recognition. Indigenous hosts hope that sharing their histories, cultures, and stories will shift visitor perceptions of them from "the Indigenous Other" to fellow human. By humanizing difference, Indigenous hosts work to dismantle *a priori* "whiteness" that permits ongoing acts of colonization and genocide. Indigenous representation taking place through tourism reveals unmarked "whiteness," shaped over time in contrast to the Indigenous Other, and replaces it with critical perception.[16] By the same token, hosts come to a better understanding of their guests, as the encounter begins to break down the ideologies that support asymmetrical power relations between Indigenous host and non-Indigenous guest.

The chapters in this volume discuss communities that have been subjugated in some shape or form, forced to abandon their ancestral lifeways to differing degrees, and compelled to follow the rule of outside governing bodies. Visitors bear witness to a version of hosts' current lives, as they are invited to imagine a past and present that often doesn't reflect the full scope of what it means to be Indigenous today. Hosts negotiate a fine line between what aspects of the contemporary Indigenous experience to reveal and what to erase from touristic representation. A failure to address lived experiences of intergenerational trauma, discrimination, poverty, and ongoing disenfranchisement implies continued suppression, but too much attention to the effects of colonization does not give guests a chance to learn about the enduring aspects of cultures that allow hosts to persevere and celebrate their unique identities. Moreover, hosts cannot afford to openly criticize their visitors' assumptions and worldviews given that guests are often the inheritors of the dominant ideologies that created the conditions for contemporary power relations. Within this context, visitors may or may not come to realize that they continue to receive the ongoing benefits of the dispossession of lands and resources once belonging to Indigenous hosts. Whether they like it or not, Indigenous hosts are a part of the late-capitalist, global economy. And as such, they need to operate within its logic while reproducing indigeneity through their products and business models. If hosts go too far in one direction – too Indigenous, or too "mainstream" – they risk losing the saleable aspects of their identity, the ability to capitalize on indigeneity or use it for other political goals.

Indigenous communities find ways to work within imposed social and economic structures that help them to shape their futures. Whereas dominant discourses posit a rigid divide between settler colonial and Indigenous worldviews, Indigenous tourism operates under a different paradigm. Rather than fitting themselves into existing Western schemas for consuming "the Other" within a global capitalist system, most Indigenous tourism compels the tourism industry complex to accept some standards drawn from a locally derived economic philosophy, as they operate according to principles that reflect a commitment to community needs and goals.[17] Instead of seeing Indigenous tourism as merely a means to alleviate poverty within the existing global-politic status quo, we should assess it by the degree to which it transmutes cultural and spiritual capital into the potential for economic gain.

In commodifying features of local culture, the landscape, or other natural resources so intimately tied to their cultural identities, Indigenous communities strive to honour the past while investing in the future. Indigenous tourism is almost always married to cultural perpetuation as part of a greater strategy to employ identity politics in larger arenas of concern, such as retaining or reclaiming history, control over representation, surface and subsurface land rights, and political sovereignty. This objective falls directly in line with Martinez Cobo's (1986) definition for "Indigenous" adopted and sanctioned by the UN: "they form at present non-dominant sectors of society and are determined to preserve, develop and transmit to future generations their ancestral territories, and their ethnic identity, as the basis of their continued existence as peoples, in accordance with their own cultural patterns, social institutions and legal systems." The shared experience made possible through the tourism encounter renders it inherently political. And the effects of building cross-cultural understanding have the potential to transform the world in ways that go far beyond the economic. As global, cosmopolitan lifeways increasingly flourish, the tourists are also Indigenous peoples exploring their own landscapes, pasts, and continuing heritage traditions. Together, hosts and guests imagine Indigenous futures.

NOTES

1 Bunten and Graburn (2009) define "Indigenous tourism" as any service or product that is (a) owned and operated at least in part by an Indigenous group and (b) results from a means of exchange with outside guests.

2 These examples are culled and paraphrased from a United Nations Permanent Forum on Indigenous Issues document, "Indigenous People, Indigenous Voices: Advances in the Recognition of Indigenous Rights since the Adoption of the UN Declaration," http://www.un.org/en/events/indigenousday/pdf/Indigenous_Advances_Eng.pdf.

3 While all of the tourism venues discussed in this volume capitalize on difference through cultural tourism offerings, not all Indigenous tourism operations follow this trend. For example, Ngai Tahu Holdings

Ltd, a Maori corporation in the South Island of New Zealand, owns a number of adventure tourism businesses that do not rely on cultural commodification as part of their business model (personal communication with Mark Solomon, former chairman of Ngai Tahu, March 2007; www. ngaitahutourism.co.nz, accessed 6 August 2016). Six thousand miles across the Pacific Ocean, Alaska Native–owned Ciri Alaska Tourism Corporation operated several lodges and excursions until it sold its tourism portfolio in 2015. Although these Indigenous-owned corporations' tourism holdings do not offer a marked "Indigenous experience" per se, they share features with all the forms of Indigenous tourism discussed in this volume. However, the case studies in this volume are concerned primarily with the kinds of tourism that capitalize upon culture, identity, and heritage.

4 Scholars such as Kirshenblatt-Gimblett (1998) and Handler and Saxton (1988) have remarked upon this "museumizing" of Indigenous groups through the paradigm of tourism, noting that heritage politics are, according to Appadurai, "remarkably uniform throughout the world" (1990, 304).

5 The cultural tourism formula requires the tourism site to have most or all of these elements: (1) the greeting, (2) the guide, (3) demonstrated use of the heritage language, (4) traditional architecture, (5) a performance, (6) a gift shop or souvenirs for sale, often (7) demonstrations of traditional Native crafts, and sometimes (8) a Westernized Native feast such as the Hawaiian lu'au or Maori Hangi meal. Typically, this format does not allow for a deeply personalized encounter with the Native host (Bunten 2010, 294).

6 Whereas many Indigenous groups' special relationship to the land crosses international boundaries, most nation states engage with their Indigenous populations through national and subnational institutions. Maybury-Lewis states, "Indigenous peoples are defined as much by their relations with the state as by any intrinsic characteristics they may possess" (1997, 54).

7 The Japanese government has fought against the idea that the Ainu of Hokkaido are Indigenous with any special rights. In the conquest of the eighteenth and nineteenth centuries, the Ainu were dispossessed of most of their land, told to become rice farmers, forbidden to use their language, and were sent to government schools. In the 1980s, the Japanese government passed a law forcing assimilation, severing most Ainu from the land and waterways that formed the basis of their cosmological and economic relations. However, the Ainu used tourism as an economic force and to maintain or teach their dances, music, crafts, and language without official recognition.

8 http://www.unesco.org/new/en/education/themes/strengthening-education-systems/inclusive-education/indigenous-people/.

9 Young scholars have begun to write about this phenomenon of nation states marketing their Indigenous peoples, considering the tourism sector in Guatemala (Devine 2009) and in Mali (Douny, this volume). Anglo, liberal democratic nation states such as Australia, Canada, New Zealand, and to some extent the United States use federal monies to develop marketing campaigns that centre on visiting Indigenous peoples as part of a larger effort to support economic development among these "Fourth World" communities.

10 For example, an American citizen can only be defined as an American Indian (Indigenous person) if he or she belongs to a federally recognized tribe. And to be federally recognized as an Indian tribe, a group must comprise a distinct community and have existed as a community from historical times, have political influence over its members, have its own membership criteria, and have a membership consisting of individuals who descend from a historical Indian tribe and who are not enrolled in any other tribe.

11 In Australian and other forms of totemism, the totem species was considered to be a mystical ancestry of the kinship group and a source of the peoples' spiritual powers and territorial rights. The same was true amongst numerous Euro-Americans who considered themselves the true inheritors of Native American Indigenous lands and cultures. This concept was put into practice by anthropologist Lewis Henry Morgan when he and his friends founded the society of the Gordian Knot to cut themselves off from their classical European origins in order to reformulate their group (which included the Iroquois leader Ely Parker and later other ethnologists such as Henry Schoolcraft) as the Grand Order and later the New Confederacy of the Iroquois.

12 The Canadarm was a mechanical arm, or crane, that was attached to and used on NASA's space shuttle. The American pavilion had the space shuttle itself, so metonymically it might have appeared that Canada was a small but useful appendage to the United States.

13 The ordinary tourist could not be sure whether the items for sale were traditional objects, replicas, or even novelties invented for the trade (Graburn 1976) or, perhaps, made by a different Indigenous group from the sellers. Recently, this problem has been compounded by the resale of objects manufactured (or handmade) in distant countries, especially China or India.

14 Stanley (1998) and LeFevre (2004) discuss these debates.

15 See also Clifford (2004).

16 Here, "whiteness" is a category that stands in for the unquestioned, dominant social group. In the case of the Batek, whiteness may be represented by a homogenous Malay national identity. However, the

process of gaining and maintaining power in relation to those who are subjugated remains the same.

17 For more discussion, see Bunten (2010).

REFERENCES

Adams, K.M. 1984. "Come to Tana Toraja, 'Land of the Heavenly Kings': Travel Agents as Brokers in Ethnicity." *Annals of Tourism Research* 11 (3): 469–85. http://dx.doi.org/10.1016/0160-7383(84)90032-X.
Appadurai, Arjun. 1990. "Disjuncture and Difference in the Global Cultural Economy." *Public Culture* 2 (2): 1–24. http://dx.doi.org/10.1215/08992363-2-2-1.
Aspelin, Paul. 1977. "The Anthropological Analysis of Tourism: Indirect Tourism and Political Economy in the Case of the Mamainde of Mato Grosso, Brazil." *Annals of Tourism Research* 4 (3): 135–60. http://dx.doi.org/10.1016/0160-7383(77)90005-6.
Bartholomew, Dean, and Jerome Levi. 2003. *At the Risk of Being Heard: Identity, Indigenous Rights and Postcolonial States.* Ann Arbor: University of Michigan Press.
Brownlie, Ian. 1992. *Treaties and Indigenous Peoples.* Edited by F.M. Brookfield. New York: Oxford University Press.
Bruner, Edward. 2005. *Culture on Tour: Ethnographies of Travel.* Chicago: University of Chicago Press.
Bunten, Alexis C. 2008. "Sharing Culture or Selling Out? Developing the Commodified Persona in the Heritage Industry." *American Ethnologist* 35 (3): 380–95. http://dx.doi.org/10.1111/j.1548-1425.2008.00041.x.
Bunten, Alexis C. 2010. "More Like Ourselves: Indigenous Capitalism through Tourism." *American Indian Quarterly* 34 (3): 285–311. http://dx.doi.org/10.5250/amerindiquar.34.3.285.
Bunten, Alexis C., and Nelson H.H. Graburn. 2009. "Guest Editorial: Current Issues in Indigenous Tourism." *London Journal of Tourism, Sport and Creative Industries* 2 (1): 2–11.
Butler, Richard, and Tom Hinch. 2007. *Tourism and Indigenous Peoples: Issues and Implications.* Amsterdam: Elsevier/Butterworth-Heinemann.
Carniero da Cunha, Manuela, and Mauro W.B. de Almeda. 2000. "Indigenous People, Traditional People, and Conservation in the Amazon." *Daedalus: Journal of the Academy of Arts and Sciences* 129 (2): 315–38.
Carr, Anna, Lisa Ruhanen, and Michelle Whitford. 2016. "Indigenous Peoples and Tourism: The Challenges and Opportunities for Sustainable Tourism." *Journal of Sustainable Tourism* 24 (8–9): 1967–79.

Clifford, James A. 2004. "Looking Several Ways: Anthropology and Native Heritage in Alaska." *Current Anthropology* 45(1): 5–30.

Clifford, James A. 2007. "Varieties of Indigenous Experience: Diasporas, Homelands, and Sovereignties." In *Indigenous Experience Today*, edited by M. de la Cadena and O. Stara. Oxford: Berg.

Comaroff, John L., and Jean Comaroff. 2009. *Ethnicity, Inc.* Chicago: University of Chicago Press. http://dx.doi.org/10.7208/chicago/9780226114736.001.0001.

Conran, Mary. 2006. "Commentary: Beyond Authenticity: Exploring Intimacy in the Touristic Encounter in Thailand." *Tourism Geographies* 8 (3): 274–85.

Cotterill, Simon 2011. "Ainu Success: The Political and Cultural Achievements of Japan's Indigenous Minority." *Asia Pacific Journal* 9 (12/2). http://apjjf.org/2011/9/12/Simon-Cotterill/3500/article.html.

DeLugan, Robin. 2012. *Reimagining National Belonging: Postwar El Salvador in a Global Context*. Tucson: University of Arizona Press.

Devine, Jennifer. 2009. "The Maya Spirit: Tourism and Multiculturalism in Post Peace Accords Guatemala." *London Journal of Tourism, Sport and Creative Industries* 2 (1): 28–42.

Durkheim, Emile. 1915. *Elementary Forms of Religious Life*. Trans. Joseph Swain. New York: Free Press.

Graburn, Nelson. 1970. "Art and Pluralism in the Americas." *Anuario Indigenista (Problemos ethnicos de la Sociedad contemporanea)* 30: 191–204.

Graburn, Nelson, ed. 1976. *Ethnic and Tourist Arts: Cultural Expressions from the Fourth World*. Berkeley: University of California Press.

Graburn, Nelson. 1977. "Tourism: The Sacred Journey." In *Hosts and Guests: The Anthropology of Tourism*, edited by Valene Smith, 17–32. Philadelphia: University of Pennsylvania Press.

Graburn, Nelson. 2015. "Ethnic Tourism in Rural China: Cultural or Economic Development." In *Ethnic and Minority Communities as Tourist Attractions*, edited by Anya Diekmann and Melanie Smith, 176–86. Bristol: Multilingual Matters.

Greenwood, Davydd. 1989. "Culture by the Pound: An Anthropological Perspective on Tourism and Cultural Commodification." In *Hosts and Guests: The Anthropology of Tourism*, 2nd ed., edited by Valene Smith. Philadelphia: University of Pennsylvania Press. http://dx.doi.org/10.9783/9780812208016.169.

Hailey, J. 1992. "In the Politics of Entrepreneurship: Affirmative Action Policies for Indigenous Entrepreneurs." *Small Enterprise Development* 3 (2): 4–14. http://dx.doi.org/10.3362/0957-1329.1992.014.

Handler, Richard, and William Saxton. 1988. "Dyssimulation: Reflexivity, Narrative, and the Quest for Authenticity in 'Living History.'" *Cultural Anthropology* 3 (3): 242–60. http://dx.doi.org/10.1525/can.1988.3.3.02a00020.

Harkin, Michael. 2003. "Staged Encounters: Postmodern Tourism and Aboriginal People." *Ethnohistory (Columbus, Ohio)* 50 (3): 575–85. http://dx.doi.org/10.1215/00141801-50-3-575.

Hinch, Tom, and Richard Butler. 1996. "Indigenous Tourism: A Common Ground for Discussion." In *Tourism and Indigenous Peoples: Issues and Implications*, edited by Richard Butler and Tom Hinch, 3–19. London: International Thomson Business Press.

Kirshenblatt-Gimblett, Barbara. 1998. *Destination Culture: Tourism, Museums, and Heritage*. Berkeley: University of California Press.

Kymlicka, W. 2007. *Multicultural Odyssey:, Navigating the New International Politics of Diversity*. Oxford: Oxford University Press.

Lee, Molly. 1999. "Tourism and Taste Cultures: Collecting Native Art in Alaska at the Turn of the Twentieth Century." In *Unpacking Culture: Art and Commodity in the Colonial and Postcolonial World*, edited by Ruth B. Phillips and Christopher Steiner, 267–81. Berkeley: University of California Press.

LeFevre, Tate. 2004. "Seizing Identity, Manipulating Globalization: The Wetr Dance Troupe in Lifou, New Caledonia." B.A. honours thesis,. Dartmouth College. Department of Anthropology, Dartmouth College.

Levi-Strauss, Claude. 1963. *Totemism*. Trans. Rodney Needham. Boston: Beacon.

Lewallen, Ann-Elise. 2008. "Indigenous at Last! Ainu Grassroots Organization and the Indigenous Peoples Summit in Ainu Mosir." *Asia Pacific Journal* 48 (6). http://apjjf.org/-ann-elise-lewallen/2971/article.html.

MacCannell, D. 1976. *The Tourist: A New Theory of the Leisure Class*. Berkely: University of California Press.

Martinez Cobo, J.R. 1986. *Study of the Problem of Discrimination against Indigenous Populations*. New York: United Nations.

Maybury-Lewis, David. 1997. *Indigenous Peoples, Ethnic Groups, and the State*. Boston: Allyn & Bacon.

Merlan, Francesca. 2009. "Indigeneity Global and Local." *Current Anthropology* 50 (3): 303–33. http://dx.doi.org/10.1086/597667.

Redfield, Robert. 1956. *Peasant Society and Culture: An Anthropological Approach to Civilization*. Chicago: University of Chicago Press.

Root, Maria P.P. 1996. *The Multiracial Experience: Racial Borders as the New Frontier*. Thousand Oaks: Sage. http://dx.doi.org/10.4135/9781483327433.

Ryan, Chris, and Michelle Aicken. 2005. *Indigenous Tourism: The Commodification and Management of Culture*. Amsterdam: Elsevier.

Ryan, Chris, and Jeremy Huyton. 2002. "Tourists and Aboriginal People." *Annals of Tourism Research* 29 (3): 631–47. http://dx.doi.org/10.1016/S0160-7383(01)00073-1.

Solfield, T. 1993. "Indigenous Tourism Development." *Annals of Tourism Research* 20 (4): 729–50. http://dx.doi.org/10.1016/0160-7383(93)90094-J.

Stanley, Nick. 1998. *Being Ourselves for You: The Global Display of Cultures*. London: Middlesex University Press.

Zeppel, Heather. 2006. *Indigenous Ecotourism: Sustainable Development and Management*. Ecotourism series no. 3, edited by D. Weaver. Wallingford: CABI. http://dx.doi.org/10.1079/9781845931247.0000.

PART ONE

Identity Movements

2 Deriding Demand: A Case Study of Indigenous Imaginaries at an Australian Aboriginal Tourism Cultural Park*

ALEXIS CELESTE BUNTEN

Tjapukai Aboriginal Cultural Park: Uniquely Formulaic?

As Australia's largest and most successful cultural tourist attraction and the Australian domestic tourism industry's largest employer of Aboriginal people, Aboriginal-owned Tjapukai Aboriginal Cultural Park is the premier destination to experience Tjapukai culture.[1] As such, visitors look to this attraction to fulfil their expectations for "Aboriginal people" with whom they are already somewhat familiar through the imaginaries of the Indigenous Other. One visitor described the Tjapukai experience:

> While I was in Australia, I was looking for an appreciation of Aboriginal culture ... What I wanted was someone to explain to me how Indigenous people lived, what they thought was important, and maybe explain to me what the "Dreamtime" was. The only place I found this was at the Tjapukai Cultural Park. The people there gave a hands-on introduction to their culture. Learn how to throw a boomerang, a spear, make bush medicine, and lots more. It was fun, informative, and entertaining. (14 June 2011)[2]

Through a series of mediated presentations and activities, Tjapukai Aboriginal Cultural Park workers demonstrate iconic aspects of Aboriginal culture that speak to imaginaries for the Indigenous Other as "close to nature," "magical," and "living relics." While park workers mostly

*An earlier version of this chapter was published in *Tourism Imaginaries: Through an Anthropological Lens*, edited by Noel B. Salazar and Nelson H.H. Graburn (Oxford: Berghahn, 2014).

Figure 2.1 Creation story in the Bulurru Storywaters Theatre. Copyright: Tjakupai Aboriginal Cultural Park

belong to the Djabugay Aboriginal community in North Queensland not far from the park's location in Cairns, presentations of Aboriginal beliefs and lifeways toggle between generic, pan-Aboriginal representations and those specific to the Djabugay people. The day tour begins in the "magic space," a museum-like room that juxtaposes "authentic stone-age artefacts"[3] alongside contemporary Aboriginal art and experience. Visitors are invited to contextualize material culture through a looped screening of a documentary about Aboriginal history. While the "magic space" showcases Aboriginal cultural continuity, it evokes a "paradigmatic fossilization," in which Aboriginal hosts are "confined to the fixed status of an object frozen once and for all in time by the gaze of the Western percipients" (Said 1985, 92).

After visitors move through the "magic space," they are escorted to an outdoor amphitheatre to watch Aboriginal guides present their culture through a narrated performance that freezes hosts into a Paleolithic past (Nesper 2003) through a fire-making demonstration and mimetic dance that highlights their connections to the animal world. The guides then break up the audience into groups and escort them to experience more cultural demonstrations that frame Aboriginal hosts as living hunter-gatherers whose specialized skills and knowledge help them to maintain a close relationship to the natural world. Finally, visitors return to the "Bulurru Storywaters Theatre," a sensory, multimedia experience that brings Tjapukai origin stories alive as live-action performers enact dreamtime visions by interacting with life-size holograms. Visitors must exit the park through the gift shop stocked with Aboriginal art, crafts, and other souvenirs to remind them of their trip.

The Tjapukai Aboriginal Cultural Park is simultaneously unique and banal. While the cultural traditions and intellectual property of the local Djabugay hosts could not faithfully be presented anywhere else or by any other people, this venue follows standard procedures for presenting culture. Typically, this takes the form of staging the world as a museum in which Indigenous cultures are experienced in a uniform, sanitized, synchronic design, regardless of location and history.[4] By touring the sites of this global "museum," tourists can ultimately affirm and reinforce what they think they already know about the world presented in a predictable format (Bruner 2005). Bunten (2010, 294) describes this phenomenon as a "cultural tourism formula" that has presented Indigenous peoples with a basic model to begin the process of taking control of their representation through tourism, albeit one designed to appeal to tourists' desires within the dominant systems of representation and consumption that underpin all cultural tourism.

This formula includes: (1) the greeting, (2) the friendly guide, (3) demonstrated use of the heritage language, (4) traditional architecture, (5) a performance, (6) a gift shop or souvenirs for sale, (7) demonstrations of traditional Native crafts, and sometimes (8) a Westernized Native feast. An assemblage of visitor reviews illustrates the formula in effect at Tjapukai:

> You start with the "Magic Space," which is a strategically lit open space with beautiful artifacts, paintings telling stories and a fantastic painting with the Rainbow Serpent ... Then you basically move from one show to another ... You also have chance to talk to someone about Aboriginal weapons & medicines. Apparently green ant is great for hangover!!! (8 October 2011)

> Dreamtime Theatre presentation was a fascinating look into the roots of Aboriginal beliefs. I really liked the live demonstrations of song, dance,

and didgeridoo playing! The gift shop has a wonderful assortment of fabric panels, boomerangs, didgeridoos, and artwork for sale. My only wish is that I had more time. (26 October 2010)

With a final warning:

Let's be clear that it is not a 'National Geographic' type experience nor are you paying for one. (13 April 2010)

This chapter unpacks the relationship between the tourist gaze and hosts' manipulation of it. Through a set of observations examining the ways that the Indigenous imaginary mediates engagements between hosts and guests, it is meant to raise more questions than it answers. It begins with a discussion of the sets of expectations that mediate the way visitor experiences are constructed and interpreted, drawing examples from Tjapukai Aboriginal Cultural Park's presentation of Aboriginal identity and visitor responses to them via online comments. Then, drawing evidence from mainly secondary sources, I argue that Indigenous hosts are sophisticated culture brokers who can play with and subvert the Indigenous imaginary to redefine the way outsiders view them. While tourism affords Indigenous peoples opportunities to influence broader discourses of indigeneity, it also binds them to categories created by the dominant society through the imaginary (such as "primitive," "childlike," and the like), making it unclear exactly how much room there is to redefine and assert Indigenous ontologies within the consumptive supply-and-demand context of tourism. Through a mini-case study of this "double bind" as it plays out at Tjapukai Aboriginal Cultural Park, this chapter engages in a larger scholarly dialogue exploring broader questions around the negotiation of Indigenous identity, and the effects of these understandings on those who self-identify as Indigenous.

The ideas introduced in this chapter are culled from my impressions visiting Tjapukai Aboriginal Cultural Park (on 25 June 2011) and those gathered though correspondence with visitors and workers, as well as primary and secondary sources. Primary sources of information about how hosts and guests present and interpret Aboriginal content provided at Tjapukai were drawn from the Trip Advisor website, the Tjapukai Aboriginal Cultural Park website, and promotional pieces. Secondary data were gathered from observations made in articles and graduate theses. This chapter is not meant as an ethnography or deep exploration; it is simply a pulling together of different evidence available to the public regarding the presentation, reception, and negotiation of imaginaries of Australian Aboriginal peoples within the context of the Tjapukai Aboriginal Cultural park from the perspective of an outside observer. Outside of correspondence with Tjapukai management about the content of this chapter, the ideas presented here are not drawn from first-hand interviews, nor are they based on any kind of long-term relationship with staff at the cultural centre. This work is not meant to represent the views of staff or members of the Djabugay community nor to unpack the inner workings of the tourism venue. Finally, my interpretation of this evidence is filtered through more than a decade of first-hand, ethnographic research on the topic of Indigenous tourism, including two years of fieldwork as an Indigenous guide myself.[5] While Tjakupai and the Aboriginal cultures it presents are unique to the people who developed it, the processes by which Aboriginal hosts have come to commodify their cultures and identities relative to imaginaries of the Indigenous Other, and to use these tropes to their advantage under a political context of increasing self-determination, play out around the world at many similar Indigenous tourism sites.

As the first Aboriginal attraction of its kind in Australia, Tjapukai was founded in 1987 by a non-Indigenous North American couple with expertise in cultural theatre in partnership with displaced Djabugay people living in and around Cairns, Australia, the hub of tropical, Great Barrier Reef tourism. Among over five hundred Aboriginal groups within the country, the Djabugay are a rainforest people, with a distinct language and ways of surviving off the land. But they share with other Aboriginal peoples experiences of marginalization, language and cultural loss in their home territory, and ongoing social, economic, and spiritual difficulties resulting from colonization. According to the 2011 Australian census, Cairns is home to about 13,400 Aboriginal peoples, who make up nearly 9.3 per cent of the city's population, in a state with the second-largest population of Aboriginal and Torres Straight Islanders (155,824 people) after New South Wales.

From humble beginnings as a touring Aboriginal dance group, the nucleus for today's Tjapukai experience took shape through a 1996 merger with Aboriginal groups and regional tourism operators, who developed it into a cultural park attraction.[6] In 2004, the Aboriginal and Torres Strait Islander Commercial Development Corporation (renamed Indigenous Business Australia [IBA]) acquired 19.93 per cent equity in the park, and later increased its ownership to 100 per cent to keep the park operating through a downturn in tourism. In accord with IBA's commitment to "increase the wellbeing of Indigenous Australians by supporting greater economic participation and self-reliance,"[7] Tjapukai cultural presentations are vetted through elder consultants to ensure cultural integrity and protection of Tjapukai intellectual property. Like other Indigenous-owned cultural tourism venues, Tjapukai has been actively involved in promoting Aboriginal culture from within, providing millions of dollars in jobs and revenue for the local Aboriginal community.[8] Despite critiques that the park is "too touristy," the cultural tourism formula clearly works for Tjapukai, garnering the park numerous tourism industry awards.

The recent expansion of Indigenous-owned and -operated tourism has been made possible through industry-wide trends, policies designed to boost economies through tourism, and reclamation of Indigenous resources through legal settlements with colonizer states. The corporation that now owns Tjapukai was founded directly following the 1989 Aboriginal and Torres Strait Islander Commission Act that established statutory corporations to manage reclamations. The act proclaims, "The [Australian] Government expects that the Corporation will enhance the opportunities for Aboriginal and Torres Strait Islander people to begin to break free from the web of dependency and achieve a significant degree of economic independence."[9] As part of the government's Indigenous Economic Development Strategy, IBA seeks to close the gap between Indigenous Australians' and other Australians' standard of living.

The Indigenous tourism sector does not just reflect a trend that capitalizes on difference as simply an opportunity for local development. Rather, Indigenous tourism should be understood as part of a larger project among subaltern communities to redefine dominant notions of the Other in a post-capitalist global economy. Indigenous cultures promoted at touristic destinations are products of the Western gaze that tends to isolate hosts' worldviews and traditions into the fixed geographic and temporal spaces that comprise the landscape of the tourist imagination. With more possibilities to make connections with potential customers, Indigenous communities are taking advantage of these discourses in developing tourism sites.

Bunten and Graburn (2009, 3) describe Indigenous tourism as "any service or product that is *a*) owned and operated at least in part by an Indigenous group and *b*) results from a means of exchange with outside guests." While Indigenous control is the defining factor of this industry, it is limited by market demand. For this kind of tourism to generate business, visitors must agree that the hosts are indeed "Indigenous" according to their own sets of criteria articulated through the discourse of "imaginaries" (and these may differ from those currently debated on the world stage).[10] Imaginaries possess dichotomous qualities; they are tacit and implicit, travelling backward and forward at the same time (Salazar and Graburn 2014). Some reflect stereotypes and fantasies about the "-ized" (Orientalized, colonized, globalized, etc.), while others are more site- and even person-specific. Transnational imaginaries tend to be more generalized, such as the concept that Indigenous peoples are "natural," whereas domestic imaginaries reflect particular colonizer-settler histories, and more personal imaginings address a range of ideas that reflect upon the individual doing the imagining.

Several scholars have pointed out that interactions between tourists and Indigenous hosts perpetuate stereotypes of the Other (Evans-Pritchard 1989; Lujan 1993; Nicks 1999; Whittaker 1999) that appease visitors' desires and aspirations. While one take on this asserts that yielding to the tourist gaze reduces hosts to inauthentic caricatures of their "real" selves (Rossel 1988), I have argued elsewhere that Indigenous hosts respond to the gaze through a carefully crafted commoditized persona that manipulates these stereotypes to subvert asymmetrical power relations (Bunten 2008). In fact, Indigenous hosts view tourism as part of a larger strategy to shape their participation in the global economy in a way that honours culturally based values (see Bunten 2010; Tucker 2003; Wiketera and Bremner 2009). They actively manipulate tourist imaginaries of the Other to shape industry trends and articulations of alterity at multiple levels. In doing so, hosts take advantage of the cyclical and reciprocal shape of the imaginary. The rest of this chapter tracks the imaginary as it circulates through a feedback loop between visitor to host and back to visitor (see Salazar 2010).

Tourist Imaginaries of the Indigenous Other

People who visit Indigenous tourism sites in one place tend to experience Indigenous attractions in other countries, suggesting that similar motivations underlie touristic desires to visit Indigenous peoples in general. A 28 August 2011 visitor to Tjapukai explained, "Having experienced some rather disappointing 'culture park' type attractions in different countries, I was a little apprehensive about visiting Tjapukai, but was very pleasantly surprised." Another had an opposite reaction: "I love the Culture Center on Oahu and expected Tjapukai to be similar. I was very much disappointed" (29 August 2010). Though Tjapukai makes no pretence that it is anything more than a place to encounter Aboriginal culture filtered through the tourism context, comparing reviews reveals contradictions in visitor satisfaction.

> The Park offered an excellent, multi-faceted portrayal of the Aboriginal experience – a play, a film, music/dance performance, didgeridoo performance, food presentation, spear-throwing, boomerang-throwing, and exhibits ... Aborigine staff members interacted with us in very small groups [and] most of the activities and answered wide-ranging questions regarding Aboriginal life (both past and present) ... We very much appreciated the opportunity to learn about this ancient culture. (11 January 2010)

> I went to the Saturday night dinner and show and was blown away with the entire experience! The entertainers were interactive, informative and incorporated the right amount of humour. Singing and dancing along to traditional tribal rituals made fun by the amazing staff! Couldn't fault the food, we tried Kangaroo, Crocodile and Emu! Thank you for a fantastic night. (29 January 2017).[11]

While some clearly appreciate an exposure to Aboriginal culture within the comfortable boundaries of the cultural tourism formula, others express disappointment.

> I know we are "tourists" and that most things are geared for us, but this one was a little too touristy for our liking. Although it gave us good insight into the Aboriginal culture, the dancing, spear throwing, it left us in a bit of a daze. (5 September 2010)

These comments reveal tourist expectations that Aboriginal hosts reflect an ancient, spiritual, low-technological, and performative culture easily consumed through exhibition, activities, and interaction. These expectations are imaginaries in the sense that they are uniformly shared across the spectrum of visitors and reproduced within the popular consciousness through mass media, museums, and other heritage sites. Several scholars have remarked upon the shaping of the tourist desire for the Other as an imaginary that cannot be met. Rossel (1988, 5) finds "exaggerations, misleading statements, and lies" that provided a certain way of understanding reality, and that offered the "tourist view." Likewise, Craik (1997) argues that tourist expectations are rooted in the tourist's origin culture rather than in the cultural offerings of the destination (see also King 1997; Nuttal 1997).

Following this logic, the tourist imaginary is always subject to the visitor's expectation of reality, an egocentric pursuit characterized by self-delusion through simulacra (Ritzer and Liska 1997, 107). In order for the imaginary to be fulfilled, visitors must suspend their knowledge that the encounter is staged expressly for them. This creates a double bind of the imaginary, in which visitors are conscious that hosts play to an imagined authenticity that can never be reached (because it doesn't exist outside of the imagination), yet hosts present heritage that is part of their lived experience within and outside the tourism context.[12] For example, Djabugay employees at Tjapukai demonstrate the didgeridoo, perhaps the greatest icon of Australian Aboriginal identity, yet performers acknowledge that their people neither made, nor played, the instrument in the past. One Tjapukai visitor wrote:

> I never really understand why people overly bash an attraction for being too touristy – Tjapukai park IS touristy – it doesn't pretend not to be, but it still delivers a pretty fun day ... No, it's not as authentic as if you tagged along on a National Geographic expedition searching for lost Aboriginees [sic], but it tries to introduce people to a culture using fun activities, shows and exhibits ... by no means is it a complete or exhaustive education of Aboriginal history, but it's not watered down either. (12 October 2009)

This feedback clearly demonstrates that visitors understand they are being presented with cultural bric-a-brac that indexes a contemporary type of cultural authenticity lived outside of the park. Despite their awareness of the constructed nature of the cultural tourism site made expressly for them, visitors use the language of authenticity as a benchmark from which to rate whether the quality of their experiences matches their expectations. While fraught with contention within academic debates, discourses of authenticity are useful inasmuch as hosts, guests, and tourism mediators frequently refer to this concept to describe the tourism experience.

Handler and Linnekin (1984) argue that authenticity is highly sought after in contexts, such as tourism, in which people's lives are packaged into discrete stories as a reaction to the alienation felt in everyday modern life. By consuming the Other within a highly proscriptive tourism format, visitors are attempting to "feel authentic" themselves. However, tourists' notions of what is "authentic" are highly mediated by their own subjective experience. Building from Leach's (1961) theory of time as marked by cycles of sacredness and profanity and Turner's (1969) notions of liminality, Graburn (1977) argues that tourists make meaning of their lives by experiencing a world outside of their own, through tourism as a pseudo-religious pilgrimage. The trope of "imperialist nostalgia" (Rosaldo 1989), or a longing for what one has destroyed in the past, is used to advertise the Indigenous tourism experience as outside the humdrum of visitors' everyday lives.

Aboriginal people are heavily marketed (both by outsiders and in self-promotion) as "the world's oldest living culture" in ways that serve dominant power dynamics. Palmer (2004, 111) states that "non-Aboriginal Australians have increasingly drawn on emblematic images of Aborigines, the 'first people,' to provide their nation with a sense of national antiquity and distinctiveness." One Tjapukai reviewer observed, "I found the show a great insight into Australia's history and culture and something that I have not particularly had an interest in the past. I hope the Tjapukai tribe continue their great work and continue to show both national and international tourists a great insight into our [Australian national] history" (5 November 2008). Akin to the United States' doctrine of "manifest destiny," the Australian government actively promoted a romanticized notion of Australian Aboriginal peoples as stuck in the "dreamtime" to justify the theft of Aboriginal resources in founding modern nationhood. Coined by early twentieth-century salvage anthropologists who translated Indigenous ontologies into colonial narratives of progress, the Western imaginary of the "dreamtime" links "authentic" Aboriginal people to "empty" land, both under the management of settler colonial agents. Though many of the inhumane policies tied to the promotion of these imaginaries are long over, the tourism industry propagates these ideas through the transmogrification of complex Indigenous beliefs into simplified images, sound bites, and ideas that can be easily consumed in highly mediated spaces, performances, and souvenirs.

Tourism tends to favour imaginaries of the Other invented during colonial periods of conquest, because they are a part of a shared consciousness that visitors actively seek out through their tourism experiences (Salazar 2012). In their efforts to meet the tourist gaze, Indigenous hosts run the risk of smothering local interpretation with these kinds of narratives of conquest that once legitimized Indigenous exploitation, and currently maintain an asymmetrical relationship between themselves and guests.[13] It is within this framework, shaped by dominant discourses and ideologies, that Indigenous tourism operates.

Meeting the Tourist Imaginary

Indigenous cultural tourism sites generally follow predictable formats that have been proven to work in similar contexts. Ryan and Huyton (2002, 42) explain that "one reason why Aboriginal communities have looked to culturally based products is because they have little business experience and tend to repeat a known successful product." As the first purpose-built Aboriginal tourism park in Australia, Tjapukai has co-opted the "model culture" format exemplified by the Mormon-owned Polynesian Cultural Center in Hawaii (Stanton 1989).[14] This format presents a sanitized version of culture that is often compared to a precolonial past, in which performers follow what appears to be culturally proscribed gender roles, don "pre-contact" clothes, and perform "traditional" songs and dances in the heritage language. All of these performative and representational elements are adapted to the constraints of the tourism environment. For example, songs and dances are shortened and accompanied by translation in the dominant language.

One visitor to Tjapukai was disappointed by the superficiality of the "model culture" on display: "We were looking forward to learning more about the Aborigines at a dinner show. The show began with a poor re-enactment of the tribe's history. The fire ceremony seemed authentic, but once dinner began, authenticity was not seen very often. The song they ended on sounded like a Disney animated movie soundtrack rather than a lesson in history" (4 August 2004). On the other hand, the "model culture" experience works for the mass tourist used to highly mediated experiences. A reviewer commented, "Our family, which includes a 4 and 6 year old visited Tjapukai today and we enjoyed ourselves ... On arrival we were given a map and info on the program and show times and in what order to do them" (30 June 2011).

While they do not allow for a deeply personalized encounter with Indigenous hosts, cultural parks such as Tjapukai successfully fulfil tourist desires for the Indigenous Other in a controlled space, where visitors know what to expect. As Barbara Kirshenblatt-Gimblett observes, "Sameness is a problem the [tourism] industry faces. Standardization is part and parcel of the economies of scale that high-volume tourism requires ... the industry requires a reliable product that meets universal standards, despite the dispersal of that product across many widely separated locations" (1998, 152). The parallels in contemporary touristic representation grew out of similar histories of colonizing objectification, epitomized in continuums of "cultural evolution" from savagery to civilization reproduced in expository texts, world's fairs, advertising, museum exhibitions, and theme park attractions, perhaps culminating in the "It's a Small World" ride at Disneyland (Bunten 2010). Within this broad context, ethnographic displays of any sort function as "trophies of conquest – command performances of manifest destiny – and as carefully bounded representations that allowed this difference to be sampled at a safe distance" (Johnson and Underiner 2001, 45). Following this logic, effecting distance through self-commoditization legitimizes structures of domination (Mieu 2011).

Under these kinds of pressures to frame touristic notions of Indigenous authenticity within the subjugator's imaginary and traditions of display (Kirshenblatt-Gimblett 1991; Stanley 1998), Indigenous hosts have a limited ability to project culturally and politically nuanced presentations of themselves to their audiences. Tjapukai's general manager acknowledges where Tjapukai representation fits within the wider scope of the industry, stating, "Cultural tourism is an important part of the Australian tourism landscape. It has been around for countless generations. At Tjapukai, cultural tourism means expressing our living culture every day to guests from all over the world. It's a responsibility we take seriously – Edu-taining guests is what Tjapukai is all about."[15] In addition to "edu-taining," which implies brevity, the "fake" villages in places like this imply that the host culture is not to be taken seriously. The constructed nature of the site combines with the fact that visitors are paying for something most Indigenous peoples deem inalienable – cultural contact forces everyone, host and guest alike, to suspend their disbelief. Those who cannot "play along" with the irony of the context find themselves disappointed. One such visitor to Tjapukai explained:

> This is one of those experiences that years later, I still laugh about and consider it one of the hokiest and strangest live action shows I have ever seen. It was like one of those really, really bad dioramas you saw when you were a kid, touring the really bad museum with your classmates. Now just imagine the dioramas coming to life. This is the Tjapukai Show ... I still can't hear a didgeridoo without having flashbacks and then bust out laughing. (2 August 2007)

Another visitor left the same performance with an earnest desire for the "magical Aborigine" of her imagination:

> Then we went off to see a live performance of traditional Aborigines and songs and didgeridoo playing. This was enjoyable but for me lacked some atmosphere, I feel the fake rocks that make up the stage and other landscaping errors took away from the overall feel. A lot of money has been spent on other things and I think this could be made a whole lot better, a real rock amphitheatre with aboriginal paintings surrounded by lush rainforest would make you feel like you were experiencing something magical. (30 June 2011)

While a cursory visit might leave the impression that Tjapukai and places like it are in the business of reproducing Western fantasies of the Other, a closer look reveals there is a lot more going on. Like other mass entertainment genres, cultural parks can be approached on many different levels. Visitors recognize the irony inherent in practices of "staging authenticity," to varying degrees of satisfaction. One disappointed Tjapukai customer complained: "The performers seemed to be having a laugh among themselves. [It] felt like a private joke onstage we weren't privy to." Another offered a less cynical response to the "double bind of authenticity" taking place at Tjapukai: "As the taxi pulled up to the Tjapukai cultural park, I was expecting something either really hokey or very serious. What I found was something in between" (11 December 2002).

Deriding Demand: Indigenous Imaginaries at Work

Emblematic of the Indigenous-owned and -operated cultural tourism industry in general, Tjapukai Aboriginal Cultural Park does not slavishly reproduce Western ontologies of difference. No pretence is made that the simulated experiences of Indigenous cultural tourism are "real," yet they construct liminal spaces where Indigenous hosts invite guests to experience local culture through a mutually respectful exchange. Martha Brim, Djabugay and a Tjapukai employee, confirmed, "Working at Tjapukai gives me the opportunity to work with my family and friends, meet people from different countries and not only share my culture with them but also learn a little about theirs." Similarly, Garina Brady, also Djabugay and an employee, explained "The most exciting thing about Tjapukai is that I get to meet people from different countries and not only share my culture with them but also learn a little about them."[16]

Indigenous employees come to work with a different sense of investment in their labour than what might be expected of workers in places that merely play to imaginaries of domination; their cultural identities are intimately tied to the workplace, a crucial site where workers' bodies, identities, ancestors, beliefs, and landscapes make up the tourist attraction.[17] In this setting, one that is at the same time both Indigenous and Western, employees seem to genuinely enjoy sharing aspects of their cultures, past and present, with their customers. They see their work as a way to celebrate their cultures and educate the mainstream public. Likewise, visitors can tell that workers are not burdened by the yoke of Western representation. One Tjapukai visitor remarked, "The Aboriginal hosts were the friendliest tour guides I have ever met. They made us feel a part of their culture in the friendliest way possible. They were smiling even when they thought we weren't watching" (23 November 2011). Another corroborated, "The staff were all excellent and clearly proud to share their background" (28 August 2011).

Through the cross-cultural tourism encounter, Indigenous hosts navigate complex, entangled tourist imaginaries, including their own expectations for what they hope to get out of the workplace experience.[18] Although they feel pressure to respond to the imaginaries implicit in the tourist gaze, Indigenous tourism professionals often adhere to their own cultural norms of representation, protocols regarding the sharing of traditional knowledge and concepts of the self. For Tjapukai hosts, this entails protecting aspects of their culture that are secret and elder approval of those that are on display. Tjapukai proudly proclaims that the shows and activities offered have been approved by the traditional Aboriginal elders as a marketing tactic to verify the authenticity of its product.[19] Backstage, these checks and balances ensure Aboriginal control over products that follow local cultural protocols, rather than "selling out" culture to the whims of the tourist gaze. By respecting their own cultural norms while meeting certain aspects of the tourist gaze, Indigenous tourism professionals maintain a sense of pride in sharing their culture, in addition to any monetary compensation.[20]

Hosts' own imaginaries about visitors are informed by their cultural attitudes towards guests and how to treat them, as well as historical relations between themselves and outsiders. For Indigenous tourism workers, this often entails rectifying negative feelings about serving and entertaining members of the dominant society, a. process that requires managing the very ideologies that allowed ethnocide, and are constantly recycled within dominant tropes of difference. Resistance is an integral aspect of this process, a self-protective mechanism that balances out acts of self-exoticization. It is almost always hidden behind a mask of compliance (Scott 1990), used as a way to live through, but not necessarily resolve, problematic power relations (see Hall and Jefferson 1989). Assuming many different forms, it is usually undetected by those to whom it is directed (Salazar 2010). Resistance expressed in the cultural tourism setting is covert, varying in gradations of agency and intensity, "continually negotiated in the discourse and practice of everyday life" (Valaskakis 1993, 283). At its most basic and unconscious level, tour guides practise resistance simply by portraying themselves through a trope of cultural persistence in the face of dominant society. At the most consciously directed level, workers actively challenge stereotypes through both rehearsed and spontaneous commentary (Bunten 2008).

Tjapukai hosts convey their own imaginaries behind a "mask of compliance" that may appear "touristy" to some visitors and highly "authentic" to others. If they pay careful attention, visitors can gain a clear sense of how their hosts see themselves in time and view their place in the world in relation to the colonizer settler nation. As at Indigenous tourism venues elsewhere (see Bunten 2008), Tjapukai workers are engaged in varied levels of covert acts of resistance, which range from looping a documentary about the effects of colonization, to explaining that didgeridoos are not part of the regional repertoire, to a live presentation that explains how the incredible diversity of Aboriginal peoples defies stereotyped generalization.

While the cornerstone of the Tjapukai experience is cross-cultural understanding, workers do not deny the intergenerational trauma of theft (of children, land, culture, ancestors, etc.) and colonization that has left Aboriginal peoples from across Australia with disparities in health, education, income, and employment. At the end of every performance, Tjapukai dancers play a song, titled "Proud to be Aborigine," that tells the story of colonization, cultural change, and reconciliation (Ellis 2007, 23). The lyrics state:

Twenty thousand years we lived in peace
a land a man was free to wander
The white man came and pulled it down under
The white man found a land he thought no one owned
Spears can't fight guns and dynamite
The white man came and pulled it down under ... The black and white

should unite
Be as brothers in the land down under
Proud to be Aborigine
We'll never die
Tjapukai
Always be our identity
Proud to be
Aborigine

Critics of cultural commoditization used to discuss cultural producers as if they experience their own cultures in the bounded and discrete
ways that they are sometimes presented on tour, or as if hosts cannot
engage in meta-discursive action (MacCannell 1973; Greenwood 1989;
Hewison 1987). In fact, most Indigenous peoples do not experience their
world as integrated culture, and may perform aspects of their identities
that reflect both tourist and local imaginaries. In line with this perspective, Fienup-Riordan (2000, 167) sees heritage as "conscious culture"
responding to demands and pressures that originate both within and
outside Native communities, "mediating new powers and attachments;
relations with the land, among local groups, with the state and with
transnational forces" (quoted in Clifford 2004, 6). While some think that
commoditizing culture reinforces stereotypes that reproduce asymmetrical power relations with the unpleasant side effect of bastardizing
"real" culture, others see cultural tourism sites as cultural border zones
(Bruner 2005), or contact zones (Pratt 1992) where people from dispa-
rate backgrounds come face to face to redefine their ongoing relations
on both personal and ideological levels (Bunten 2008; Ellis 2007, 28).

The mandatory performance of the Other in the tourism context is a
critical activity that reflects a double bind implicit within the representation of identity. Tourism workers' performances are in dialogue with
tourist imaginaries, but they also reflect their own imaginaries about
heritage, colonization, work, and the visitors themselves (see Salazar
2010). Around the world, Aboriginal development within the ethno-
cidal context of settler colonial economic and social structures poses
unique challenges and opportunities for Indigenous entrepreneurs.
Indigenous tourism workers face opposition from factions within their
own communities, who see the cultural representation within a capi-
talistic context as an extension of colonial domination. According to
this viewpoint, playing to the tourist imaginary becomes an implicit
form of acceptance of narratives of conquest. As long as workers dress

up in leather and play the didgeridoo, they reproduce stereotypes that uphold unequal power structures. Another faction within the Aboriginal community sees playing to the tourist imaginary as an important way to open up meaningful dialogue between hosts and guests, ultimately erasing imaginaries inherited from a previous era.

As the first Aboriginal tourism presentation of its kind in Australia, Tjapukai faced multiple sources of opposition to the staging of Aboriginal culture. According to a case study written for Indigenous Tourism Australia:

When Tjapukai began their Aboriginal theatre, they weren't even sure if the audience would be there. They had to win over a local community (both black and white), and a tourism industry unsure where to place a product like this; they also had to win the hearts and minds of an audience who had never before been exposed to anything like this. Where Tjapukai encountered prejudice, they answered it with humour and talent. When they found barriers, they charmed them out of existence with their passion and vision of what they wanted so much to achieve.[21]

Indigenous tourism operators recognize that tourism can provide a means to heal intergenerational wounds through cross-cultural dialogue in a mediated setting that applauds cultural difference while improving the basic conditions for individual workers and the local community. One Tjapukai worker explained:

My experience with tourism has changed my life. I now own 20 acres of land, my own house, and four-wheel drive. My standard of living and that of my family has been lifted dramatically ... The economic and social benefits have flowed on to the entire community in increased respect for my people and greater integration between the white and black community. (quoted in Ryan and Huyton 2002, 60)

Comparing examples of Indigenous tourism from around the world, Bunten (2010) argues that profitability, while important, is not the overriding factor driving tourism business operations. Rather, Indigenous tourism is nearly always aligned with cultural perpetuation, ecological preservation, and promoting international peace as part of an overall community development vision. Jon Altman, former director for the Center for Aboriginal Economic Policy, writes:

Aboriginal interests often consider development options in a context that includes social and cultural as well as economic components. Within this perspective, development is not limited to issues like material expansion, increased cash income, and high formal employment, but also involves social and cultural issues, the potential for increased political power, and the possibility of widened future options. (1989, 460)

Similarly, Notzke observes, "For the [Canadian] Inuvialuit in embracing tourism, the challenge is twofold: to protect the integrity of their land-based economy and way of life from trespass and interference of the tourism industry; and to engage in tourism activities in a way which enables the industry to fit into, nurture, and benefit community mixed economies to an optimum degree" (1998, 67).

There is a difference between tourism that accommodates a perceived tourist gaze at the expense of cultural integrity and tourism that is carefully crafted to appeal to tourists while upholding local values. Tourists can sense the internal colonization in the former. They comment to the effect that what they are seeing is "fake" or "quaint." On the contrary, those who experience the latter seem to reflect on the humanity they share with their hosts, sometimes with tears, or by embracing their new friends on their way out. Ultimately, visitors want to make a connection with their hosts.

This chapter has presented visitors' reviews at both ends of this continuum, analysing the complex nature of the tourism experience through the concept of the imaginary. For Indigenous communities, tourism is one of the primary settings in which their people are valued for their unique cultures and heritages in relation to the outside world. Through thoughtful planning, tourism can be a means for Indigenous communities to take control of power expressed through imaginaries by providing an instrument to determine what to share and not share with visitors. At this early stage of critical research on the topic of Indigenous tourism, many other questions remain to be explored, such as the role of state policy in limiting the scope and reach of Indigenous tourism sites and whether or not these destinations can serve as a catalyst to support social movements. Is tourism really the context from which to construct new discourses of alterity? I think it is.

NOTES

1 "Tjapukai" culture may be a misnomer for some. According to the park's website (http://www.tjapukai.com.au/cairns-cultural-centre, accessed

28 November 2011), "Tjapukai" refers to the Aboriginal peoples of the rainforest in Queensland, northeast Australia, though many have been forcibly removed due to colonization. While the website mentions that the "culture" is that of the Djabugay people, the park's official term for the culture is "Tjapukai"; therefore, this is the term I will use to refer to the Aboriginal culture portrayed at this venue.

2 All of the visitor reviews discussed in this chapter were culled from the TripAdvisor website. I have presented them in their original form, including spelling and grammatical errors, to reflect the voices of the reviewers. While I acknowledge that the things people write on websites may not be true, and may even be generated by the hosts themselves, I assume they are accurate representations of users' experiences at Tjapukai.

3 The phrase "stone-age artefacts" was taken from the park's website, http://www.tjapukai.com.au/tjapukai-by-day/ (accessed 28 November 2011).

4 Others (Handler and Saxton 1988; Kirshenblatt-Gimblett 1998) have commented upon this "museumizing" of Indigenous groups through the paradigm of tourism, noting that heritage politics are, according to Appadurai (1990, 304), "remarkably uniform throughout the world."

5 For more on my prior research and expertise on the topic of Indigenous tourism, see Bunten (2008, 2010, 2013).

6 Prior to this merger, the Djabugay people had very little control over the operations at the park, resulting in community needs and desires going unfulfilled (Schuler 1999). Despite the fact that it displayed Tjapukai culture to visitors, Tjapukai was not an Aboriginal business until owned by Aboriginal interests.

7 Retrieved from http://www.iba.gov.au/about-us/our-commitment/ (accessed 3 December 2011).

8 Tjapukai's "education fact sheet 4, tourism and marketing," www.tjapukai.com.au/documents/FactSheet4.pdf (accessed 15 January 2012), states that "since we began, we have returned over more than $25 million dollars [AUD] in wages, profits, royalties and art sales to the Aboriginal community. We support many local schools, businesses, and organizations with donations and offer free off site performances. We value our local visitors and offer them specials throughout the year." This and other web pages consulted in earlier stages of my research no longer exist. Browsers are sometimes redirected to http://www.tjapukai.com.au/cairns-cultural-centre, which does not include the same text quoted in this chapter. Below, I provide the original site consulted, with date accessed.

9 IBA website, http://www.iba.gov.au/about-us/our-history/ (accessed 24 January 2012).

10 In a United Nations study, Martinez Cobo (1986, 5) defines "indigeneity" in terms of "those which, having a historical continuity with pre-invasion and pre-colonial societies that developed on their territories, consider themselves distinct from other sectors of the societies now prevailing in those territories, or parts of them. They form at present non-dominant sectors of society and are determined to preserve, develop, and transmit to future generations their ancestral territories, and their ethnic identity, as the basis of their continued existence as peoples, in accordance with their own cultural patterns, social institutions, and legal systems."

11 While all other reviews were culled from TripAdvisor, this review was taken from the Tjapukai Facebook page, https://www.facebook.com/tjapukai/ (accessed 3 July 2017).

12 A double bind of the imaginary results in a paradox in which visitors measure their experiences against expectations for authenticity that are lost once commoditized through tourism (Harkin 1995). Once it is indexed, however, the signifier ceases to be authentic.

13 Nash (1977) argues that touristic interactions between host and guest endorse Western imperialism by replaying colonial relationships of dominance and servility inherent in tourist imaginaries of the Other.

14 Bunten (2010) has written about other cultural tourism parks around the world, including the Saxman Village in Alaska and the Tamaki Maori Village in New Zealand, that also resemble the Polynesian Cultural Center. Ellis designed her master's thesis analysis around the similarities between Tjapukai Aboriginal Cultural Park and the Polynesian Cultural Center, explaining that "both sites serve similar functions: that is, to educate and entertain primarily Western (European and American) tourist audiences with both broad and more localized notions of 'native culture' through interactive displays, activities and dance performances. Both sites are located near major tourism centers – Waikiki in Honolulu, Hawaii and Cairns, North Queensland, Australia respectively – and require indigenous involvement, whether as performers, collaborators, or board members" (2007, 3).

15 Tjapukai website, http://www.tjapukai.com.au/david-hudson/ (accessed 24 January 2012).

16 Tjapukai website, http://www.tjapukai.com.au/tjapukai-the-culture/dancer-profiles/ (accessed 12 December 2011).

17 However, the author of one piece about the park noted that for "many, the experience was one of powerlessness. Over the years of its operation, there has been tension between Djabugay staff and the Cultural Park

Management, and on occasion, employees have gone on strike over their working conditions ... There was also concern that an agreement to give priority to the employment of Djabuguy people in the park was not being honoured. Djabuguy people feared that other Aboriginal people, more ready and able to performing the style of speech and bodily demeanor that the management considered to be more attractive to tourists, would slowly and insidiously replace Djabugay employees" (Henry 2012, 208).

18 The concept of a "host gaze" that is at the same time both independent of and in response to the tourist gaze contests this notion of passive capitulation to dominant economies and systems of cultural representation (Bunten 2013). Just as tourists size up and coerce their hosts with the power of the tourist gaze, hosts interact with visitors based on a set of systematized beliefs about their guests. Like the tourist gaze, which can change over the course of the touristic experience, the host gaze is not static. As the tourist gaze is informed by long-held imaginary motifs about the culture being consumed, the host gaze is generated well before the tourist encounter. The host gaze changes through interaction with guests, and over the course of a tourism season. Ultimately, it becomes a memory of visitors long gone, and expectations for those to come.

19 From TripAdvisor: "Thank you very much for visiting Tjapukai Aboriginal Cultural Park. We are very pleased you enjoyed your Tjapukai by Day experience. The shows and activities we offer at Tjapukai have been approved by the Traditional Aboriginal Elders, hence why your experience was authentic and educational. We appreciate your support and we hope you return in the future" (30 August 2011).

20 While many cultural norms are observed, Indigenous patterns of speech are often suspended within the tourism context. Fordham (1994, 17–19) and McGarvie (1985, 12–15) have listed Djabugay communicative norms, including proscriptions against eye contact, the use of silence, and indirect communication, that are cultural barriers to communicating with English-speaking members of the dominant culture. As is the case among many other Indigenous groups, these barriers must be surmounted in order to operate a tourism business. However, other cultural norms, such as gratuitous concurrence (agreeing to something out of politeness while harbouring reservations), storytelling, and humour, lend themselves well to the kind of cross-cultural encounter made possible through tourism.

21 Indigenous Tourism Australia, http://www.indigenoustourism.australia. com/casestudies.asp?sub=0604 (accessed 22 December 2011).

REFERENCES

Appadurai, Arjun. 1990. "Disjuncture and Difference in the Global Cultural Economy." *Public Culture* 2 (2): 1–24. http://dx.doi.org/10.1215/08992363-2-2-1.

Bruner, Edward. 2005. *Culture on Tour: Ethnographies of Travel.* Chicago: University of Chicago Press.

Bunten, Alexis C. 2008. "Sharing Culture or Selling Out? A Case Study of Self-Commodification in the Native-Owned Cultural Tourism Industry along the Northwest Coast of North America." *American Ethnologist* 35 (3): 380–95. http://dx.doi.org/10.1111/j.1548-1425.2008.00041.x.

Bunten, Alexis Celeste. 2010. "More Like Ourselves: Indigenous Capitalism through Tourism." *American Indian Quarterly* 34 (3): 285–311. http://dx.doi.org/10.5250/amerindiquar.34.3.285.

Bunten, Alexis C. 2013. "You Never Know Who Is Going to Be on Tour: Reflections on the Indigenous Host Gaze from an Alaskan Case Study." In *The Host Gaze in Global Tourism*, ed. Omar Moufakkir and Yvette Reisinger, 111–124. Wallingford: CABI.

Bunten, Alexis C., and Nelson Graburn. 2009. "Guest Editorial: Current Issues in Indigenous Tourism." *London Journal of Tourism, Sport and Creative Industries* 2 (1): 2–11.

Clifford, James A. 2004. "Looking Several Ways: Anthropology and Native Heritage in Alaska." *Current Anthropology* 45 (1): 5–30.

Craik, Jennifer. 1997. "The Culture of Tourism." In *Touring Cultures: Transformations of Travel and Theory*, edited by C. Rojek and J. Urry. New York: Routledge.

Ellis, Tiffany M. 2007. *Going Native: Tourism, Negotiable Authenticity, and Cultural Production in the Polynesian Cultural Center and Tjapukai Aboriginal Cultural Park.* Master's thesis, Institute for Social and Cultural Anthropology, University of Oxford.

Evans-Pritchard, Deirdre. 1989. "How 'They' See 'Us': Native American Images of Tourists." *Annals of Tourism Research* 16 (1): 89–105.

Fienup-Riordan, Ann. 2000. *Hunting Tradition in a Changing World: Yup'ik Lives in Alaska Today.* New Brunswick: Rutgers University Press.

Fordham, H. 1994. "Cultural Difficulties in Defense of Aboriginal Clients: Guidelines to Assist Lawyers in Dealing with Aboriginal Clients." *Proctor*, March, 17–19.

Graburn, Nelson. 1977. "Tourism: The Sacred Journey." In *Hosts and Guests: The Anthropology of Tourism*, ed. Valene Smith. Philadelphia: University of Pennsylvania Press.

Greenwood, Davydd. 1989. "Culture by the Pound: An Anthrlogical Perspective on Tourism and Cultural Commodification." In *Hosts and Guests: The Anthropology of Tourism*, 2nd ed., edited by Valene Smith. Philadelphia: University of Pennsylvania Press. http://dx.doi.org/10.9783/9780812208016.169.

Hall, Stuart, and Tony Jefferson, eds. 1989. *Resistance through Rituals: Youth Subcultures in Post-war Britain*. London: Unwin Hyman.

Handler, Richard, and Jocelyn Linnekin. 1984. "Tradition, Genuine or Spurious?" *Journal of American Folklore* 97 (2): 273–90.

Henry, Rosita. 2012. *Performing Place, Practising Memories: Aboriginal Australians, Hippies, and the State*. Oxford: Berghahn.

Handler, Richard, and William Saxton. 1988. "Dyssimulation, Reflexivity, Narrative, and the Quest for Authenticity in Living History." *Cultural Anthropology* 3 (3): 242–60. http://dx.doi.org/10.1525/can.1988.3.3.02a00020.

Harkin, Michael. 1995. "Modernist Anthropology and Tourism of the Authentic." Annals of Tourism Research, 25: 650–70.

Hewison, Robert. 1987. *The Heritage Industry: Britain in a Climate of Decline*. London: Methuen.

Johnson, Katie, and Tamara Underiner. 2001. "Command Performances: Staging Native Americans at Tillicum Village." In *Selling the Indian: Commercializing and Appropriating American Indian Cultures*, ed. Carter Jones Meyer and Diana Royer. Tucson: University of Arizona Press.

King, John. 1997. "Marketing Magic: Process and Identity in the Creation and Selling of Native Art and Material Culture." In *Present Is Past: Some Uses of Tradition in Native Societies*, ed. Marie Mauzé. Lanham, MD: University Press of America.

Kirshenblatt-Gimblett, Barbara. 1991. "Objects of Ethnography." In *Exhibiting Cultures: The Poetics and Politics of Museum Display*, ed. Ivan Karp and Steven D. Lavine. Washington, DC: Smithsonian Institution Press.

Kirshenblatt-Gimblett, Barbara. 1998. *Destination Culture: Tourism, Museums, and Heritage*. Berkeley: University of California Press.

Leach, Edmund. 1961. *Rethinking Anthropology*. London: Athlone Press.

Lujan, Carol C. 1993. "A Sociological View of Tourism in an American Indian Community: Maintaining Cultural Integrity at Taos Pueblo." *American Indian Culture and Research Journal* 17 (3): 101–20.

MacCannell, Dean. 1973. "Staged Authenticity: On Arrangements of Social Space in Tourist Settings." *American Journal of Sociology* 79 (3): 589–603.

Martinez Cobo, J.R. 1986. *Study of the Problem of Discrimination against Indigenous Populations*. New York: United Nations.

McGarvie, Neil. 1985. *Inservice/Induction Kit for Use with Teachers of Aboriginal and Islander Students in Queensland Schools*. Brisbane: Department of Education.

Mieu, George Paul. 2011. "On Difference, Desire and the Aesthetics of the Unexpected: The White Masai.' in Kenyan Tourism." In *Great Expectations: Imagination and Anticipation in Tourism*, edited by Jonathan Skinner and Dimitrios Theodossopoulos, 96–115. New York: Berghahn.

Nash, Dennison. 1977. "Tourism as a Form of Imperialism." In *Hosts and Guests: The Anthropology of Tourism*, ed. Valene Smith. Philadelphia: University of Pennsylvania Press.

Nesper, Larry. 2003. "Simulating Culture: Being Indian for Tourists in Lac Du Flambeau's Wa-Swa-Ga Indian Bowl." *Ethnohistory* 50 (3): 447–72.

Nicks, Trudy. 1999. "Indian Villages and Entertainments: Setting the Stage for Tourist Souvenir Sales." In *Unpacking Culture: Art and Commodity in Colonial and Postcolonial Worlds*, ed. Ruth B. Phillips and Christopher B. Steiner. Berkeley: University of California Press.

Nuttal, Mark. 1997. "Packaging the Wild: Tourism Development in Alaska." In *Tourists and Tourism; Identifying with People and Places*, edited by Simone Abram, Jacqueline Waldren, and Donald MacLeod. Oxford: Berg.

Palmer, Lisa. 2004. "Bushwalking in Kakadu: A Study of Cultural Borderlands." *Social and Cultural Geography* 5 (1): 109–27.

Pratt, Mary Louise. 1992. *Imperial Eyes: Travel Writing and Transculturation*. New York: Routledge.

Ritzer, George, and Allan Liska. 1997. "'McDisneylandization' and 'Post-Tourism': Complementary Perspectives on Contemporary Tourism." In *Touring Cultures: Transformations of Travel and Theory*, ed. Chris Rojek and John Urry. London: Routledge.

Rosaldo, Renato. 1989. "Imperialist Nostalgia." *Representations* 26: 107–22.

Rossel, Pierre. 1988. "Potlatch and the Totem: The Attraction of America's Northwest Coast." In *Tourism: Manufacturing the Exotic*, ed. Pierre Rossel. Copenhagen: International Work Group for Indigenous Affairs.

Ryan, Chris, and Jeremy Huyton. 2002. "Tourists and Aboriginal People." *Annals of Tourism Research* 29 (3): 631–47. http://dx.doi.org/10.1016/S0160-7383(01)00073-1.

Said, Edward. 1985. *Orientalism*. Middlesex: Penguin.

Salazar, Noel B. 2010. *Envisioning Eden: Mobilizing Imaginaries in Tourism and Beyond*. Oxford: Berghahn.

Salazar, Noel B. 2012. "Tourism Imaginaries: A conceptual approach." *Annals of Tourism Research* 39 (2): 863–882.

Salazar, Noel B., and Graburn, N.H. eds. 2014. *Tourism Imaginaries: Anthropological Approaches*. Oxford: Berghahn.

Scott, James. 1990. *Domination and the Arts of Resistance: Hidden Transcripts*. New Haven: Yale University Press.

Schuler, Sigrid. 1999. "Tourism Impacts on an Australian Indigenous Community: A Djabugay Case Study." MA thesis, University of the Sunshine Coast, Australia.

Stanley, Nick. 1998. *Being Ourselves for You: The Global Display of Cultures*. London: Middlesex University Press.

Stanton, Max E. 1989. "The Polynesian Cultural Center: A Multi-Ethnic Model of Seven Pacific Cultures." In *Hosts and Guests: The Anthropology of Tourism*, 2nd ed., ed. Valene Smith. Philadelphia: University of Pennsylvania Press.

Tucker, Hazel. 2003. Living with Tourism: Negotiating Identities in a Turkish Village. London: Routledge.

Turner, Victor. 1969. "Liminality and Communitas." In *The Ritual Process: Structure and Anti-Structure*. Chicago: Aldine.

Valaskakis, Gail. 1993. "Parallel Voices: Indians and Others." *Canadian Journal of Communication* 18: 283–98.

Whittaker, Elvi. 1999. "Indigenous Tourism: Reclaiming Knowledge, Culture and Intellectual Property in Australia." In *Tourism and Cultural Conflicts*, ed. Mike Robinson and Priscilla Boniface. Wallingford: CABI.

Wiketera, Keri Ann, and Hamish Bremner. 2009. "Maori Cultural Tourism or Just Being Ourselves? Validating Cultural Inheritance." *London Journal of Tourism, Sport and Creative Industries* 2 (1): 53–61.

3 The Maasai as Paradoxical Icons of Tourism (Im)mobility

NOEL B. SALAZAR

The word was passed round that the Masai had come … Passing through the forest, we soon set our eyes upon the dreaded warriors that had been so long the subject of my waking dreams, and I could not but involuntarily exclaim, "What splendid fellows!" as I surveyed a band of the most peculiar race of men to be found in all Africa.

Joseph Thomson (1885)

The Maasai, speakers of the Eastern Nilotic Maa tonal language, are a widely dispersed Indigenous group living across southern Kenya and northern Tanzania – an area collectively known as Maasailand. The Maasai people, currently estimated to number around 1.3 million, have attracted enormous interest since the first reports of contact with Europeans in the nineteenth century (such as the one by Thomson, quoted above). They act as proud ambassadors of both Indigenous tourism and the global Indigenous movement, and almost represent the whole of Africa for those who know little about the continent. Through a powerful stereotyped image, the Maasai have become true icons of (an imagined) Indigenous "traditionalism," unwitting symbols of resistance to modernist values (Galaty 2002). Paradoxically, in the way they are being depicted, "exoticisation and demonization of the Maasai (or who the Maasai are imagined to be) manifest as two sides of the same coin" (Hughes 2006b, 4).

For early European explorers who came across this "nomad warrior race," young *ilmurran* represented the epitome of a wild and free lifestyle.[1] By publishing embellished accounts of these encounters, the Europeans reinforced the mythical image of Maasai as icons of wildest Africa and enhanced their own reputation for bravery and boldness (Hodgson 2001).[2] Knowles and Collett (1989) sketch how the warrior archetype, one of several possibilities found in early explorers' texts, was elaborated in ways that justified colonial policies, and later became the basis for post-colonial development initiatives. In part due to these historical (mis)representations, Maasai are now considered an integral part of the African wilderness, an image that corresponds with a stereotyped Western idea of the primitive, sexual, and violent African, or the romanticized image of the noble savage (Hughes 2006a). Bruner nicely summarizes the representational narrowing of Maasai culture as follows: "the basic story about the Maasai ... is a gendered Western fantasy of the male warrior – proud, courageous, brave, aristocratic, and independent, the natural man, and the freedom-loving pastoralist. Associated with this warrior narrative are artifacts and adornments – shield and spear, beads, earrings, red ochre, sandals" (2002, 387). The Maasai "props" are so iconic that they are widely recognized across the globe (Salazar 2009a).

Based on long-term ethnographic fieldwork in Tanzania (home to around five hundred thousand Maasai), this chapter discusses how the Maasai are variously represented and represent themselves as "Other" and how Maasai youth in particular try to reconcile their own aspirations of social mobility with the persistent outsider perception of a Maasai life world that develops little or not at all.[3] It is aptly situated in the section of the book that deals with those who seek an encounter with the Other through tourism, and it illustrates how this encounter goes both ways. As such, this chapter confirms the premise of this volume that "the cross-cultural encounters made possible through Indigenous tourism do not take place on value-neutral ground."

My findings show that Maasai culture is simultaneously both reproduced and subtly contested, going against the lingering representations of immutable and unreasoning Maasai rigidity. Relying on data obtained from participant observation, in-depth interviews, and secondary sources, gathered with the invaluable help of my Maasai research assistant, Joseph Ole Sanguyan, I show in this chapter how the double-edged imagery of Maasai culture as both attractive and repugnant is profoundly affecting the daily life of many Maasai communities as well as neighbouring ethnic groups in the country. While the globally circulating cultural representations of Maasai may remain largely "frozen in time," the Maasai themselves are increasingly on the move, in ways that diverge widely from their stereotypical image as obstinate semi-pastoralists.[4]

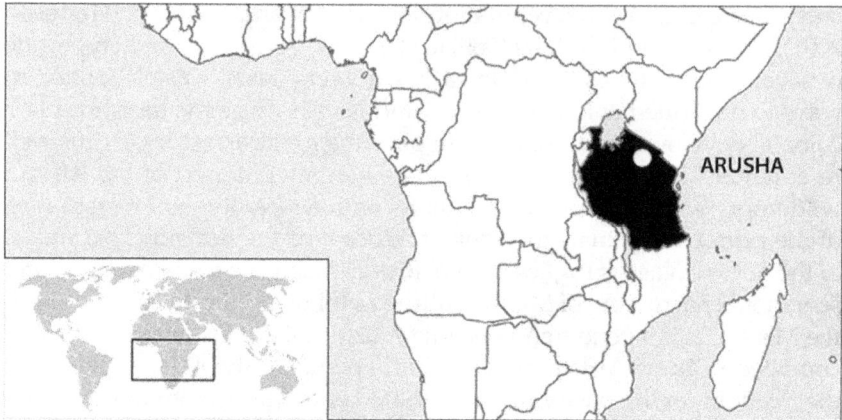

Figure 3.1 Map of Tanzania showing the Arusha region, where most Maasai live. (Multi-licence with GFDL and Creative Commons)

Imagined Maasai Indigeneity

Due to cultural representations that are circulating across the globe in countless coffee-table books, movies, snapshots, and websites, everybody seems to "know" the Maasai (Bruner 2001; Bruner and Kirshenblatt-Gimblett 1994; Salazar 2009a). The sight of a virile Maasai warrior dressed in colourful red blankets and beaded jewellery evokes the romantic image of a modern noble savage – a priceless tourism attraction. In fact, until recently Maasai were virtually the only ethnic group extensively used to represent the Tanzanian people on the one hand (e.g., in the global "Tanzania, Authentic Africa" campaign of the Tanzania Tourist Board) and to fulfil tourists' expectations to see "authentic" Africans on the other hand. Although over 120 different Indigenous groups populate the country, most foreign visitors only think of the Maasai as "local people" (Bachmann 1988; Spear and Waller 1993). As my participant observation and short interviews during safari tours through northern Tanzania confirmed, tourists want to catch a glimpse of *ilmurran* with their lion-hunting equipment (spears, clubs, and knives) and women decorated with beads and a child on their back in their most traditional "habitat." They not only want to set eyes on the Maasai, "as seen on television," but also want to immortalize the experience by taking pictures of or filming them and buying tangible souvenirs to be reminded of the "historical" encounter.

In conventional tourism circles, the Maasai have been represented as a unique and esoteric community that represents the essence of real Africa, namely as a people who have managed to resist Western influence and to retain their "exotic" culture. Ironically, it is the contact with Westerners that created this image in the first place. In earlier work (Salazar 2009a), I have detailed how contemporary representations draw heavily on colonial ones (cf. Salazar and Graburn 2014). The latter are constantly recycled in popular culture media forms (particularly books and movies and, increasingly, the Internet), which in turn influence tourism marketing. The large number of safari outlets drawing inspiration for their promotional materials or even their name from Karen Blixen's novelturned-into-movie *Out of Africa* nicely illustrates the representational overlap. Joseph Thomson's travelogue *Through Masai Land* (1885) has played a major role in disseminating the iconic image of the Maasai. In his book, which was translated into a number of languages, Thomson declared that large areas of Maasailand were uninhabited, ignoring seasonal transhumance by the Maasai migrating with their livestock. He condemned the Maasai for their apparently aimless wandering, a label that stuck and fatally influenced the colonial administration's view of pastoralists, yet the Maasai rightly saw Thomson as the aimless rover. Thomson's great ambivalence towards the Maasai – admiration and attraction (not least sexual) mingled with repugnance – would become a constant in many representations of the Maasai, including in tourism (Bruner 2001; Bruner and Kirshenblatt-Gimblett 1994).

Overseas tour operators and travel agents (and not only Western ones) keep marketing the Maasai as one of those extraordinary, mysterious Indigenous African communities that have remained untouched by the global forces of modernization. In most instances, foreign tourists, particularly those from North America and Europe, want to see Africans and the African landscape in the same way as they "saw" it during their formative years of image-moulding, when images of the black continent were usually based on information dating back to the colonial period (Wels 2002, 64). Akama (2002), who did a historical analysis of the development of the Maasai image and the representation of their culture in tourism, argues the latter has taken over colonial images to use Maasai culture as "additional anecdotes" in the safari experience. The romance of the safari pairs the viewing of wildlife with the scenes of nomadic Maasai.

Because of their worldwide image and their presence near the most popular game parks in the Serengeti-Mara ecosystem and tourism hotspots such as Arusha (Tanzania's "safari capital") and Moshi (foot of Mount Kilimanjaro), the Maasai are being both pushed and pulled into the front stage of tourism. This results in the apparent freezing or standstill of their culture. Their lasting place in tourists' imagination is partly due to the common belief that they still live in harmony with nature. While perhaps true to a degree, this idea leads to the attitude, reinforced by tourism advertising, that Maasai are part of the landscape, not so unlike wildebeest and zebras. Such representations of Indigenous Africans as a prototype of the "animal" were a creation of the colonizer's imagination. Based on racist ideologies (including social Darwinism) that were in vogue at the end of the nineteenth century, they underlay stereotypical "us" versus "them" categorizations.

Not treating Maasai as individuals is common practice among other ethnic groups in Tanzania. In one of the tour guide schools I frequented in Arusha, a tense discussion ensued one day when a Maasai student formally requested to be called by his name instead of being addressed always as "Maasai." Tanzanian tour guides (often from entrepreneurial ethnic groups such as the Chagga or the Haya) jokingly say that foreign visitors do not come to see the "Big Five" – a hunting term historically used to denote the five most dangerous African animals: lion, leopard, rhinoceros, elephant, and buffalo – but the "Big Six": the big five plus the Maasai. In reality, the same protected areas that draw tourists to view wildlife were often created by removing Maasai people from their previously inhabited lands (Neumann 1998).[5]

International tourism has quickly turned Maasai traditions into a cultural commodity, part of an all-inclusive package (Van der Cammen 1997). Many Maasai now portray "customary" versions of themselves for tourists, "to invoke the idea of a 'traditional' idyll which has been shattered by modernization" (Hughes 2006b, 4). Those not wanting to take part in the tourism game, often motivated by a strong desire to protect their culture, are forced to retreat to locations that are distant from the tourism circuit and are hard to reach (although no place is safe from "off the beaten track" travellers). One of the major predicaments is that so many of the traditional Maasai activities are now against the law, and precisely those illegal activities are most appealing to tourists.[6] Many Maasai, like other Indigenous groups, seem to be selling their own marginality. The fact that tourism stakeholders see them as an auxiliary to wildlife viewing strengthens the marginality argument regarding the Maasai as an object of tourism attraction. Were they not marginal to and (maximally) different from the visiting tourists, they would not have attracted the latter's attention (cf. Comaroff and Comaroff 2009).

In order to sustain such commodity status and to continue attracting visitors, Maasai have to maintain the difference (Bruner and Kirshenblatt-Gimblett 1994). They conceal blue jeans, watches, and cell phones behind spears, feathers, and other ornaments, or they take them off for the duration of the tourism performance. However, such a show, in order to sustain itself over time, has to be well disguised: it would be self-defeating if it were too blatant (Bruner 2001). Spears, clubs, jewellery, and artwork were initially just part of the Maasai culture. They normally produced them only for their own use but eventually discovered that it is worthwhile selling these objects to tourists. Nowadays, an extensive manufacturing system is set up to produce tourist art. They even sell used machetes and leaking calabashes used to transport milk to eagerly paying visitors. While Maasai artistry is being harnessed to meet the growing tourist souvenir market, age-old ceremonies are being turned into visitor shows. Culture has become a flexible form of capital to be used profitably and has to yield a return. As a result, an interlocking Maasai community with tourism maintains, defends, or contests some key societal institutions.

Some Maasai themselves have been accused of peddling falsehoods as a means of enticing foreign visitors (Salazar 2013). It is partly because of poverty, but more and more Maasai are exploiting the situation and, as some confessed to my Maasai research assistant, they do not mind fabricating untruths about their culture to make money. People in some areas have resorted to begging or seeking to be photographed for cash. They have become so aware of how to extract money from tourism that foreign visitors on occasion have been horrified at the boisterous and frantic attempts to be photographed and videoed, in exchange for hard currency. Although some Maasai certainly benefit from wildlife tourism revenues, "these riches have not been equitably shared beyond the county councils which manage the game parks in Maasai territory and powerful individuals and families, though some tourism profits are distributed to the community via Maasai-run wildlife associations" (Hughes 2006b, 175). Most of the profits go to the government (in the form of taxes) and an ever-increasing number of safari companies, many of which are foreign owned.

Maasai on the Move

The ancestors of the Maa-speaking people came to "settle" in Kenya and, later, in Tanzania from southern Sudan sometime during the first millennium CE (Hughes 2006b). Despite persisting images that heavily romanticize the Maasai's perceived freedom from authority and closeness to nature, they were forcibly relocated a number of times by the British colonial powers in Kenya (Hughes 2006b). Specialized pastoralism, historically at the core of Maasai cultural identity, has declined throughout the twentieth century (Homewood, Kristjanson, and Trench 2009; Spear and Waller 1993). While in the pre-colonial era, pastoralist migrations (ranging from daily herd movement to seasonal transhumance) were limited principally by disease and more occasionally by insecurity, colonial and post-colonial policies added the occupation of land by cultivators, wildlife, and new borders that impede "free" passage (Schneider 2006).

In addition to restrictive (post-)colonial policies that constrained Maasai movements (e.g., due to the creation and expansion of national parks), tourism has (economically) pushed many Maasai to lead a more sedentary life. For instance, a new development within *boma* (settlements) along heavily trodden touristic circuits is the permanent presence of warriors. The *ilmurran* play an important role in performing dances and seem to be extending their interests into the marketplace, whereas traditional practice stipulated that they live together in their own *manyatta*, a temporary camp in surrounding bush areas – a kind of liminal phase of life allowing them to detach themselves from their family and become independent, mature individuals (Ritsma and Ongaro 2002, 132). Nowadays, young Maasai men hang around the *bomas* and show off their recently gained social mobility and cosmopolitan capital by wearing socks and shoes, smoking cigarettes with filters, putting on watches, or, the ultimate symbol of mobility, using cell phones (all items that are habitually hidden the moment tourists show up). Paradoxically, their aspirations to upward social mobility – by becoming more modern and Western – can only materialize if they represent their life world to tourists as developing little or not at all (Salazar 2006).

While for semi-nomadic pastoralists such as the Maasai, herd mobility traditionally did not imply household mobility, entire Maasai families are now exploring new horizons. Environmental conditions, government policies, new technologies, and public services affect contemporary migration patterns. Some Maasai head south, going as far as Zambia, where they try to sell their medicines and their services as traditional healers; many more travel towards the big urban centres. In the coastal town of Dar es Salaam and on the beaches of Zanzibar, the places where most of the package tourists stay, there are many young Maasai. Attracted by potential employment opportunities, unemployed up-country Maasai have journeyed to these coastal areas to find risky, poorly paid, unskilled, casual work. Benefiting from their colonial image as fearless and warrior-like, they take up jobs as night watchmen or security guards, sell artefacts and adornments along the beach or in towns, and perform traditional dances in hotels.

In Zanzibar's Stone Town, for example, there are plenty of Maasai tourist art traders. They all migrated from the northern districts of Arusha and Kilimanjaro, following the tourist movements. Many of them were first employed as *walinzi* (guardians) in hotels. However, being extremely popular with tourists who tour the national parks, they became an attraction themselves and now perform for tourists. Most of them work in the souvenir trade and travel regularly between the mainland and Zanzibar. Quite a number of Maasai got into tourism in the mid-1990s, impelled by livestock losses from disease, severe drought, and land alienation. Interestingly, Zanzibari people produce most of Stone Town's Maasai or Maasai-style tourist art. Maasai men who produce beaded jewellery are a cultural oddity, because beading is a woman's task in Maasai culture. Recently, Tanzanian Maasai women also started migrating from Maasailand to Dar es Salaam and other cities, even as far as Zanzibar, Kampala, and Nairobi, producing and selling beads and traditional medicines for cash to support their families.

The new phenomenon of labour-related mobility and migration is indicative of an overall intensifying impoverishment of the Maasai (Coast 2002). Many Maasai blame the recent decline in economic circumstances on their generation's lack of schooling. Historically, Maasai shunned formal education, due both to their mobile lifestyle and because its relevance to pastoralism was not evident. This explains why so few Maasai end up working as tour guides, for instance, because this requires specialized education after finishing secondary school.

Young Maasai men who travel to the coast to become "beach boys" may expand the sense of roaming adventure long associated with their age grade, but elders are concerned about their moral decline from encounters with Western tourists (Hodgson 2001). These youngsters are often seen by other Maasai as deviants, likely to stay in town and become "lost" to the more traditional Maasai community (May 2003, 17). The new migrants usually profess little knowledge of and interest in the government's doings, a profound dislike for life in the city, and an expressed goal to earn enough to replenish their shrunken livestock herds and return home – a wish to remain pastoralists and politically as well as socio-culturally independent (Salazar 2011). Despite the strong Maasai cultural identity, they may cease to be pastoralists, at least in economic terms. As well as a lack of opportunities, perceptions of shame may constrain unsuccessful migrants from returning to their natal home or family.

Other Tanzanians express condescending views of Maasai migrants, typifying them as "unmodern" and as curious young warriors who are lazy, naive, drunk, and dirty (May and Ole Ikayo 2007). In Tanzania, as elsewhere, different categories of mobile people are clearly valued differently.[7] Although various policies have been developed over the last century to try to "develop" and settle the Maasai (Schneider 2006), their nomadic image is widely used as part of an instrumentalist agenda (including tourism advertising). Their marginalization has been at once material and discursive, because efforts by elites to disenfranchise Maasai and label them as "second-class citizens" have been buttressed by disparaging stereotypes of "the Maasai" as backwards, "traditional," and culturally conservative (Hodgson 2001).

Lacking political or social capital, many Maasai themselves manipulate and reinforce their Indigenous identity by continuing to wear traditional garments and engaging in practices that emphasize their difference from other Tanzanians. Maasai culture, while retaining its distinctiveness in stressful circumstances (e.g., by creating new forms of old "traditions" in urban settings), exhibits a multiple as well as a flexible nature. It is simultaneously both reproduced and contested, going against the lingering imaginaries of immutable and unreasoning Maasai "rigidity." Mirroring patterns of other migrant or subaltern groups throughout the world, Maasai are now intermarrying, adopting the languages and livelihoods of neighbouring communities, and participating in various national and international development activities. Increasing numbers of Maasai children are attending primary (and sometimes secondary) school and there is a rapidly growing group of well-educated urban(ized) Maasai, although there is still a very clear gender bias (Coast 2002).

Meeting "the Maasai"

Foreign tourists usually remain unaware of the broader political, economic, and sociocultural context in which contemporary Maasai are embedded. For them, the Maasai are simply part of the safari package they bought. If they meet Maasai, it is usually in lower-paid jobs, not as tour guides or safari drivers (strategic occupations because these people get to spend most time with foreign tourists, offering plenty of opportunities to subtly contest the imaginaries and ideas they have). During their stay, however, tourists are exposed to various types of "Maasainess." It already starts at the door of their lodge or hotel, where Maasai warriors (or, at least, men dressed like *ilmurran*) guarantee the safety of the property and its visitors. At a Maasai museum along the safari circuit, the museum guide dressed as an *ilmurran* takes visitors through the exhibition. His looks and the way he indexically shifts in his narrative from "we" to "they" and back indicate he is faking his identity.

My fieldwork observations confirmed that tourists usually do not realize that most of the "authentic" Maasai settlements they visit were specifically built for tourism purposes. Only the disproportionately large souvenir stalls somehow mark them as tourism places. These tourism *boma* were built by Maasai who live in neighbouring homesteads. In order to spread the tourism revenues more equally, some Maasai communities have worked out a rotating scheme determining who can stay when at the *boma*. In and around the Ngorongoro Crater, the Ngorongoro Conservation Area Authority controls the tourism activities of *boma*. Visits in this area along the safari highway often start with intense negotiations between Maasai and drivers or tour guides about the entrance fee (even if an agreement was reached a couple of years ago about a fixed price).

Then there are the cultural tours to Maasailand. In the summer of 2007, I accompanied a group of American tourists on a typical three-day visit to the area. On their first day, the group had a walking safari through the savannah. Their tour guide was not a Maasai but a Meru (an ethnic group, originally farmers, settled around the base of Mount Meru) from a neighbouring village. He never identified himself as such. One of the tourists was a general medical practitioner and very interested in knowing more about how the Maasai use local plants for medicinal purposes. The guide told her that the plants "they" (the Maasai) use have no real healing values but are just used because of tradition. When visiting a Maasai *boma*, he was unable to explain how the settlement is structurally organized. After a very brief introduction, he invited the group to "walk around and take pictures." Since the guide spoke no Maa and the Maasai present spoke little Swahili, an exchange of information was hardly possible. The next day, the group went on a camel safari. At the start, the Meru tour guide introduced all the camels by name. The accompanying Maasai men (one per camel), on the contrary, were never mentioned, let alone properly introduced.

The negative attitude of Meru people towards the Maasai has much to do with growing tensions over the fact that the land they share around the mountain is becoming overcrowded and overstocked. Meru working in tourism have an ambivalent relation to the Maasai. While some depend on commoditizing Maasai culture for a living, others try to carve out a separate Meru tourism niche in which they stress how different (read: more civilized) Meru are from Maasai. Neighbouring ethnic groups, such as the Arusha people, try to benefit from the tourist (mis)perception that they are Maasai.[8] During a cultural tour to an Arusha settlement, the European tourists I accompanied noticed red blankets on the bushes around the houses. They assumed these were Maasai garments that the women had just washed and were drying in the sun. Little did they know that neither the women who had washed the blankets nor the men who occasionally wear them in this village are actually Maasai. Once inside the hamlet, the Arusha guide explained to the group about the daily life and activities of the villagers that the visitors erroneously thought of as Maasai. The difference between Arusha and Maasai people and culture was never spelled out.

In fact, foreigners are curious to know whether the Maasai still exist, since news of their imminent extinction has been broadcast since the 1900s – via Sidney and Hildegarde Hinde's *The Last of the Masai* (1901) – and still abounds today (e.g., Taylor 2011). Some Maasai deliberately invoke this idea when calling for special protection as an Indigenous community within the nation state (Hughes 2006b). International cultural advocates have been struck by their adamant refusal to abandon their culture, and naturalists laud their ability to sustain balance with the environment, which allows them to coexist with their cattle and wild game. Ideas of Maasai traditionalism and conservatism are closely bound together with imaginaries of the Maasai male, alternately as a fierce warrior or obstinate pastoralist (Coast 2001). The portrayed ideal of people living exclusively from livestock keeping has always been difficult to achieve and tenuous to maintain. Nevertheless, it remains an essential element of Maasai identity, especially as projected to outsiders (Igoe 2006).

This globally circulating imaginary has helped the Maasai to become ambassadors of the global Indigenous movement (Hodgson 2011).

They are "by far the most prominent actors in Indigenous rights movements of East Africa, yet they are not, nor claim to be, 'first peoples' in the region since they migrated south into Kenya and northern Tanzania probably only in the last several hundred years" (Hodgson 2002, 1087). The first African Indigenous group to attend the United Nations Working Group on Indigenous Populations in 1989 was a Maasai group from Kenya. As Igoe explains, Indigenous identity in Africa "reflects the convergence of existing identity categories with shifting global structures of development and governance. Specifically, it reflects a combination of 'cultural distinctiveness' and effective strategies of extraversion in the context of economic and political liberalization" (2006, 399). It is thus not surprising that the Maasai, who are "culturally distinct," and who have a long tradition of enrolling outsiders in their cause, naturally lead this movement. In Tanzania, there can be no doubt that the pastoral ideal dominates the movement, even though increasing numbers of Maasai now practise agriculture – and many have for generations. Maa-speaking groups such as Parakuyo and Arusha who often previously sought to distinguish themselves from Maasai, now, at least in the company of foreigners (NGO workers and tourists alike), assert that they are "Maasai" (Hodgson 2002).

Indigenous Trap?

Through both tourism and the pursuit of Indigenous rights, many Maasai have discovered their culture's capacity to have an impact upon the global scene. Paradoxically, in the case of tourism, this has partially resulted in a loss of some of that culture's characteristics, mainly because tourism development is deeply embedded in Maasai cultural factors. Cultural narratives are ambivalent and can no longer exist without reference to tourism. Instead of providing an accurate representation of Maasai history and culture, tourism has continued to present the colonial images and stereotypes portraying the Maasai as a backward community that provide additional anecdotes to tourists seeking exoticism and adventure in the African wilderness. These kinds of imaginary are so powerful because "they not only enact but also construct peoples, places, and stories" (Bruner 2002, 387). The incorporation of *ilmurran* into an "economy of performance" for tourists evidences how the self-exploitation of one's own culture – "being-themselves-for others" – predominates where few economic alternatives prevail (Bruner and Kirshenblatt-Gimblett 1994).

When people occupy a contested space that they are striving to legitimize, they reproduce their identity through the confirmation of cultural imaginaries that speak to their conceptions of themselves and their interpretation of what they perceive to be outsiders' perceptions of them (Salazar and Graburn 2014). Therefore, uncoordinated tourism development presents an immense potential power to destroy Indigenous identities. According to Akama, "it can be argued that instead of tourism assisting to ameliorate social and economic problems that are confronting the Maasai, it has become part of the process of marginalization of the Maasai and the distortion of their historical and cultural values" (2002, 43). At the same time, tourism as well as the upholding of Indigenous rights has proved to be an integral part of the Maasai cultural process, and both provide institutionalized and prestigious forms through which these cultural and ideological processes can be mediated.

In tourism, culture is always reworked, repackaged, and reproduced for new audiences (Bruner 2001). This mediation of culture need not lead to homogenization (the "end of history" approach) but can instead create hybridization (whereby cultures learn and adapt from each other). While it ushers in modernization of local traditions, often making destinations unattractive to cultural tourists, tourism also leads to a movement of identity affirmation, variously called traditionalization, indigenization, or, in this case, Maasaiization. Besides, as this chapter has shown, tourism is far from being the only factor influencing Maasai culture and identity. History, politics, tourism, and Indigenous rights are all closely intertwined. While the Maasai outsider image remains relatively "immobile" (and this across the globe), the Maasai themselves are increasingly "on the move," in ways that go far beyond their stereotyped mobility as nomadic pastoralists.

There may be a monolithic romanticized, distorted, and exoticized image of the Maasai in international tourism and Indigenous rights discourses, but what is crucial for an understanding of Maasai culture and identity is to examine ethnographically the reality on the ground to determine how those global discourses and images are locally enacted and contested. Everybody seems to "know" the Maasai – with spears and shields dancing or charging across the open plains – at a time when these Indigenous communities are faced with political marginalization and are often being dispossessed of their land. The silent assertions that are partners of the explicit images through which they are conveyed suggest, wrongly, that pastoralists are unready to grasp the opportunities of modernization, are unproductive in their use of the rangelands, and represent unworthy trustees of the environmental resources of the great East African savannah (Galaty 2002).

NOTES

1 *Ilmurran* describes the stage in a Maasai youth's life when he has been circumcised and incorporated into the newest age set of junior warriors.
2 Anthropologists too have had their share in creating the image of Maasai culture as we know it. Representative colonial ethnological writings on the Maasai comprise Hollis's *The Masai: Their Language and Folklore* (1905), Merker's *The Masai: Ethnographic Monograph of an East African Semite People* (1910), Leakey's *Some Notes on the Masai of Kenya Colony* (1930), Fosbrooke's *An Administrative Survey of the Masai Social System* (1948) and Huntingford's *The Southern Nilo-Hamites* (1953).
3 This chapter is part of a larger research project in which I examine how local tourism actors and intermediaries in Tanzania represent their heritage to a global audience of tourists (Salazar 2006, 2009a, 2009b, 2010, 2012, 2013).
4 In 1959, with the establishment of Serengeti National Park, the Maasai who lived there were evicted and moved to the Ngorongoro Conservation Area. In 1974, they were forced to evacuate some parts of Ngorongoro as well, because their presence was believed to be detrimental to wildlife and landscape. In the 1980s, they faced further restrictions as the conservationist attitude of the government stiffened. In 2006, the Tanzanian government even gave an ultimatum to Maasai communities living inside Ngorongoro – around sixty thousand people – to vacate the area by the end of the year.
5 Other factors that have greatly contributed to transforming the Maasai way of life are trade, missionary activities, and, increasingly, new information and communication technologies (e.g., the use of mobile phones and the Internet).
6 The British banned, unsuccessfully, the practices of the *ilmurran* in 1921, and the post-colonial East African governments all have laws against lion hunting, cattle raiding, and female circumcision.
7 On the one hand, minority ethnic groups such as the Chagga (Mount Kilimanjaro area) and the Haya (area west of Lake Victoria) are looked up to for their lucrative trading networks across the country. On the other hand, colonial as well as post-colonial policies have equated pastoral nomads with backwardness – very similar to how the Romani and other Traveller people are treated in Europe or the Fulbe, Fulani, or Peul in West Africa.

8 The Arusha people are originally from the foothills of Mount Meru too. They are Maasai-related in that they have Maasai ancestry and they still use the Maasai age system and other elements of Maasai social organization. However, they have different clans and have long abandoned livestock herding in favour of settled cultivation.

REFERENCES

Akama, John S. 2002. "The Creation of the Maasai Image and Tourism Development in Kenya." In *Cultural Tourism in Africa: Strategies for the New Millennium*, edited by John S. Akama and Patricia Sterry, 43–53. Arnhem: Association for Tourism and Leisure Education.

Bachmann, Philipp. 1988. "The Maasai - Choice of East African Tourists - Admired and Ridiculed." In *Tourism: Manufacturing the Exotic*, edited by Pierre Rossel, 47–64. Copenhagen: International Work Group for Indigenous Affairs.

Bruner, Edward M. 2001. "The Maasai and the Lion King: Authenticity, Nationalism, and Globalization in African Tourism." *American Ethnologist* 28 (4): 881–908. http://dx.doi.org/10.1525/ae.2001.28.4.881.

Bruner, Edward M. 2002. "The Representation of African Pastoralists: A Commentary." *Visual Anthropology* 15 (3): 387–92.

Bruner, Edward M., and Barbara Kirshenblatt-Gimblett. 1994. "Maasai on the Lawn: Tourist Realism in East Africa." *Cultural Anthropology* 9 (4): 435–70. http://dx.doi.org/10.1525/can.1994.9.4.02a00010.

Coast, Ernestina. 2001. *Colonial Preconceptions and Contemporary Demographic Reality: Maasai of Kenya and Tanzania*. London: University College, Human Ecology Research Group.

Coast, Ernestina. 2002. "Maasai Socioeconomic Conditions: A Cross-Border Comparison." *Human Ecology* 30 (1): 79–105. http://dx.doi.org/10.1023/A:1014567029853.

Comaroff, John L., and Jean Comaroff. 2009. *Ethnicity, Inc*. Chicago: University of Chicago Press. http://dx.doi.org/10.7208/chicago/9780226114736.001.0001.

Galaty, John G. 2002. "How Visual Figures Speak: Narrative Inventions of "the Pastoralist" in East Africa." *Visual Anthropology* 15 (3-4): 347–67. http://dx.doi.org/10.1080/08949460213910.

Hodgson, Dorothy L. 2001. *Once Intrepid Warriors: Gender, Ethnicity, and the Cultural Politics of Maasai Development*. Bloomington: Indiana University Press.

Hodgson, Dorothy L. 2002. "Precarious Alliances: The Cultural Politics and Structural Predicaments of the Indigenous Rights Movement in Tanzania."

American Anthropologist 104 (4): 1086–97. http://dx.doi.org/10.1525/
aa.2002.104.4.1086.

Hodgson, Dorothy L. 2011. *Being Maasai, Becoming Indigenous: Postcolonial Politics in a Neoliberal World*. Bloomington: Indiana University Press.

Homewood, Katherine, Patricia Kristjanson, and Pippa Trench. 2009. *Staying Maasai? Livelihoods, Conservation, and Development in East African Rangelands*. London: Springer.

Hughes, Lotte. 2006a. "'Beautiful Beasts' and Brave Warriors: The Longevity of a Maasai Stereotype." In *Ethnic Identity: Problems and Prospects for the Twenty-First Century*, edited by Lola Romanucci-Ross, George A. de Vos, and Takeyuki Tsuda, 246–94. Lanham: Altamira.

Hughes, Lotte. 2006b. *Moving the Maasai: A Colonial Misadventure*. Basingstoke: Palgrave Macmillan.

Igoe, Jim. 2006. "Becoming Indigenous Peoples: Difference, Inequality, and the Globalization of East African Identity Politics." *African Affairs* 105 (420): 399–420. http://dx.doi.org/10.1093/afraf/adi127.

Knowles, Joan, and David Collett. 1989. "Nature as Myth, Symbol and Action: Notes towards a Historical Understanding of Development and Conservation in Kenyan Maasailand." *Africa: Journal of the International Africa Institute* 59 (4): 433–60. http://dx.doi.org/10.2307/1159941.

May, Ann. 2003. Maasai migrations: Implications for HIV/AIDS and social change in Tanzania. In *Population Aging Center Working Paper*. Boulder: University of Colorado, Institute of Behavioral Science.

May, Ann, and Francis N. Ole Ikayo. 2007. "Wearing Illkarash: Narratives of Image, Identity and Change among Maasai Labour Migrants in Tanzania." *Development and Change* 38 (2): 275–98. http://dx.doi.org/10.1111/j.1467-7660.2007.00412.x.

Merker, M. 1910. *The Maasai: Ethnographic Monograph of an East African Semite People*. Berlin: Dietrich Reimer. http://dx.doi.org/10.5479/sil.120833. 39088000479063.

Neumann, Roderick P. 1998. *Imposing Wilderness: Struggles over Livelihood and Nature Preservation in Africa*. Berkeley: University of California Press.

Ritsma, Nanda, and Stephen Ongaro. 2002. "The Commodification and Commercialisation of the Maasai Culture: Will Cultural Manyattas Withstand the 21st Century?" In *Cultural Tourism in Africa: Strategies for the New Millennium*, edited by John S. Akama and Patricia Sterry, 127–36. Arnhem: Association for Tourism and Leisure Education.

Salazar, Noel B. 2006. "Touristifying Tanzania: Global Discourse, Local Guides." *Annals of Tourism Research* 33 (3): 833–52. http://dx.doi.org/10.1016/j.annals.2006.03.017.

Salazar, Noel B. 2009a. "Imaged or Imagined? Cultural Representations and the "Tourismification" of Peoples and Places." *Cahiers d'Études Africaines* 49 (193–4): 49–71.

Salazar, Noel B. 2009b. "A Troubled Past, a Challenging Present, and a Promising Future? Tanzania's Tourism Development in Perspective." *Tourism Review International* 12 (3–4): 259–73.

Salazar, Noel B. 2010. *Envisioning Eden: Mobilizing Imaginaries in Tourism and Beyond; New Directions in Anthropology.* Oxford: Berghahn.

Salazar, Noel B. 2011. "Tanzanian Migration Imaginaries." In *Migration and Culture*, edited by Robin Cohen and Gunvor Jónsson, 673–87. Cheltenham: Edward Elgar.

Salazar, Noel B. 2012. "Community-Based Cultural Tourism: Issues, Threats and Opportunities." *Journal of Sustainable Tourism* 20 (1): 9–22. http://dx.doi.org/10.1080/09669582.2011.596279.

Salazar, Noel B. 2013. "Seducation: Learning the Trade of Tourism Enticement." In *Tourism and the Power of Otherness*, edited by David Picard and Michael A. Di Giovine, 110–23. Bristol: Channel View.

Salazar, Noel B., and Nelson H.H. Graburn, eds. 2014. *Tourism Imaginaries: Anthropological Approaches.* Oxford: Berghahn. http://dx.doi.org/10.1007/978-3-319-01669-6_267-1.

Schneider, Leander. 2006. "The Maasai's New Clothes: A Developmentalist Modernity and Its Exclusions." *Africa Today* 53 (1): 101–31. http://dx.doi.org/10.1353/at.2006.0063.

Spear, Thomas T., and Richard Waller. 1993. *Being Maasai: Ethnicity and Identity in East Africa.* London: James Currey.

Taylor, Darren. 2011. "Pastoralists of Northern Tanzania Face Extinction, Say Activists." *Voice of America*, 8 April 2011. Available from https://www.voanews.com/a/pastoralists-of-northern-tanzania-face-extinction-say-activists--119488944/160053.html (accessed 4 July 2017).

Thomson, Joseph. 1885. *Through Masailand.* London: Sampson Low, Marston, Searle and Rivington.

Van der Cammen, Sylvia. 1997. "Involving Maasai Women." In *The Earthscan Reader in Sustainable Tourism*, edited by Lesley France, 162–3. London: Earthscan.

Wels, Harry. 2002. "A Critical Reflection on Cultural Tourism in Africa: The Power of European Imagery." In *Cultural Tourism in Africa: Strategies for the New Millennium*, edited by John S. Akama and Patricia Sterry, 55–66. Arnhem: Association for Tourism and Leisure Education.

4 The Alchemy of Tourism: From Stereotype and Marginalizing Discourse to Real in the Space of Tourist Performance

KAREN STOCKER

A multigenerational secret society of academics devised the fictional realms of "Tlön, Uqbar, Orbis Tertius" in Jorge Luis Borges's short story by the same name. Their meticulously woven encyclopedic writings on the existence of this fabricated region eventually took over official history in school curriculum, thus obscuring its invention and rendering the place real in collective consciousness. Inhabitants of Tlön are familiar with "*hrönir*," a made-up concept referring to copies of lost items, with the unique characteristic that the duplicate seems more real to people than the original might have (Borges 1962, 30). I argue that this sort of cultural alchemy and corresponding conversion of scholarly representation into impetus for cultural genesis occurs in the space of heritage tourism for the Chorotega of Costa Rica. Through presentation of choreographed performances of indigeneity originally created for tourist audiences, and through documentation of those presentations, such performances have transformed images drawn from the social sciences, media, other Indigenous peoples, and stereotypes into meaningful symbols taken as emblematic of Chorotega indigeneity and broadcast as current reality.

For this group, courting tourism as a viable economic alternative to more exploitative sources of employment has entailed the use of stereotypical images drawn from the media, from conquistadors' chronicles, and from social science discourse. While such images have not always resonated with realities lived by inhabitants of the Chorotega Indigenous Territory, through performance for tourist audiences these emblems of indigeneity have become meaningful to insiders. This stereotypical imagery-turned-real, in keeping with outsider expectations of what indigeneity might look like, adorns a meeting hall originally crafted for tourists that has since become the site of nation building, community building, solidarity with a pan-Indian community, cultural revival, and transformative performance. In the crucible of cultural tourism, or at least the hope of it, discourses written by outsiders and wrought with stereotype have morphed into actuality as they have been performed as real and have taken on meaning by insiders. Through these changes, and in keeping with theoretical considerations of the transformative nature of performance, the Chorotega have managed to recentre powerful discourses about themselves and use those to present a strategic public image.

Focusing on active exertion of agency and the Chorotegas' efforts towards self-representation, this chapter engages a decolonizing framework. It focuses on "Indigenous representation taking place through tourism" (Bunten and Graburn, this volume) and touristic movements, given that it is tourism, broadly envisioned, that has provided the space for self-representation. Initially, this context held promise for economic benefits, and led to a strategic display of Indigenous identity in keeping with tourist expectations of what that might look like. In some ways, this has required a reduction from the complexity of performers' lives to the presentation of stereotype. Yet it may also allow for locals to refashion the popular imaginary of Indigenous peoples today. Moreover, these efforts to draw from intellectual and media portrayals of themselves, but to turn those to the their own interests, thereby informing popular ideas about their indigeneity, in turn have provided the springboard for entering into a social movement geared towards Indigenous autonomy. In short, the tourist context did not deliver the economic benefits locals expected of it, but it did allow for the mobilization of a strategic public identity. Moreover, it turned a space built for tourism into a site of political mobilization, self-representation, self-discovery, and cultural innovation and revitalization.

Representing Indigeneity

For the Chorotega of Costa Rica, Indigenous identity was not always tantamount to economic opportunity. In fact, for most of the group's post-colonial existence, the Indigenous label has led to discrimination and exploitation, and for that reason, many locals masked Indigenous tradition and identity.[1] The Costa Rican government demarcated Indigenous Territories (akin to reservations) in the 1970s, thus countering predominant historical presentations of the nation as devoid of

Indigenous peoples since prior to colonization. Through establishment of the reservation system, the government recognized eight tribes, including the Chorotega. For all practical purposes, however, federal recognition of Indigenous peoples is accorded only to those who reside within the official Indigenous Territories, rather than their relatives or individuals of similar ethic heritage residing outside the official territories. As well, while community members are federally recognized as Indigenous, legally speaking, the nation's museums and history books tend to relegate them to the past, thus denying them recognition as contemporary, living Indigenous peoples. This has had serious implications for their access to resources, the pan-Indigenous community of Costa Rica, and political processes. In recent years, following decades of exclusion rooted in that same erasure, they have been included in and participate in pan-Indigenous movements and activities on a national scale.

As of 2014, the Chorotega Indigenous Territory is home to approximately fifteen hundred people, although this number fluctuates in accordance with urban migration for purposes of employment. While in the pre-contact era the Chorotega enjoyed high status, as evident in an archaeological record rich in objects denoting leadership and wealth, in the current era the community has struggled against widespread discrimination (see Stocker 2005) and lack of economic opportunities. Their economic standing, mixed with a long history of marginalization by neighbouring communities and, until recently, the pan-Indigenous community, has led to a state of marginalization.

I have been witness to this history of marginalization and recent changes throughout my interactions with this community over the course of more than twenty years. My relationship to the collaborators in this research began over two decades ago as a professional one. From 1993 to the present, that research connection has become thoroughly infused with, if not superseded by, deep friendships and kin-like relationships. However, when I am specifically collecting ethnographic data, I am careful to abide by the ethical practices of my discipline in obtaining informed consent. In keeping with the wishes of a community damaged long ago by written documentation trumping verbal agreements (and in a decision supported by the internal review boards of the universities that approved my research), I have obtained verbal (rather than written) informed consent. The majority of the research documented in this chapter stems from ethnographic fieldwork carried out in 2009, for which I conducted interviews and participant observation of the tourist context specifically. I have continued to follow up on this line of research annually, through 2013.

This research showed that in contrast to the Chorotega Indigenous Territory's history of masking indigeneity as a survival strategy for self-defence against discrimination, a context of international tourism has led to a revaluing of indigeneity on both national and regional levels. The neighbouring town that for years discriminated most consistently against inhabitants of the Chorotega Indigenous Territory now courts its residents' performances to enhance touristic offerings. It was this lure of economic promise (as yet unrealized) that led leaders of the Indigenous Territory to keep tourists in mind in community-planning efforts. Most small communities in Costa Rica have a meeting hall in which to hold dances, community-wide meetings, and other events. The Chorotega Indigenous Territory is no different in that regard. Yet while this space constitutes a site for nationalistic civic acts, it is also home to events specific to Indigenous heritage. The latter use, however, is relatively new.

In 1998, when the light-blue paint was peeling off the wooden building that served as a gathering space, its corrugated tin roof was rusted, and the place was proving too small for the community's population growth, the local leadership decided to replace it. Local leaders opted to hold an *empajo* – something akin to a barn raising – not only to build a new hall but to give it a thatched roof. Community members came out in force, from all factions of the village, to offer labour, sweat, traditional knowledge (of building thatched roof *ranchos* and of cooking Chorotega foods for builders), and community spirit. The results included both an enormous meeting hall built and thatched in the fashion traditional to the Chorotega and the renewed interjection of traditional knowledge into circulation for a younger generation. This was perhaps the springboard for a nascent cultural revival that gained momentum in later years. When the thatched roof of that hall was beginning to decay, in 2004, the leadership reconvened to discuss the shape a new meeting hall might take.

The elected leadership sought the expertise of artist Mario Guitiérrez Garita, known as Mario Garita, whose vision has kept Indigenous imagery present in sculpture and public spaces throughout the region. Garita provided not only artistic vision and skill but also historical knowledge to the community. At the same time as he worked on sculpting adorned columns and friezes on the building, he met with youth from the Indigenous Territory. In those sessions, he distributed and discussed social science articles, historical sources, and the conquistadors' chronicles of the region. His lessons – both considering the community as written about by outsiders and urging youth to take pride in their indigeneity – were influential among the Indigenous Territory's young people. In my interviews of them in 2009, several of those who had participated in Garita's sessions made clear that his teachings had a notable effect on the ways in which they viewed themselves and their community. His influence was an important element in shifting the general tenor of the community from stigma to pride in Indigenous heritage. His views on the matter are also evident in the artistic renderings of indigeneity that adorn the new meeting hall.[2]

Images sculpted in cement and intermingling with the very structure of the building include some drawn from other Indigenous peoples of the Americas, some from commonly held (and at times stereotypical) beliefs about Indigenous peoples in general, and some that speak to local Chorotega and *mestizo* experiences. Many members of the community wanted to put a new thatched roof on the hall, but external constraints (such as relative scarcity and high cost of palm) rather than internal identity have made that impossible so far. Taken as a whole – stereotypical assumptions, inaccessibility to traditional resources, and all – these images speak to the realities of the current-day Chorotega of Costa Rica. Like the *hrönir* of Borges' invented realm, more of these images acknowledge outsider expectations of what Indigenous experience and arts ought to look like than they do the experiences of those who reside in the Indigenous Territory. This array of images also reflects the desire of some community members to be associated with pan-indigeneity. Other community members may see them more or less uncritically, accepting them as the vision of a single artist rather than as the representation of a people.

Sculpted images of plants and animals convey the oft-held belief (true or not) that Indigenous peoples are closer to nature than non-Indigenous peoples.[3] Guarding the door is a jaguar, said by Garita to symbolize the "spirit of conservation" of Indigenous peoples, at the same time that it evokes imagery mentioned in the chronicles written by conquistadors (Figure 4.1).[4] The writings of chronicler Francisco Oviedo y Valdés describe the pre-Colombian Chorotega men as tattooed with the image of a jaguar on one shoulder, a tradition long since gone (Fernández Guardia 1913, 7–8; León Fernández 1975, 37). Emblems from Aztec, Mayan, Olmec, and Toltec traditions and from an unspecified South American shamanic tradition also adorn the building (Figures 4.2 and 4.3).

Figure 4.1 Sculpted jaguar, by Mario Garita. (Copyright: Karen Stocker)

Figure 4.2 Sculptor Mario Garita's representations of indigeneity of the Americas through the use of Mayan glyphs and the Aztec deity Quetzalcoatl. (Copyright: Karen Stocker)

These emblems seemingly place the Chorotega within a larger, pan-Indian context at the same time as they present imagery more recognizable to outsiders as Indigenous than images drawn from actual Chorotega imagery might be. Indeed, only three images speak specifically to Chorotega tradition, and these will likely not be apparent as such to outsiders. The image of a plant from which is derived the Indigenous Territory's Mangue-language name, a traditional kitchen scene common not only to inhabitants of the Indigenous Territory but also to *mestizo* rural dwellers of this area, and an Olmec jade pendant like those common to the region's archaeological record and to the Chorotega through pre-Colombian trade make tacit reference to this place's own history. Yet in greater proportion, artistic renderings of indigeneity speak to Indigenous traditions native to other regions or tribes or to a generalized, stereotypical notion of indigeneity. In a similar vein to symbols of proximity to nature, images of topless women (Figure 4.2)

Figure 4.3 Sculptor Mario Garita's representation of a South American shaman figure. (Copyright: Karen Stocker)

and men in loincloths speak to stereotypical images that members of this community battled for years.

Like Borges' *hrönir*, the symbols that are less close to the actual experience of the Chorotega are those more likely to be read by outsiders as emblematic of Indigenous experience. Writing of Native Americans of North America, Melissa Meyer (1999, 241) alludes to romanticized images having replaced realistic depictions in the minds of non-Native Americans. Likewise, images drawn from more publicized and more readily recognized Mesoamerican Indigenous peoples, and icons that resonate with outsiders' stereotypes, are more likely to seem "real" to visitors. Indeed, as Urry (2002, 77) warns, they may seem "more real than the real." Were this building with its array of images to exist outside an official Indigenous Territory, perhaps viewers would question its veracity as Indigenous. Placed within an Indigenous Territory, however, it takes on an air of less-questionable reality.

Cultural Gatherings and Performances: Nationalistic and Autonomous Uses of Communal Space

Just as the meeting hall evokes Borges' *hrönin*, it also conjures up another concept from Borges' fabricated universe. Borges' secret academic society conspiring to bring into existence a fiction taken as truth wrote also of the *ur*, which represents the hope of an imagined future (Borges 1962, 30). When local leadership first entertained discussions of the new meeting hall, they intended it to draw tourists. This plan informed the reasons that a community that for so long had masked Indigenous practice and imagery would come to place it centre stage. A pamphlet distributed at the inauguration of the meeting hall in 2004 explained the style of the meeting hall as an attempt to value the community's Indigenous roots and place the community in a position of "rescuing the roots of our culture, to identify it as such, and to place this reservation in a Historical, Cultural, and Touristic position on a global scale." Clearly, cultural maintenance and revival existed as complementary goals to touristic development and to the attainment of global renown or recognition. The brochure also reveals that leadership hoped that promotion of tourism, through the building of this meeting hall in a way that might attract outsiders, would "facilitate [meeting] the needs of the rest of the community."

Although the hope of tourism spurred the construction of the meeting hall in a particular style, and while it also inspired the revitalization of some dance practices and new choreography of others, tourism has yet to come about in the Chorotega Indigenous Territory. Local dancers have performed for tourist audiences outside of the Indigenous Territory (hired by a nearby coffee plantation tour), a smattering of domestic tourists have attended festivals in the Indigenous Territory, and approximately four student groups from the United States have visited for educational and volunteer tourism. However, the global economic downturn led to a dramatic decline in tourism throughout Costa Rica just as heritage tourism and rural tourism were gaining currency within the nation's official institute of tourism (ICT). Had the recession not been as devastating to tourism in Costa Rica as it was, perhaps heritage tourism in the Chorotega Indigenous Territory might have gotten off the ground. As it stands, plans for tourism within the Chorotega Indigenous Territory remain indefinitely inchoate. In the meantime, visits by other Indigenous groups from Costa Rica have increased, as have uses of that communal space more in keeping with the sort that occurs inside any rural Costa Rican meeting hall as well as those specific to Indigenous experiences. Thus, while tourists have yet to visit the community in any kind of consistent manner or with reliable frequency, this building has served as a place to meet community needs in a variety of ways.

The paired goals of cultural revival and economic gain, though not yet fully realized, have already been enacted. In this space, community members have engaged in nationalistic activities (such as the celebration of Independence Day in ways that it might also be celebrated throughout the country, in non-Indigenous settings) as well as events more closely tied to this specific Indigenous community. Community-building events have taken various forms. In 2009, I observed numerous occasions on which that hall served to bring people together in ways that cultivated respect for and revival and maintenance of cultural practices.

A festival of corn sponsored by local leadership provided a context in which local educators elaborated on the importance of corn in Chorotega history, citing social science discourse on the matter alongside ancestral experience. Also at that event, activists encouraged local farmers to continue to plant seed corn from their own harvest and avoid transgenic varieties. Although the activists in question were not from the Indigenous Territory, locals were receptive and in agreement.[5] Women from the Indigenous Territory, experts in Chorotega culinary tradition based on corn, sold foods there. Artists from the area also marketed wares infused with local imagery (as I shall discuss shortly). In a later event, a regional offshoot of the Ministry of Culture and Youth, in conjunction with local leadership, organized an annual festival of Chorotega culture in which similar themes and products were displayed and celebrated. While these two events were for the benefit of both insiders and outsiders, other gatherings benefited locals alone.

In 2009, the regional director of the Ministry of Culture and Youth organized a presentation by bank officials in a meeting about microlending to support small-scale entrepreneurs (sometimes to enable their production of traditional goods or foods prepared in a traditional manner). In subsequent years, the hall has provided space for classes promoting good nutrition and physical fitness. These classes, sponsored by the national health care service, instructed locals on ways to combat growing health concerns such as diabetes and obesity, and offered lectures for women on self-esteem. The meeting hall has also constituted a classroom for a course about local culture.[6] Also held there in 2009 was a community-wide meeting led by the locally elected government to inform the community of its actions and plans and seek community input on these. Although such meetings are standard for locally elected governments throughout Costa Rica, a unique element of this one was that the president of the Indigenous Territory's governing body repeatedly used an emergent language of sovereignty. This reflects a change in local leadership as well as participation in a current movement within Costa Rica's pan-Indigenous community. In particular, recent mentions of sovereignty are linked to Indigenous efforts in recent years to pressure legislators to approve a law regarding Indigenous autonomy.

In that space, too, in addition to solidifying community plans and enacting their role as part of both the nation and an Indigenous movement seeking autonomy, inhabitants of the Chorotega Indigenous Territory have engaged with other Indigenous communities or their representatives. In so doing, they are seeking solidarity within the pan-Indian community from which they were long excluded.[7] This is evident in use of the hall as a meeting ground for representatives of different Indigenous groups, but also performances of other Indigenous traditions, as took place during the annual cultural festival, in which the oral histories of the Cabécar Indigenous community were performed through puppetry. In the midst of that performance, a community member sidled over to me and whispered that the Chorotega could do the same using oral histories I recorded and wrote down years ago (Stocker 1995). The Chorotega's location within the pan-Indian community of Costa Rica was also apparent in discussions of the salience of corn in Indigenous narrative during the festival of corn. One of these drew tacitly from oral histories about corn from the Bribrí Indigenous Territory, and from conversations with me about the same.

The Transformative Nature of Performance

Through building a structure in order to attract tourists to a place where traditional goods are sold and practices performed, and by infusing that building with imagery meant to display indigeneity easily recognized by outsiders, it is as if the community meeting hall possesses performative qualities. Through this building, as well as through the events that have taken place within it, the transformative nature of performance has been evident. Existing anthropological literature regarding the potential of performance (in the case of narrative practices) to bring about change in the society it describes may be applied to the realm of performance of culture for a touristic audience. In the sphere of narrative practice, storytelling may "change people's ideas about themselves," leading to change in behaviour (Basso 1996, 60). Furthermore, the context of performance and the relationship among performers and audience may undergo a shift. According to Briggs (1988, 15), "Performance features do not merely reflect situational factors; rather, they interpret the social interaction, thus opening up the possibility of transforming its very nature." By invoking social science and historical discourse about their own people in events held inside the meeting hall, local educators and speakers may draw from relationships shot through with power differentials, such as those of conqueror to descendants of the conquered or academician to the people studied. Presenters thus turn on their head such differences in power, reclaiming subjectivity as authorship.

Along similar lines, and also focusing on the performative sphere, Bauman (2001, 183) writes about a man of marginal status who, through oral performance, situates himself at the centre of social structure. As Bauman (1990, 76) notes of verbal art, "to decontextualize and recontextualize texts is thus an act of control." Translating this dynamic to the realm of performance in which local life is exhibited for outsider or tourist audiences (as it is in the meeting hall, and as the meeting hall itself may do), it is here that we see a community exerting agency and developing and engaging a decolonizing framework. By virtue of creating a space that uses visual imagery to contextualize the Chorotega among more widely known Indigenous peoples of the Americas, the artist and the community members that sought and approved the artist's work reposition themselves. No longer are they placed on the margins of a pan-Indigenous community; rather, they are central to it. By extension, through hosting other Indigenous communities, they solidify this strategy.

Bauman (1990, 69) calls upon scholars to attend to the "multiplicity of indexical connections that enable verbal art to transform, not simply reflect, social life." Through the community's current and deliberate use of symbolism that were once deemed stereotypical images to be overcome, inhabitants of the Chorotega Indigenous Territory are doing just this. They are actively transforming and resituating their social location within the Costa Rican pan-Indigenous community. On a regional level this has resulted in that pan-Indigenous community beginning to invite Chorotega participation rather than deride it. Such efforts began with the appointment of a local teacher of culture in 2000, funded by the Ministry of Education's Department of Indigenous Education, and her connections to teachers of culture from other Indigenous Territories.[8] In subsequent years, this intercultural exchange has been supported by the Ministry of Culture and Youth as well as spearheaded by local leaders and by youth through the use of social media. On an international level, this recontextualization places the Chorotega in a better position to draw in tourists than their neighbouring villages might enjoy. Indeed, it was the promise of tourism that led to this reconfiguration to begin with, and it is within this realm that we might see, as Bauman urges us to do, that "performance is a mode of social production" (Bauman 1990, 76).

Other authors, attending to the realm of tourism specifically, have noted that performances invented, reinvented, or staged for tourist audiences may indeed take on a real quality or become meaningful, over time, for performers of local life. For many toured Indigenous peoples, performances of traditional customs may boost revival of those practices (Brandes 2006, 70; Bruner 2005, 79, 119; Chambers 2000, 55, 81; Deloria 1998, 146–8; Erikson 2003, 537; Hiwasaki 2000, 396; Ingles 2010, 240–4; Nesper 2003, 464; Stronza 2010, 299; WTO 1998, 129; Yamashita 2003, 109). Moreover, various authors note that performing culture may lead to a renewal of ethnic pride among performers or those of the same background as performers (Bruner 2005, 48; Stronza 2010, 299; WTO 1998, 129). Both of these observations have held true in the Chorotega Indigenous Territory. At the same time that a revival of arts and customs is afoot, some of the imagery that is evident in the building itself also infuses arts performed or sold at events in the meeting hall. These images, too, draw from social science and historical discourse and are mediated through the lens of television imagery, including stereotypes. Yet they have taken on new meaning when used deliberately by artists representing themselves and their own people rather than being depicted by outsiders.

Artistic Licence and the Refashioning of Stereotypes through Dance and Visual Arts

At the 2009 annual cultural festival, a young man performed a stylized dance choreography inspired by a ritual from the past in which people used fire to purify their homes and their bodies. He performed dressed in a loincloth adorned with earthy, nature-based imagery, and with body paint in the style of Hollywood Western (mis)representations of US Plains Indians. While the chronicles do describe the Chorotega in the time of European contact as painted, the descriptions available to the choreographer were less thorough, and it is probable that more accessible images of painted Indians (such as those presented on television) influenced this interpretation.[9] An audience member's shout of "Geronimoooo!" upon seeing the dancer come on stage suggested that US media also influenced that Chorotega man's interpretation of this visual imagery. A local singer-songwriter, whose song about the Chorotega Indigenous Territory has lent it status, accompanied the dancer's performance. Furthermore, the singer and dancer carried out this performance in front of a banner from the Ministry of Culture that depicted this same dancer performing this same dance, thereby doubly enforcing its legitimacy as official culture. While the dancer was, in fact, performing stereotype, it was an image that may have become meaningful to some locals through its ability to index and embody expectations of indigeneity (even if not their lived reality).

Former members of the same dance group offered varied reflections on this choreography. One young man recognized that inside the Indigenous Territory, people might not respond with great enthusiasm to this dance. When they performed it outside that territory, however, he had seen it bring people to tears. It appeared to be transformative for audience members just as it transformed local dancers. Another former performer, who listed technological advances and modern conveniences that made her question whether the community still counted as

Indigenous, alluded to this one dance as evidence of Chorotega herit-age. Although she had been part of the dance group when the dance was first choreographed, and therefore saw its beginnings, to her the dance had become real, and seemingly rooted in the distant past. There, as in the realm described by Borges, "Such was the first intrusion of the fantastic world into the real one" (Borges 1962, 32). The dance had become emblematic of ethnic persistence in the Chorotega Indigenous Territory. This was the alchemy of performance.

A choreographed piece performed by someone from an Indigenous Territory appeared to verify the assumption that a person from there would dress in that way. It was a self-reinforcing cycle of authenticity: place – by virtue of official status of the land, as an Indigenous Ter-ritory, on which its performers reside – made this dance Indigenous (whereas enacted by anyone else, it might be seen as parody). In turn, the dance came to legitimate that place as Indigenous. For that reason, young people from the community, who were not performers but audi-ence members, had mixed reviews.

Some worried that the dance would solidify people's stereotypical assumptions that people from the Indigenous Territory wear loincloths or live in a way dramatically different from people in neighbouring communities. Whether performing in loincloths would affirm stereo-types or be seen merely as a costume worn for the sake of performance, the transformative potential of this performance, as presenting reality to outsiders in a way that did not conform to insider views of lived experience, was clear. Some disapproved out of a fear that it could bring into being a distorted perception of reality. Another young person did not claim to know if the dance reflected truth or not. She recognized that the choreographer drew from social science and historical articles to lend veracity to the rendition; her uncertainty was rooted in televised media. She said she didn't have an opinion on the dance because she had never seen a "real Indian," except on US television. Though she herself identified as Indigenous, it was television that defined what that ought to look like, and not matching that image somehow made her own experience less "real." This phenomenon of media-based images and those from social science making their way back into present real-ity also became evident through visual arts.

In the festival of corn, more than one local artist sold carved gourds. Among the hollowed, dried gourds carved by a certain artist was one hand-engraved with the image of a bare-breasted Indigenous woman grinding corn on a *metate*. Had the woman depicted been fully clothed, as women in the community are when they carry out this task, she might not have been recognizable as Indigenous to viewers beholden to particular (inaccurate) visual cues of indigeneity. Another gourd crafted by the same artist bore the image of a shaman, in keeping with designs apparent on pottery from the pre-Columbian era. This image may well have come from photocopies of archaeological works distributed by the sculptor, as his packet of materials included such sources. Another carver of gourds sold one that depicted a man looking across a field at a ghost, drawn not as ghosts are described in Chorotega oral histories, but as they are often depicted in US cartoons – as a person covered in a sheet. Also engraved on the gourd was a phrase remarkably similar to the title of my book about oral histories from the Chorotega Indigenous Territory.[10] In these cases, as with the design of the community's meeting hall, it seemed that social science discourse purporting to reflect past culture was infusing present manifestations of it, and was embellished in conformity with outsiders' expectations in order to make it more readable as Indigenous imagery. Like Borges' *hrönir*, the duplicates were made to seem more real to an outsider audience than the originals.

Mediated Indigeneity

I have argued elsewhere (Stocker 2009, 67) that the same media that shape tourists' expectations of what Indigenous people look like or do also influence local views of indigeneity in this context in which local practices were forcibly curtailed in the colonial era. In 2007, I saw a child in the Chorotega Indigenous Territory watch the television show *Survivor*, complete with a "tribal council" that represents "tribalness" in a way that is foreign to this Indigenous community. In fact, I saw a child watch this scene while an actual meeting of the Indigenous Territory's tribal council was taking place in the meeting hall, without any of television's artifice or visual cues of tribal belonging. Three years later, the same young girl talked about her DVD of *The Three Stooges*, noting that the funniest episode is "the one with the Indians," no doubt rife with exaggerated visual stereotypes to get that point across.

This juxtaposition of television-based, "mediated" Indians and living ones was apparent once again in 2011. I had just participated in a discussion of a recent newspaper article about the supposed disappearance of the Chorotega, a conclusion the journalist seemingly reached based on a lack of stereotypical expectations of Indianness among the

Chorotega. Minutes later, I joined members of a family interviewed for the article and critical of it – themselves very much present and showing no signs of imminent disappearance – in watching the Mexican comedy *El Chapulín Colorado*. This particular episode portrayed the sneaky resurgence of an Indigenous group presumably "lost" five hundred years earlier. The tribe, identifiable to viewers as Indigenous through war paint and costumes conveying a generic Indianness common to televised media, threatened the Mexican superhero and his damsel in distress. In keeping with the show's favourite trope, she was more endangered by *el Chapulín*'s clumsiness than other circumstances, but nonetheless she appeared worried about lascivious looks by the chief and about the tribe's other unknown but distrusted motives. In these examples (*Survivor, The Three Stooges*, and *El Chapulín Colorado*), it appears that television Indians may be invented and resurrected with the stroke of a war paint brush. At the same time, the contrast between real Indigenous people watching television in their home and those fictionalized on *El Chapulín Colorado* shows an instance in which living Chorotega people are rendered invisible (or "lost") as Indigenous if they do not bear markers of ethnic belonging popularized, if not invented, by media and believed by its consumers.

In fact, television-based media, among other "mediascapes" (Appadurai 1990, 299), has served to provide a standard of measure for indigeneity for many of the Indigenous Territory's youth. In interviews in 1999, as in 2009, young people explained to me that they had seen Indigenous peoples on National Geographic, and since they themselves looked nothing like those televised people with their unique clothing and practices, they must not be truly Indigenous. I have known the children in two generations of one Chorotega family to "play Indian," drawing from the sounds they had heard on television to give that game a credible (albeit fully fictional) soundtrack.

Although television may seem to delegitimize Chorotega culture as Indigenous to some youth from the Indigenous Territory, in some instances it has had the opposite effect. News cameras filmed the festival of corn, broadcasting current representations of the Chorotega Indigenous Territory that rest on past media images of indigeneity. At the annual festival of culture in 2009, videographers from the National University filmed the elders talking about the past. An official in charge of this production later described it as a resource for the community itself, to be used in schools, and also to make the Chorotega Indigenous Territory known at an international level. The latter goal mirrors that held by the community, as expressed in the brochure produced for the inauguration of the meeting hall in 2004.

For the community, this goal of global recognition is linked to the development of heritage tourism and may be the springboard for a revaluing of indigeneity by non-Indigenous Costa Ricans. For the videographer, the goal seems to be to seek for the Chorotega the same status and respect accorded to more widely recognized Indigenous groups. For both, the goal of international renown counters the marginalization that has marked so much of Chorotega history to this point. Indeed, globalization has been useful in completing the cycle of making sure local knowledge, filmed by outsiders, makes it back to the community. In 2010, a friend not from the Chorotega Indigenous Territory sent me a YouTube clip of the documentary, which I sent back to youth from there.[11] And finally, my own social science articles describe current realities influenced by past social science writing in that I am writing about the gourd that depicts my previous written accounts of the community's oral histories. In this decidedly Borgesian cycle of representations, each one feeds on previous iterations. Each description passes back and forth between outsiders prone to depicting the Chorotega through visual images or written word based on what locals revealed to them, and locals who later adopt and reintegrate these descriptions. Through this process, ultimately, all of these sources – experiential, historical, academic, televised, and others – have been folded into a new version of reality made to look old.

Cultural Alchemy in the Spectre of Tourism

In all of this, the hope or general context of tourism has been the crucible for such cultural alchemy, for this cyclical repositioning of discourse and recentring of actors within it. Tourism has provided the (as yet unfulfilled) promise of economic stability in exchange for performing life as Indigenous people. In that regard, tourism has been the Borgesian *ur*, the "object brought into being by hope" (Borges 1962, 30). The meeting hall – complete with Indigenous imagery or at least imagery that will be read as Indigenous, then recorded as such by televised media and scholarly discourse so that it becomes real to insiders that draw from these authenticating discourses – was designed to bring tourism into being in the Chorotega Indigenous Territory. To that end, locals also began reviving, reinventing, or unmasking and dusting off customs that would be believable as Indigenous perhaps less because they stem from Indigenous people's practices than because they look the part. But in their performance, and the various forms of documenting those performances, these practices have become meaningful as Indigenous to insiders and outsiders alike.

In presentations created within a context of tourism, the transformative nature of performance has led practices once stigmatized to become the source of pride for many, and locals have been able to draw from written discourses to renegotiate their own placement within social science discourse as authors, co-authors, or active participants in their own representation. Even while stereotypes infuse some of the iconography that assures, to outsiders, the legitimacy or authenticity of this Indigenous group's heritage, insiders are able to twist and turn these representations to their own benefit, taking control of them, and deploying them in the space of performance where they might underscore transformation in ways beneficial to the current-day Chorotega.

NOTES

1 See Stocker (2005, 2007).
2 For a more detailed account of this process and this building, see Stocker (2009, 2013).
3 This has been debated in anthropological circles. For thorough considerations of origins of and contemporary writing on this issue, see Redford (1990, 25–9) and Hames (2007). However, the notion extends well beyond academia and is deeply entrenched in the popular imaginary (as acknowledged also by Hames 2007, 182).
4 No Borgesian homage would be complete without a smattering of scholarly footnotes presenting some mix of academic certainty, uncanny reality, and (in Borges's work, not mine), outright fiction. For years I studied the stigma surrounding residence within this Indigenous Territory and the discrimination faced by its inhabitants. In the book I wrote expressly about this topic (Stocker 2005), I created a pseudonym for that. I chose one that harkened back to the Mangue language no longer used in the area except in place names and plant names, including the actual name of the Chorotega Indigenous Territory. In looking through Mangue language word lists, I decided upon "Nambué," the word for "jaguar," because of this identifying feature from the pre-Colombian era. During a five-year absence from the reservation, while I wrapped up past research projects and started a new job, the community began its shift from stigma to pronounced pride

in indigeneity, and began planning and building the meeting hall. When I returned to the Chorotega Indigenous Territory after five years, I was surprised not only by this turn of events, but also by the figure of Nambué at the entrance of the hall that stands for the whole community, and that embodied the name I had given the community in my book.

5 This agreement stems from pride in heritage to some degree, but also from past experience with government requirements to plant particular varieties of seeds and to destroy certain crops (coffee, in particular) intended for subsistence use. Since that time, members of the community have weighed in on the debate via social media.

6 In this class on culture, according to one community member, it was unclear who was teaching whom. Presumably it was convened to teach residents about traditional practices, but it seems that inhabitants of the Indigenous Territory – experts on the cultural practices that constitute the backbone of the course curriculum – were engaged in discussions of traditional practices to the benefit of the supposed instructor. Even so, such conversations may well be of use to participants in maintaining and validating the cultural practices discussed.

7 For a more thorough assessment of this exclusion, see Stocker (2005).

8 This job appointment resulted from the efforts of a local elementary school teacher following conversations about my research on discrimination in the nearby high school in 1999.

9 The choreographer was not alone in this vision of how to present indigeneity through body paint. In a 2009 "corn pageant" (a pageant meant to honour an Indigenous past, but that invoked stereotypical images to accomplish this), at least one contestant competing for the title of Corn Princess had stripes of paint on her cheeks, also in keeping with images offered through US movies. Other images used included artefacts from a variety of different Indigenous groups, corn, and props such as dolls strapped to the contestant's back, as well as clay plates on which tortillas would be cooked. In a later year, boys participated in this activity, previously limited to girls. Several of the boys vying for the title of Corn Prince wore loincloths and body paint seemingly modelled after the performer of the fire dance. See also Grünewald (2009, 24–25) for an Amazonian case in which touristic inquiry led an Indigenous group (the Pataxó) to create dances and songs, and in which these cultural innovations spurred by tourism came to promote self-affirmation.

10 See Stocker 1995. Another carver of gourds gifted one to me. Her artwork included a mix of designs common to pre-Columbian pottery unearthed in the region, as well as geometric shapes of my own design that she had

seen me draw years before, when I lived with her family while carrying out research. In this less direct way, too, the influence of a social scientist has made its way into Chorotega wares.

11 While the video production discussed here is done by outsiders to the reservation, among current research interests regarding this community is the local use of social networking media and other forms that allow simultaneously for self-representation and cultural revitalization. In other Indigenous communities, video production by Indigenous peoples has served this purpose (see Ginsburg 1991; Turner 1992). Ginsburg (1991, 104) discusses "ethnographic media," in general, and their use in presenting cultural identity in keeping with modes of self-representation. Extending her term more broadly, we might consider artistry as described in this chapter and other forms of self-representation, even if they include imagery and discourse from outsiders, as acts of self-determination. See Ginsburg 1991 and Turner 1992 for thorough discussions of how Indigenous media takes a Western form of media expression and twists it successfully to serve the needs of Indigenous peoples.

REFERENCES

Appadurai, Arjun. 1990. "Disjuncture and Difference in the Global Cultural Economy." *Theory, Culture & Society* 7 (2): 295–310. http://dx.doi.org/10.1177/026327690007002017.

Basso, Keith. 1996. *Wisdom Sits in Places: Landscape and Language among the Western Apache*. Albuquerque: University of New Mexico Press.

Bauman, Richard. 1990. "Poetics and Performance as Critical Perspectives on Language and Social Life." *Annual Review of Anthropology* 19 (1): 59–88. http://dx.doi.org/10.1146/annurev.an.19.100190.000423.

Bauman, Richard. 2001. "Verbal Art as Performance." In *Linguistic Anthropology: A Reader*, edited by Alessandro Duranti, 165–88. Malden: Blackwell.

Borges, Jorge Luis. 1962. "Tlön, Uqbar, Orbis Tertius." Translated by Alastair Reid. In *Ficciones*, 17–35. New York: Grove.

Brandes, Stanley. 2006. *Skulls to the Living, Bread to the Dead: The Day of the Dead in Mexico and Beyond*. Malden: Blackwell.

Briggs, Charles. 1988. *Competence in Performance: The Creativity of Tradition in Mexican Verbal Art*. Philadelphia: University of Pennsylvania Press.

Bruner, Edward M. 2005. *Culture on Tour*. Chicago: University of Chicago Press.

Chambers, Erve. 2000. *Native Tours*. Long Grove: Waveland.

Deloria, Philip J. 1998. *Playing Indian*. New Haven: Yale University Press.

Erikson, Patricia Pierce. 2003. "Welcome to This House: A Century of Makah People Honoring Identity and Negotiating Cultural Tourism." *Ethnohistory (Columbus, Ohio)* 50 (3): 523–47. http://dx.doi.org/10.1215/00141801-50-3-523.

Fernández, León. 1975. *Historia de Costa Rica durante la dominación española 1502–1821*. San José: Editorial Costa Rica.

Fernández Guardia, Ricardo. 1913. *History of the Discovery and Conquest of Costa Rica*. New York: Thomas Y. Cromwell.

Ginsburg, Faye. 1991. "Indigenous Media: Faustian Contract or Global Village?" *Cultural Anthropology* 6 (1): 92–112. http://dx.doi.org/10.1525/can.1991.6.1.02a00040.

Grünewald, Rodrigo de Azeredo. 2009. "Indigenous, Tourism and Cultural Revival among the Pataxó People in Brazil." In "Current Themes in Indigenous Tourism," special issue, *London Journal of Tourism, Sport and Creative Industries* 2: 21–7.

Hames, Raymond. 2007. "The Ecologically Noble Savage Debate." *Annual Review of Anthropology* 36 (1): 177–90. http://dx.doi.org/10.1146/annurev.anthro.35.081705.123321.

Hiwasaki, Lisa. 2000. "Ethnic Tourism in Hokkaido and the Shaping of Ainu Identity." *Pacific Affairs* 73 (3): 393–412. http://dx.doi.org/10.2307/2672026.

Ingles, Pamela. 2010. "Performing Traditional Dances for Modern Tourists in the Amazon." In *Tourists and Tourism: A Reader*, edited by Sharon Bohm Gmelch, 237–47. Long Grove: Waveland.

Meyer, Melissa L. 1999. "Blood Is Thicker Than Family." In *Over the Edge: Remapping the American West*, edited by Valerie J. Matsumoto and Blake Allmendinger, 231–49. Berkeley: University of California Press.

Nesper, Larry. 2003. "Simulating Culture: Being Indian for Tourists in Lac Du Flambeau's Wa-Swa-Gon Indian Bowl." *Ethnohistory (Columbus, Ohio)* 50 (3): 447–72. http://dx.doi.org/10.1215/00141801-50-3-447.

Redford, Kent H. 1990. "The Ecologically Noble Savage." *Orion* 9: 25–9.

Stocker, Karen. 1995. *Historias Matambugueñas*. San José, Costa Rica: Emprenta de la Universidad Nacional.

Stocker, Karen. 2005. *"I Won't Stay Indian, I'll Keep Studying": The Effects of Schooling on Ethnic Identity in a Rural Costa Rican High School*. Boulder: University Press of Colorado.

Stocker, Karen. 2007. "Identity as Work: Changing Job Opportunities and Indigenous Identity in the Transition to a Tourist Market." In "Work and Anthropology in Costa Rica," theme issue, *Anthropology of Work Review* 28: 18–22.

Stocker, Karen. 2009. "Authenticating Discourses and the Marketing of Indigenous Identities." In "Current Themes in Indigenous Tourism," special issue, *London Journal of Tourism, Sport and Creative Industries* 2: 62–71.

Stocker, Karen. 2013. *Tourism and Cultural Change in Costa Rica: Pitfalls and Possibilities*. Lanham: Lexington.

Stronza, Amanda. 2010. "Through a New Mirror: Tourism and Identity in the Amazon." In *Tourists and Tourism: A Reader*, edited by Sharon Bohm Gmelch, 279–304. Long Grove: Waveland.

Turner, Terence. 1992. "Defiant Images: The Kayapo Appropriation of Video." *Anthropology Today* 8 (6): 5–16. http://dx.doi.org/10.2307/2783265.

Urry, John. 2002. *The Tourist Gaze*. Los Angeles: SAGE.

WTO (World Trade Organization). 1998. *Guide for Local Authorities on Developing Sustainable Tourism*. Geneva: WTO.

Yamashita, Shinji. 2003. *Bali and Beyond: Explorations in the Anthropology of Tourism*. Trans. J.S. Eades. New York: Berghahn.

PART TWO

Political Movements

5 Indigenous Tourism as a Transformative Process: The Case of the Emberá in Panama

DIMITRIOS THEODOSSOPOULOS

In this chapter I discuss how Indigenous tourism has affected the representational self-awareness of the residents of an Emberá community in Panama. I approach Indigenous tourism as a transformative process that inspires the Emberá to experiment and creatively develop pre-existing cultural practices, but also to articulate their identity to audiences of outsiders. In line with the editors and contributors of this volume, I argue that Indigenous tourism has the potential to deeply shape the political representation of Indigenous societies, and as such deserves special attention as a distinctive variant of cultural tourism. Unlike top-down homogenizing processes that rely on national narratives, Indigenous tourism provides opportunities for developing cultural representation at the local level, often by calling attention to cultural difference. Even in nations where multiculturalism is promoted as an official discourse, Indigenous tourism may encourage the articulation of Indigenous identity in previously unexplored directions.

In fact, I argue, there is a distinctive dynamic in Indigenous tourism that sets it apart from other types of tourism encounters. This dynamic relates to the peripherality of many Indigenous groups, their minority status and, often, their diminished representation. Indigenous tourism circumvents these discrepancies – or disjunctions (Appadurai 1996) – and provides new avenues for the Indigenous groups to "reach out to the world" in search of new allies and supportive connections (Strathern and Stewart 2009; Theodossopoulos 2009). As a result, Indigenous tourism can enhance the global visibility of local cultural difference – and swiftly change its status from a liability to an asset – encouraging small, significant, or even dramatic transformations in the host society. The effects of such transformative processes – regardless of how positively or negatively these are perceived by local actors – are more evident among Indigenous groups that experiment, or have not yet articulated a standard narrative to negotiate their representation; that is, among groups without a written, official or nationally endorsed identity discourse.

It is in terms of these effects – and the unique political and representational conditions that they generate – that Indigenous tourism can be treated as a special subfield of tourism studies: one that acknowledges the usual economic and cultural ramifications of tourism exchange, but also pays special attention to the representational transformations tourism generates within Indigenous societies. In the ethnographic case I examine in this chapter, I shed some light on the consequences of Indigenous tourism for Emberá cultural representation in Panama. I focus on Parara Puru, an Emberá community that has recently developed tourism as the mainstay of their livelihood. I explain how tourism has enabled its residents to continue living within a National Park – with restrictive regulations on accessing natural resources – and has encouraged them to engage with renewed enthusiasm and confidence in Indigenous cultural practices that were until recently in decline. I also stress the contribution of Indigenous tourism in providing the Emberá hosts with opportunities to develop their representational self-awareness and skill in articulating their Indigenous identity (see also Bunten 2008; Peers 2007).

The potential of tourism to reconstitute local cultural practices has been highlighted by the anthropology of tourism more generally (Abram and Waldren 1997; Boissevain 1996; Coleman and Crang 2002) and acknowledged in studies of other Panamanian ethnic groups (Guerrón-Montero 2006; Pereiro Pérez 2010; Salvador 1976; Swain 1989; Tice 1995). Indigenous tourism, in its capacity to inspire change in the host society, shares many characteristics with tourism in non-Indigenous settings: it revitalizes local traditions, strengthens the local economy, and provides new jobs and occupational specializations and new standards for negotiating authenticity (see Abram and Waldren 1997; Bruner 2005; Coleman and Crang 2002; Franklin 2003; Graburn 1976; Leite and Graburn 2009; Nash 1996; Salazar 2010; Selwyn 1996; Skinner and Theodossopoulos 2011; Smith 1989). With respect to its low environmental impact and small-scale orientation, Indigenous tourism – in the form developed by the Emberá – shares similarities with ecotourism (West and Carrier 2004) or alternative tourism (Stronza 2001).

In comparison to other types of tourism, however, Indigenous tourism more closely addresses issues of Indigenous representation, with indigeneity being simultaneously an attraction – exoticized or commodified – and a vehicle for escaping political and economic peripheralization. Here, the issue of how much control is maintained by the Indigenous community is of critical importance (Hinch and Butler 1996). Indigenous groups deprived of control over the tourism exchange can feel alienated and complain that their culture has been "taken away" (Kirtsoglou and Theodossopoulos 2004). In contrast, the community I examine in this chapter controls the content and form of the Indigenous culture that is made available in tourism, and its residents share several opportunities to experiment with their self-representation, negotiating a marketable identity – a type of self-commodification (Bunten 2008) – that does not seem alienating to them. Following Sahlins (1999, 2000) and Stanley (1998), I do not always see in commodification the decline of Indigenous authenticity. On the contrary, and inspired by Bruner (2001, 2005), I acknowledge Emberá tourism performances as self-conscious and dynamic negotiations of their performers' identity. It is from this perspective that Indigenous tourism can be seen as a deeply transformative process.

In the sections that follow, I explore some of the transformations effected by Indigenous tourism on Parara Puru, an Emberá community that has developed tourism as its main productive activity. My account is based on seventeen months of fieldwork – spread over seven years from 2005 to 2012 – during which I examined social change in a variety of topics, such as the use (or not) of Indigenous attire (Theodossopoulos 2012a, 2016), the Emberá dancing tradition (Theodossopoulos 2012b), the elusive concept of authenticity (Theodossopoulos 2013), the perception of Indigenous culture (but also of the tourists themselves) as "resources" in tourism (Theodossopoulos 2010), and the response of the Emberá to tourist expectations (Theodossopoulos 2011, 2016). I have also been concerned with the exoticization of indigeneity in the tourism imaginary and the parallel exoticization of tourists by their Indigenous hosts (Theodossopoulos 2014). All these topics illuminate different dimensions of Emberá Indigenous tourism. In this chapter, I will focus on the representational awareness stimulated by Indigenous tourism, which I also see as one of the potentialities that set the "Indigenous" variety of cultural tourism apart from other types of tourism exchange.

Entering the Tourism Economy

There was a time not that long ago when the Emberá used to live in dispersed settlements. They built their houses on stilts close to a river and cultivated the adjacent land, planting fruit trees in their yards and plantains, rice, or maize in cleared plots further away but always close to the river and the domestic compound. They also liked to hunt and fish, and this is why they preferred – as my older Emberá respondents recall – to live at distance from each other, so that there was enough game and land for all. Families, as they grew, spread along particular river sectors, and when no more land or marriageable partners were available, some family members would move to a new sector or even a different river (Faron 1962; Herlihy 1986; Kane 1994; Velásquez Runk 2009). In this gradual manner, the Emberá – following an adaptive strategy of dispersal and retreat to inaccessible rainforest locations (Williams 2004; see also Isacsson 1993, Kane 1994) – spread from the department of Chocó in Colombia to Darién in Panama (Pineda and Gutiérrez de Pineda 1999; Torres de Araúz 1966), an ongoing movement that started in the late eighteenth century (Herlihy 2003, 318; Howe 1998, 214; Williams 2004, 224).

By the mid-twentieth century, and as the Emberá population in Darién increased, small numbers of Emberá moved to uninhabited locations closer to Panama City and the Canal area (Caballero and Araúz 1962; Herlihy 1986). This is how the first Emberá arrived at river Chagres, where Parara Puru is now located, and the forested areas that now comprises the Chagres National Park. They first established themselves in dispersed settlement and enjoyed an initial period of relative freedom from external control, a time – as they remember – when game, fish, and lumber were abundant. Their uncontrolled access to natural resources was curtailed by the foundation of a national park in 1985, which imposed restrictions on hunting and cultivation. Throughout the twentieth century, the cultivation of plantains (primarily), rice and maize (to a smaller extent), and lumber provided the Emberá in Panama with cash to buy commodities from the market (see Herlihy 1986; Loewen 1975). Deprived of these economic opportunities, and for a decade following the establishment of the national park, the Emberá of Chagres had to resort to paid labour in the non-Emberá world. However, the experimental introduction of tourism to the area in the early and middle 1990s provided the Emberá of Chagres with an income.

In the meantime, the larger Emberá population in Darién considered the possibility of resettling in concentrated communities with elected representatives and primary schools. This movement started in the 1950s and took off in the 1960s and 1970s (Herlihy 1986), leading to the foundation of a semi-independent reservation (the Comarca Emberá-Wounaan). Although approximately half of the Emberá population in Panama remained outside the borders of this reservation (Colin 2010), the overwhelming majority resettled in concentrated villages, with political representatives, small shops (with basic commodities), and cement-built schools. Community formation facilitated the integration of the Emberá into the national political structures and led to the decline of certain cultural and economic practices associated with life in a dispersed settlement (see Herlihy 1986; Kane 1994). The initial decision to resettle in concentrated communities was taken by Emberá who wanted to send their children to school and enhance their political representation – a decision that was welcome, and subsequently encouraged, by the state.

Tourism provided many Emberá in Chagres with opportunities to organize themselves along similar lines, that is, to establish ethnically homogenous concentrated communities with elected representatives. The foundation of Parara Puru is a representative example: in the early 1990s a group of Chagres-born Emberá started experimenting with developing presentations for tourists in an accessible forested location on river Chagres. At first, they built a "model" Indigenous village for the purpose of entertaining groups of tourists visiting from the city, but the park authorities, who carefully monitor and regulate human activity within the park, did not allow the Emberá to reside permanently in this location. The success of the initial experiment with tourism, however, was so immediate – and in line with Panama's policy towards tourism development (cf. Guerrón-Montero 2006) – that the Emberá were granted permission, in 1998, to found a new community on a different site further up the river Chagres. During the same period, five other Emberá communities in Chagres and the general Canal area started to engage with tourism.

For the Emberá of Chagres, who were born at the fringes of Emberá society – the northwestern edge of its geographical distribution and surrounded by a non-Indigenous majority – the establishment of homogenous Emberá communities was an issue of vital importance for maintaining a distinctive cultural identity.[1] During the difficult years that followed the establishment of the national park, and under the pressure of the park restrictions, several families of Chagres-born Emberá moved closer to impoverished Latino communities. The children played with non-Emberá children and the men worked for non-Indigenous employers. Nowadays, several Emberá who evaluate this period retrospectively – after having experienced life in the new homogenous Emberá communities – identify disadvantages in residing in ethnically mixed communities. As some of them point out, the children of those Emberá who live in the city or in small Latino communities do not speak or understand Emberá and behave like non-Emberá (*kampunia*). For this reason, they explain, "living in [a homogenous] Emberá community like Parara Puru, is better than living with the Latinos."

Seen from this perspective, the development of Indigenous tourism in Chagres signalled the organization of many local Emberá in ethnically homogenous communities. Tourism provided a sustainable occupation for the inhabitants of these new communities, an occupation with a low environmental impact, enabling the Emberá to remain in the park without violating the environmental regulations that inhibit economic activities involving the extraction of natural resources. In this respect, Indigenous tourism was in harmony with the green discourse promoted by both the park authorities and the ministry of environment, and solidified the position of the Emberá in Chagres and their residence in the park.

The Emberá have now developed cultural presentations to entertain groups of tourists for one to two hours.[2] After the presentations the tourists typically return to their resorts or cruise ships. There are no hotels within the park, and those few travellers who wish to stay overnight sleep in thatched-roofed Emberá houses, examples of Emberá traditional architecture that add to "the Indigenous experience." The overall aesthetics of the built environment in the Emberá communities that entertain tourists represents a conscious attempt to minimize the visible effect of modernity in Emberá everyday life. The traditional Emberá houses – as seen by the first-time visitor – emerge through the rainforest, a view that reinforces Western expectations of Indigenous life in a pristine "natural" ecosystem (Theodossopoulos 2011; see also West and Carrier 2004).[3]

Nowadays, a number of competing tourist agencies based in Panama City advertise half-day excursions to Chagres among tourists residing in hotels and resorts in and close to that city, or tourists transiting the Canal in cruise ships. In the advertisements, the use of the terms "nature" (e.g., "adventures in nature") and "Indigenous" (e.g., "visit an Indigenous tribe") are intended to entice a tourist audience that imagines Indigenous authenticity in static terms, isolated from modernity, unaffected by time, and located in the rainforest (Theodossopoulos 2013, 2014, 2016). Indigenous people are thus emplaced in nature to enhance this very perception of isolation (e.g., "meet the Emberá, an Indigenous people in the rainforest"). Although, as I will shortly explain, the cultural aspects of this particular tourist experience far outweigh its "green" dimension, tourism advertisements – developed by non-Indigenous tourist agencies and government officials – locate Emberá indigeneity in "nature" to appeal to tourists interested in eco-tourism, alternative tourism, and Indigenous tourism, varieties of cultural tourism that share an eco-friendly orientation (Stronza 2001; West and Carrier 2004).

The tourism agencies transport tourists to Chagres (in buses), provide guides who accompany them for the duration of the trip (and translate the presentations from Spanish to English, French, German, or Italian), collect money from the tourists, and pay the Emberá community a fee per visitor. The leaders of the Emberá distribute this money among the members of their community according to their role or the degree of their participation in the tourism venue. In the following section, I discuss the cultural component of their contribution.

Emberá Culture, Representation, and Indigenous Tourism

We have seen how tourism provided the Emberá with a new occupation within the Chagres National Park, a prospect and justification for remaining in the park, and an opportunity to organize themselves politically in concentrated communities. The model and structure of concentrated village formation was already available in Panamanian Emberá society (Herlihy 1986; Kane 1994). Parara Puru and the other Emberá communities at Chagres followed this pre-existing model in most structural respects – for example, they elected leaders, acquired a primary school, and built communal buildings for community gatherings. But they also organized their communities to facilitate tourism. As mentioned previously, special attention was paid to Indigenous architectural principles. Apart from the standard roles of the community leader (nokó) and secretary, additional elected positions were introduced, such as that of the leader responsible for tourism – a position considered as important as that of the nokó.[4]

Beyond the level of structural or practical adaptations, however, tourism encouraged the Emberá in Chagres to think about the representation of their culture. Frequent participation in cultural presentations for tourists provided the Emberá working in tourism with opportunities to practice and reintroduce dimensions of Emberá culture that were in decline until recently. As a consequence, many Emberá became increasingly interested in the knowledge and memories of their parents and grandparents, and started collecting information about their history. As a man from Parara Puru puts it, by working in tourism (or "with the tourists"), "we also work for Emberá culture" and "we learn more about our culture." From their point of view, practices that in the early 1990s were considered outdated – and were heavily stereotyped by non-Indigenous Panamanians – regained, through their respectful reception by the tourist audience, part of their appeal.

A good example of the cultural revitalization encouraged by tourism is the reintroduction of traditional Emberá dances in the context of presentations for tourists. The Emberá have a distinctive music and dance tradition,[5] which is still practised in community festivals in Darién, but in Chagres – that is, further away from the main concentration of Emberá population in Panama – only a few men and women knew how to perform the dances and the music in the early 1990s. The introduction of tourism brought about a momentous change in this respect. The dances became a central part of the cultural presentations offered to the tourists, and the Emberá of Chagres acquired, through frequent practice, remarkable performative skill; they increased their repertoire of dances and music, learned to pay attention to detail, collected information from the elderly or relatives living in other communities, and embellished their performances with small stylistic innovations that contribute to what the Emberá see as more authentic and spontaneous performances. In other words, tourism inspired the overall revitalization of Emberá dance as an art form, in Chagres but also in Darién, where leaders aspiring to develop tourism encourage the young to improve their dance skills (Theodossopoulos 2012b).

Another interesting example concerns the use of the Emberá attire in relation to tourism. The traditional code of dress – which was widespread until the 1960s – attracted the exoticized admiration of early-twentieth-century explorers and anthropologists (Howe 1998, 2009), and is nowadays received with enthusiasm by many contemporary tourists-cum-consumers of the exotic. Yet, in the last quarter of the twentieth century, the men of Parara Puru, like the Emberá men of all communities in Panama, replaced their traditional loincloths with shorts and T-shirts. The Emberá women, who in the past remained bare-breasted, now systematically cover their torso with inexpensive tops bought in the market. Despite their persistent use of the Emberá skirt (*paruma*[S], *wa*[E]) – which has become a strong identifier of Indigenous identity – the women now resort to mixed Indigenous and non-Indigenous clothing combinations or dress in Western clothes when travelling outside their communities.

During presentations for the tourists, the Emberá of Parara Puru wear the full traditional attire – loincloths and *parumas*, with additional adornments such beaded necklaces, bracelets, and body painting[6] – and carefully avoid using mass-manufactured items of clothing. When the tourists depart, they put aside their adornments until the next day. The men put Western clothes back on and the women keep their *parumas* but combine them with tops. The full Emberá attire, the inhabitants of Parara Puru explain – in an attempt to justify their shifting dress codes – has always been for special occasions, such as to honour the visitors. However, some Emberá in Parara Puru admit that back in the 1990s, when they first started working for tourism, they felt embarrassed wearing the loincloth. Nowadays, they add, "the Latinos know that we are working for tourism and do not bother us," "we can dress like our grandparents within our community, everyday." Similarly, the women of Parara Puru explain that due to their participation in tourism they are now more accustomed to toplessness (or less ashamed than before). At the same time, an increasing number of Parara Puru women wear their *parumas* outside the community, in non-Indigenous towns but also in the City.

It is in this respect that a choice of dress in a particular context – such as wearing a *paruma*-skirt in the central commercial street in the city (Avenida Central) – becomes a statement of indigeneity (cf. Conklin 1997; Ewart 2007; Gow 2007; Santos-Granero 2009). In 2009, groups of Emberá from Chagres participated, along with other Indigenous people of Panama, in pro-Indigenous rights demonstrations in Panama City, where they danced while dressed in traditional attire in the streets of the capital. Such acts of Indigenous identification in public would have been unthinkable for the Emberá of Chagres in the early 1990s. Their new confidence in making their Emberá identity more widely visible is closely related to their full-time involvement with tourism; and it is positively reaffirmed by their increased performative skill (developed through daily cultural presentations), but also by the enthusiastic reception of Emberá culture among an international audience of tourists.

On an almost daily basis, the Emberá of Parara Puru see their culture being admired by foreigners from economically developed countries. Consequently, they come to appreciate their Indigenous identity not only as an economic resource made possible by tourism (see Theodossopoulos 2010), but also as a political asset. They have now joined a wider political initiative (*tierras collectives*) of Emberá and Wounaan communities that remain outside the Indigenous reservation and work towards acquiring land titles to secure their position in the national park. The main ideas and political vocabulary employed in this protest – for example, the idea of living within a semi-autonomous reservation – have come into existence during a wider process of Emberá and Wouanan political self-determination that originated five decades ago (Colin 2010; Herlihy 1986; Kane 1994; Velásquez Runk 2009). Nevertheless, in the case of the Emberá of Chagres, tourism has assisted the local communities in participating in this political process from a position of improved economic power and representational self-awareness.

The improved economic position of the Emberá in Parara Puru does not merely provide the resources and time to think about embarking on political projects – such as pursuing land titles – but also consolidates an awareness of Indigenous tourism as an asset, not only for the Emberá but for the Panamanian economy more widely. Through tourism, the Emberá of Chagres have escaped the poverty threatened by the national park restrictions. They have acquired a small stream of income that is more regular than the seasonal earnings of cash crop cultivation, and are in a position to direct the future of their communities within the national park through self-determination. The encouraging stance of the Panamanian government towards Indigenous tourism helps the Emberá realize that they can now renegotiate their land rights in Chagres from a position that reflects their contribution to the national economy.

Hence, we can easily appreciate the contribution of tourism to the representational self-awareness of the Emberá. This is not merely enhanced by the admiration of the tourist audience, or the recent national and international visibility of Emberá culture in tourism campaigns, but is constantly augmented by the practice of "working for tourism" on a daily basis. Year after year, new individuals, men and women, step in to take a more active role in cultural presentations in Parara Puru (see, Theodossopoulos 2011, 2016). Younger men assist the busier older

men in guiding tourists around the community or the nearby rainforest, explaining buildings, artefacts, and natural species. In Parara Puru,
the women now participate in the explanatory speech delivered by the
leaders of the community to the tourists,[7] taking over the part of this
presentation that explicates the art of basketry and women's attire.[8]

Through this gradual process of interacting with tourists – and as
more Emberá participate more actively in the cultural presentations –
the residents of Parara Puru have developed an awareness of their
responsibility as cultural ambassadors. They are concerned about representing their culture well and accurately in an understandable and
systematic manner, and see their role in this process as more akin to
that of a teacher who educates an audience than that of a performer
(cf. Bunten 2008). "We are like school teachers (maestros)," one of the
leaders of the community explained, "we teach the tourists what is
Emberá culture … we learn how to educate the tourists better and
better every year." "And we are happy to see that the tourists want to
learn," added his wife.

In the seven-year period that I conducted fieldwork in Parara Puru, I
have seen several younger men and women assume a more active role
in presentations to the tourists and improve their skill in describing
the particulars of their culture or acquire confidence in public speaking. This process has encouraged them to think about the representation of their culture and invest some time and effort in developing a
vocabulary in Spanish and a personal style in articulating their ideas in
a narrative they create themselves, about themselves.[9] Approximately
twenty years since their first engagement with tourism, the Emberá of
Parara Puru have learn how to speak about their culture and identity
(in many words), transforming their cultural difference from a liability
(and an object of stereotyping) to a political, economic. and representational asset.

From Stereotypes to Admiration

Indigenous tourism has encouraged the Emberá of Chagres, a marginalized cluster of Emberá communities that were until the early 1990s
increasingly assimilating to non-Indigenous influences, to re-evaluate
the potential of their Indigenous culture, regroup, and reorganize
themselves by focusing on their Emberá identity. They founded new
concentrated (and ethnically homogenous) communities, such as Parara Puru, that specialize in delivering presentations for tourists, elected

leaders to represent their communities politically (but also to organize the tourism exchange), and started engaging with renewed enthusiasm in cultural practices that were previously in decline.

Among the many impacts Indigenous tourism has had on the lives of the Emberá in Chagres, I have underlined those that have involved increased representational self-awareness. The residents of Parara Puru have experienced a dramatic transformation of their representational status in a period of less than twenty years. From being stereotyped and peripheralized because of their cultural difference, they now receive the admiration of international audiences who valorize Emberá cultural distinctiveness. Indigeneity, which was until recently the target of stereotyping as equivalent to primitiveness (see Theodossopoulos 2014) is now celebrated by tourists, but also the Panamanian government, as adding to the uniqueness and (touristic) attractiveness of the nation. This remarkable change has not only increased the visibility of Emberá culture (Theodossopoulos 2010, 2011, 2016) but has encouraged the Emberá who work for tourism to improve their self-presentational skills and develop new ways of articulating their cultural identity.

It is in this respect that Indigenous tourism has played a significant role in transforming the Emberá of Chagres from a "muted" group (Ardener 1975) to globally visible Indigenous actors reaching out to the wider world (Theodossopoulos 2009). As peripheralized Indigenous people who increasingly realize the popularity of indigeneity among Western audiences (Conklin 1997; Conklin and Graham 1995; Ramos 1998; Turner 2002, 2006), the Emberá feel inspired to revitalize Indigenous practices, partially responding to tourist imaginaries (Salazar 2010) or expectations (Theodossopoulos 2011). The idealizing, or exoticizing, orientation of the tourists' concern with indigeneity – a topic I have explored elsewhere (Theodossopoulos 2014) – should not hide from view the fact that Indigenous hosts make important steps towards consciously re-articulating (or articulating for the first time) their cultural identity. Indigenous tourism makes a significant contribution in this direction. It puts in motion processes that encourage Indigenous hosts to renegotiate their position and representation.

For this reason, I have argued that Indigenous tourism deserves special analytical attention, as a unique type of cultural tourism that generates a dynamic that can lead to an increased representational self-awareness. The promotion of Indigenous identity in the marketplace – for example, the tourism market – can devalue cultural difference (through mass marketing) but can also "(re)animate cultural subjectivity ... (re)charge collective self-awareness ... forge new patterns of sociality" (Comaroff and Comaroff 2009, 26, 142). My work among the Emberá has encouraged me to see those new socio-cultural patterns that emerge in the tourism exchange not as simulacra or imitations of an imagined (static) Indigenous identity, but as unique and original cultural productions (Bruner 2005); not reinventions or mechanical reproductions, but a testament to the "inventiveness" of Indigenous actors (Sahlins 1999). It is in this broader sense that Indigenous tourism shapes the future of Emberá cultural representation and, more generally, the political, symbolic, and representational value of cultural difference.

NOTES

1 Already by the 1960s, Caballero and Araúz (1962) reported that the Emberá of Chagres – who lived closer to a non-Indigenous majority – adopted non-Indigenous habits at a faster rate than the Emberá living in relatively inaccessible locations in Darién.
2 For a detailed description of the content of these presentations see Theodossopoulos (2011, 2012b, 2016).
3 And sharply contrast with the active and dynamic transformations effected by the Emberá on their immediate environment (through slash-and-burn cultivation or selective favouring of particular plant and animal species) (cf. Herlihy 1986).
4 In Parara Puru an additional position has been introduced, that of the "fiscal," the person who oversees those Emberá who work in tourism, ensuring they perform their duties well and ideally with enthusiasm.
5 This is a tradition featuring "dances with animal names," in which a line of women dancers imitates some characteristic of an animal, plant, or other object, and rumba- and cumbia-Emberá, in which both men and women dance accompanied by Emberá musicians. For a detailed description of these dances, see Theodossopoulos (2012b).
6 For more information on full traditional Emberá attire, its adornments, and Emberá body painting, see Theodossopoulos (2012a, 2016).
7 Although the leaders of the Emberá are usually men, there have been occasions of women being elected to political office. For example, the leader (nokó) of the community of Ella Puru in Gamboa was, at the time of writing, a woman, while I am aware of three other women who held such a position in the last ten years in other Emberá communities in Panama.

8 Despite the exceptions mentioned in the previous note, the Emberá attach importance to a clear-cut gendered division of labour. As Emberá women increase their participation in cultural presentations – from dance performers or producers of artefacts to guides and narrators of Emberá culture – they feel more confident in talking about those cultural practices that relate to women's work and women's experience.

9 And I have also contributed to this development – as "their" anthropologist – offering ideas about how to portray particular aspects of their culture or by indicating certain aspects or sets of knowledge that tourists might find interesting (see Theodossopoulos 2015).

REFERENCES

Abram, Simone, and Jacqueline Waldren. 1997. "Introduction: Identifying with People and Places." In *Tourists and Tourism: Identifying with People and Places*, edited by S. Abram, J. Waldren, and D.V.L. Macleod, 1–11. Oxford: Berg.

Appadurai, Arjun. 1996. *Modernity at Large: Cultural Dimensions of Globalization*. Minneapolis: University of Minnesota Press.

Ardener, Edward. 1975. "Belief and the Problem of Women." In *Perceiving Women*, edited by S. Ardener. London: Dent.

Boissevain, Jeremy, ed. 1996. *Coping with Tourists: European Reactions to Mass Tourism*. Oxford: Berghahn.

Bruner, Edward M. 2001. "The Maasai and the Lion King: Authenticity, Nationalism, and Globalization in African Tourism." *American Ethnologist* 28 (4): 881–908. http://dx.doi.org/10.1525/ae.2001.28.4.881.

Bruner, Edward M. 2005. *Culture on Tour: Ethnographies of Travel*. Chicago: University of Chicago Press.

Bunten, Alexis C. 2008. "Sharing Culture or Shelling Out? Developing the Commodified Persona in the Heritage Industry." *American Ethnologist* 35 (3): 380–95. http://dx.doi.org/10.1111/j.1548-1425.2008.00041.x.

Caballero, Vicente, and Bolivar Araúz. 1962. "Inmigración de indios Chocoes en Río Pequeni y algunos aspectos de su cultura." *Hombre y Cultura* 1 (1): 44–61.

Coleman, Simon, and Mike Crang, eds. 2002. *Tourism: Between Place and Performance*. Oxford: Berghahn.

Colin, F.-L. 2010. *"Nosotros no solamente podemos vivir de cultura"*: Identity, Nature, and Power in the Comarca Emberá of Eastern Panama." Ph.D. diss., Carleton University.

Comaroff, John L., and Jean Comaroff. 2009. *Ethnicity, Inc.* Chicago: University of Chicago Press. http://dx.doi.org/10.7208/chicago/9780226114736.001.0001.

Conklin, Beth A. 1997. "Body Paint, Feathers, and VCRs: Aesthetics and Authenticity in Amazonian Activism." *American Ethnologist* 24 (4): 711–37. http://dx.doi.org/10.1525/ae.1997.24.4.711.

Conklin, Beth A., and Laura R. Graham. 1995. "The Shifting Middle Ground: Amazonian Indians and Eco-politics." *American Anthropologist* 97 (4): 695–710. http://dx.doi.org/10.1525/aa.1995.97.4.02a00120.

de Araúz, Torres, Reina. 1966. *La cultura Chocó: Estudio ethnológico e historico.* Panama: Centro de Investigaciones Antropológicas, University of Panama.

Ewart, Elisabeth. 2007. "Black Paint, Red Paint and a Wristwatch: The Aesthetics of Modernity among the Panará in Central Brazil." In *Body Arts and Modernity*, edited by E. Ewart and M. O'Hanlon, 36–52. Wantage: Sean Kingston.

Faron, Louis C. 1962. "Marriage, Residence, and Domestic Group among the Panamanian Choco." *Ethnology* 1 (1): 13–38. http://dx.doi.org/10.2307/3772926.

Franklin, Adrian. 2003. *Tourism: An Introduction.* London: Sage. http://dx.doi.org/10.4135/9781446220108.n2.

Gow, Peter. 2007. "Clothing as Acculturation in Peruvian Amazonia." In *Body Arts and Modernity*, edited by E. Ewart and M. O'Hanlon, 53–71. Wantage: Sean Kingston.

Graburn, N., ed. 1976. *Ethnic and Tourist Arts: Cultural Expressions from the Fourth World.* Berkeley: University of California Press.

Guerrón-Montero, Carla. 2006. "Tourism and Afro-Antillean identity in Panama." *Journal of Tourism and Cultural Change* 4 (2): 65–84. http://dx.doi.org/10.2167/jtcc074.0.

Herlihy, Peter H. 1986. "A Cultural Geography of the Emberá and Wounaan (Choco) Indians of Darien, Panama, with Emphasis on Recent Village Formation and Economic Diversification." Ph.D. diss., Louisiana State University.

Herlihy, Peter H. 2003. "Participatory Research: Mapping of Indigenous Lands in Darien, Panama." *Human Organization* 62 (4): 315–31. http://dx.doi.org/10.17730/humo.62.4.fu05tgkbvn2yvk8p.

Hinch, Tom, and Richard Butler. 1996. "Indigenous Tourism: A Common Ground for Discussion." In *Tourism and Indigenous Peoples*, edited by Richard Butler and Tom Hinch, 3–19. London: International Thomson Business.

Howe, James. 1998. *A People Who Would Not Kneel: Panama, the United States and the San Blas Kuna.* Washington: Smithsonian Institution Press.

Howe, James. 2009. *Chiefs, Scribes, and Ethnographers: Kuna Culture from Inside and Out*. Austin: University of Texas Press.

Isacsson, Sven-Erik. 1993. *Transformations of Eternity: On Man and Cosmos in Emberá Thought*. Göteborg: University of Göteborg.

Kane, Stephanie C. 1994. *The Phantom Gringo Boat: Shamanic Discourse and Development in Panama*. Washington: Smithsonian Institution.

Kirtsoglou, Elisabeth, and Dimitrios Theodossopoulos. 2004. "' They are Taking our Culture Away': Tourism and Culture Commodification in the Garifuna Community of Roatan." *Critique of Anthropology* 24 (2): 135–57. http://dx.doi.org/10.1177/0308275X04042650.

Leite, Naomi, and Nelson Graburn. 2009. "Anthropological Interventions in Tourism Studies." In *The Sage Handbook of Tourism Studies*, edited by M. Robinson and T. Jamal, 35–64. London: Sage. http://dx.doi.org/10.4135/9780857021076.n3.

Loewen, Jacob A. 1975. *Culture and Human Values: Christian Intervention in Anthropological Perspective*. Pasadena: William Carey Library.

Nash, Dennison. 1996. *The Anthropology of Tourism*. Oxford: Pergamon.

Peers, Laura. 2007. *Playing Ourselves: Interpreting Native Histories at Historic Reconstructions*. Lanham: Alta Mira.

Pereiro Pérez, Xerardo. 2010. *Estudio estratégico del turismo en Kuna Yala: Primera versión del informe de investigación 2008–2010*. Panama: SENACYT.

Pineda, Roberto, and Virginia Gutiérrez de Pineda. 1999. *Criaturas de Caragabí: Indios Chocoes, Emberáes, Catíos, Chamíes y Noanamaes*. Medellín: Editorial Universidad de Antioquia.

Ramos, Alcida R. 1998. *Indigenism: Ethnic Politics in Brazil*. Madison: University of Wisconsin Press.

Sahlins, Marshall. 1999. "Two or Three Things That I Know about Culture." *Journal of the Royal Anthropological Institute* 59 (3): 399–421.

Sahlins, Marshall. 2000. "'Sentimental Pessimism' and Ethnographic Experience; or, Why Culture IS NOT a Disappearing 'Object.'" In *Biographies of Scientific Objects*, edited by L. Daston, 158–202. Chicago: University of Chicago Press.

Salazar, Noel B. 2010. *Envisioning Eden: Mobilizing Imaginaries in Tourism and Beyond*. Oxford: Berghahn.

Salvador, Mari Lyn. 1976. "The Clothing Arts of the Cuna of San Blas, Panama." In *Ethnic and Tourist Arts: Cultural Expression from the Fourth World*, edited by Nelson H.H. Graburn, 165–82. Berkeley: University of California Press.

Santos-Granero, Fernando. 2009. "Hybrid Bodyscapes: A Visual History of Yanesha Patterns of Cultural Change." *Current Anthropology* 50 (4): 477–512. http://dx.doi.org/10.1086/604708.

Selwyn, Tom, ed. 1996. *The Tourist Image: Myths and Myth Making in Tourism.* Chichester: Wiley.

Skinner, Jonathan, and Dimitrios Theodossopoulos. 2011. "Introduction: The Play of Expectation in Tourism." In *Great Expectations: Imagination and Anticipation in Tourism,* ed. J. Skinner and D. Theodossopoulos, 1–26. Oxford: Berghahn.

Smith, Valene, ed. 1989. *Hosts and Guests: The Anthropology of Tourism.* Philadelphia: University of Pennsylvania Press. http://dx.doi. org/10.9783/9780812208016.

Stanley, Nick. 1998. *Being Ourselves for You: The Global Display of Cultures.* London: Middlesex University Press.

Strathern, Andrew, and Pamela J. Stewart. 2009. "Shifting Centers, Tense Peripheries: Indigenous Cosmopolitanisms." In *United in Discontent: Local Responses to Cosmopolitanism and Globalization,* edited by Dimitrios Theodossopoulos and Elisabeth Kirtsoglou, 20–44. Oxford: Berghahn.

Stronza, Amanda. 2001. "Anthropology and Tourism: Forging New Ground for Ecotourism and Other Alternatives." *Annual Review of Anthropology* 30 (1): 261–83. http://dx.doi.org/10.1146/annurev.anthro.30.1.261.

Swain, Margaret B. 1989. "Gender Roles in Indigenous Tourism: Kuna Mola, Kuna Yala and Cultural Survival." In *Hosts and Guests: The Anthropology of Tourism,* edited by Valene L. Smith, 83–104. Philadelphia: University of Pennsylvania Press. http://dx.doi.org/10.9783/9780812208016.83.

Turner, Terence. 2002. "Representation, Polyphony and the Construction of Power in a Kayapo Video." In *Indigenous Movements, Self-Representation, and the State in Latin America,* edited by K.B. Warren and J.E. Jackson, 229–50. Austin: University of Texas Press.

Turner, Terence. 2006. "Political Innovation and Inter-Ethnic Alliance." *Anthropology Today* 22 (5): 2–10.

Theodossopoulos, Dimitrios. 2009. "Introduction: United in Discontent." In *United in Discontent: Local Responses to Cosmopolitanism and Globalization,* ed. Dimitrios Theodossopoulos and Elisabeth Kirtsoglou, 1–19. Oxford: Berghahn.

Theodossopoulos, Dimitrios. 2010. "Tourism and Indigenous Culture as Resources: Lessons from Emberá Cultural Tourism in Panama." In *Tourism, Power and Culture: Anthropological Insights,* edited by Donald V.L. Macleod and James G. Carrier, 115–33. Bristol: Channel View.

Theodossopoulos, Dimitrios. 2011. "Emberá Indigenous Tourism and the World of Expectations." In *Great Expectations: Imagination and Anticipation in Tourism,* edited by Jonathan Skinner and Dimitrios Theodossopoulos, 40–60. Oxford: Berghahn.

Theodossopoulos, Dimitrios. 2012a. "Indigenous Attire, Exoticisation and Social Change: Dressing and Undressing among the Emberá of Panama." *Journal of the Royal Anthropological Institute*. 18 (3): 591–612.

Theodossopoulos, Dimitrios. 2012b. "Dance, Visibility, and Representational Self-Awareness in an Embera Community in Panama." In *Dancing Cultures: Globalization, Tourism and Identity in the Anthropology of Dance*, edited by Hélène Neveu Kringelbach and J. Skinner, 121–40. New York: Berghahn.

Theodossopoulos, Dimitrios. 2013. "Laying Claim to Authenticity: Five Anthropological Dilemmas." *Anthropological Quarterly* 86 (2): 337–60. [Online]. http://dx.doi.org/10.1353/anq.2013.0032.

Theodossopoulos, Dimitrios. 2014. "Scorn or Idealization? Tourism Imaginaries, Exoticisation and Ambivalence." In *Tourism Imaginaries*, edited by Noel Salazar and Nelson Graburn. New York: Berghahn.

Theodossopoulos, Dimitrios. 2015. "Embera Indigeneity and Cultural Representation: A View from Engaged Anthropology." In *Indigenous Studies and Engaged Anthropology: The Collaborative Moment*, edited by Paul Sillitoe, 33–54. Surrey: Ashgate.

Theodossopoulos, Dimitrios. 2016. *Exoticisation Undressed: Ethnographic Nostalgia and Authenticity in Emberá Clothes*. Manchester: Manchester University Press.

Tice, Karin E. 1995. *Kuna Crafts, Gender, and the Global Economy*. Austin: University of Texas Press.

Velásquez Runk, Julie. 2009. "Social and River Networks for the Trees: Wounaan's Riverine Rhizomic Cosmos and Arboreal Conservation." *American Anthropologist* 111 (4): 456–67. http://dx.doi.org/10.1111/j.1548-1433.2009.01155.x.

West, Paige, and James Carrier. 2004. "Ecotourism and Authenticity: Getting Away from It All?" *Current Anthropology* 45 (4): 483–98. http://dx.doi.org/10.1086/422082.

Williams, Caroline A. 2004. *Between Resistance and Adaptation: Indigenous Peoples and the Colonisation of the Chocó, 1510–1753*. Liverpool: Liverpool University Press. http://dx.doi.org/10.5949/UPO9781846312670.

6 San Cultural Tourism: Mobilizing Indigenous Agency in Botswana

RACHEL F. GIRAUDO

The cultural tourism industry is well known for (re)producing differ-ence through the marketing and commodification of unique cultural experiences. While cultural tourism often misappropriates a cultural group's heritage and infringes on their intellectual property rights, it also has potential to enable economic, social, and political empow-erment. This chapter examines how cultural tourism contributes to the political recognition of the San as indigenous in the Republic of Botswana.[1] While many human rights groups and non-governmental organizations (NGOs) consider the San as *the* indigenous peoples of southern Africa, the government of Botswana does not recognize any ethnic group as more indigenous than another.[2] This chapter under-scores how the commodification of San cultural heritage through tour-ism helps to reaffirm their indigenous subjectivity within the public sphere using examples from tourism encounters and news media in the country.

Tourism has fast become a crucial industry in Botswana's bid to diversify its economy, which remains largely dependent on diamond and other mineral mining. Although most tourism income is from wild-life- and nature-based tourism, cultural tourism is becoming more wide-spread as a means to alleviate poverty within rural Botswana. In fact, the government supports proposals for community-based cultural tourism projects that are often initiated by NGOs and through public-private partnerships. Several of these tourism projects target San peoples, who are culturally, linguistically, and phenotypically distinct from the numerous Bantu ethnic groups. Their unique cultural heritage, shrink-ing population, and global portrayal as indigenous make the San attrac-tive to foreign and domestic tourists alike. Then again, it is precisely their difference as well as the international attention they receive that contribute to their extreme, ongoing marginalization by the state.

Because cultural tourism is a means of economic empowerment and visibility for the San, and due to Botswana's increasing reliance on tourism development, it has the potential to become a political tool and space for protest in Botswana, especially regarding the contentious issues of indigeneity and indigenous rights. The idea of indigeneity is now more frequently discussed in Botswana, in large part because of the importance of tourism to the country. However, tourism is also an arena that continues to fuel tensions concerning the relative significance of nature and culture as political and economic resources. One example discussed in this chapter is a national debate that erupted when the human rights group Survival International called for a tourism boycott in 2010 to draw attention to the government of Botswana's treatment of San peoples in the Central Kalahari Game Reserve. These circumstances are therefore necessary to examine because while the government supports local tourism as a sustainable development opportunity, tourism potentially empowers the most marginalized ethnic group, and at the same time helps to reshape the country's dialogue of recognition. Cultural tourism is a venue in which the San can re-articulate an indigenous identity nationally, and, due to the nature of the international tourism industry, solidify their participation in a global indigenous movement.

San Indigenousness and Botswana's Ethno-Class Hierarchy

The San are widely considered the "first peoples" of southern Africa. Archaeologists and historians have shown that hunter-gatherer-herders – the ancestors of modern-day San peoples – inhabited the southern African region, including what is now Botswana, for thousands of years before Bantu peoples migrated southward about fifteen hundred to two thousand years ago (Mitchell 2002), bringing with them pastoralism, agriculture, and iron-smelting technologies. Most Bantu peoples continued migrating southward to what is now South Africa due to the uninhabitability of the Kalahari Desert.[3] Ancestors of modern-day Tswana only moved northward to what is now northern South Africa and southern Botswana in the fifteenth century, as they formed stronger polities that would fissure and spread outward (Tlou and Campbell 1997). The San are linguistically distinct from neighbouring ethnic groups, and historical linguists have demonstrated the longevity of San peoples in southern Africa

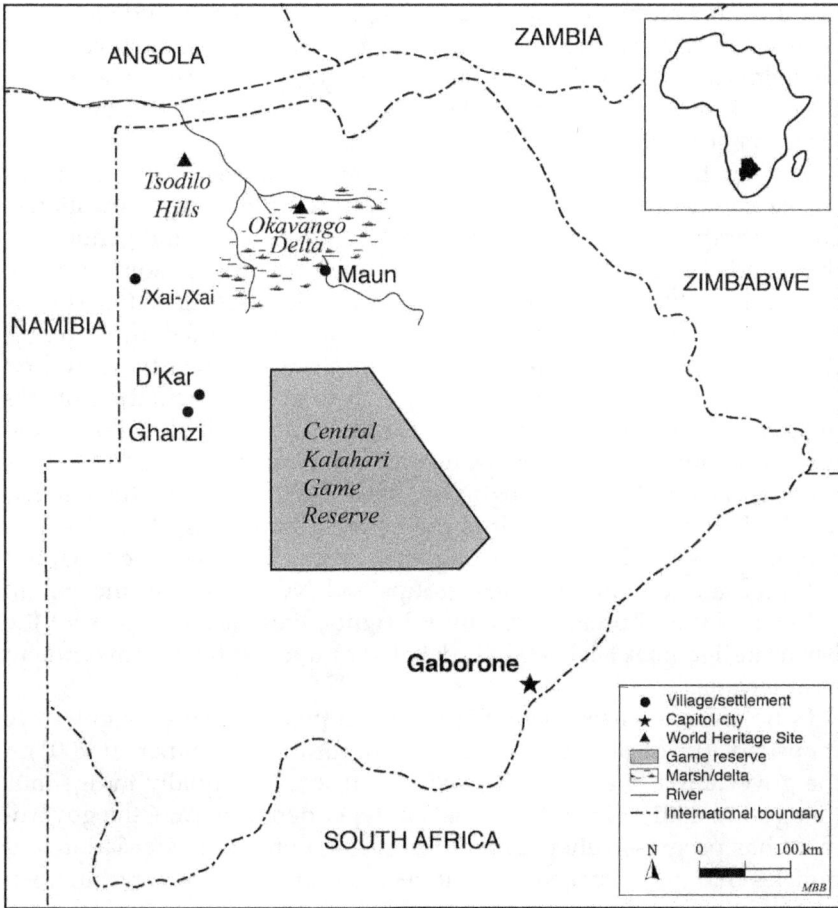

Figure 6.1 Map of Botswana featuring several locations discussed in this chapter. (Copyright: Rachel F. Giraudo)

and the more recent arrival of Bantu peoples (Güldemann and Stoneking 2008). Genetic research also points to the San as being the first peoples of southern Africa given that they have the most genetically diverse DNA in the world, even suggesting that they may be *the* first peoples on the planet (Schuster et al. 2010; see also Mitchell 2010).

The "first peoples" argument references a San presence in southern Africa before the arrival of Bantu peoples or Europeans. Additional, equally important factors to the San's being declared indigenous are their traditional livelihoods (primarily foraging, though some are also herders), egalitarian social structure, and socio-political status as marginalized by the state. Descriptions and romantic ideas of the San produced by explorers, anthropologists, and others for over two hundred years have reached a global audience through the circulation of this imaginary in print, film, and other media. San peoples have been featured in ethnographies, novels, magazines, documentary and popular films, and commercial photography; these media forms continue to fixate the San as "primitive." It is the extreme marginalization that San communities continue to face long after official decolonization that has led international human rights groups and NGOs to enter the fray in defence of their human and cultural rights; these actors represent the San as indigenous, a label that is debated or ignored by the government of Botswana.

In Botswana, where the majority of San peoples live – roughly fifty thousand out of about one hundred thousand (see Suzman 2001) – the government maintains that *all* its citizens are equally indigenous (Saugestad 2001). Since Botswana's independence in 1966, the government has progressively pursued non-racial, non-ethnic legislation and policies that are mistakenly presumed to represent a post-racial, post-ethnic Botswana society. Using nation-building ideals, the country's first president, Seretse Khama, advocated that individuals in Botswana identify themselves first as citizens and not as members of ethnic tribes (*merafe*). This pronouncement became highly gestural and merely symbolic as, in time, the government pursued policies that reflected the cultural worldview of the pastoral Tswana, therefore disregarding the new country's diverse cultural citizenry (i.e., section 15[4][*d*], section 15[9], and sections 77–9 of the Constitution of Botswana, section 2 of the Chieftainship Act, and the Tribal Territories Act [see Nyati-Rama-hobo 2008]). The cultural hegemony of the Tswana – "Tswanafication" (Solway 2002) – has made it incredibly difficult for the San to gain any footing in modern-day Botswana.

Since Independence, government legislation and policies have had an overwhelmingly negative impact on San peoples. For example, until late 2015 only Tswana tribes were legally recognized (and as of mid-2017, just the Basubiya and Wayeyi – two of about thirty-seven non-Tswana tribes in the country – are also formally recognized by the government of Botswana), and land in Botswana was primarily divided between the eight Tswana tribes (governed by tribal land boards). The traditional land tenure systems of San peoples were not taken into account, and as a result they lost most of their traditional land (Hitchcock and Holm 1993; Saugestad 2001). Cattle rearing and conservation policies and initiatives further hindered access to land. The government promoted cattle rearing throughout the 1970s and 1980s as both a land use strategy and a way to assimilate ethnic minorities into the national economy. Wildlife conservation through tightly controlled hunting laws also prohibited many San peoples from employing their traditional livelihoods, making them dependent on government handouts for fear of being imprisoned (Hitchcock 2001). This situation was exacerbated by a nationwide hunting ban imposed in 2014, the ramifications of which are yet to be thoroughly analysed. To some extent, even the gathering of wild products, such as ostrich eggshells that San women make into jewellery to sell to tourists, was prohibited. In the 1970s, the government unveiled its Bushmen Development Programme meant to help assimilate San peoples. It was renamed the Remote Area Dweller Programme (RADP), and participants are known as Remote Area Dwellers, or "RADs." Through the RADP, San peoples are given food handouts (e.g., maize meal, tea, and sugar) and some money, and RAD children are boarded in hostels at schools often far from their families. The inadequacies of these provisions have been scrutinized by researchers and development agencies alike, who argue that RADP does not do nearly enough to keep San peoples from impoverishment according to Botswana's own standard of living and that it perpetuates dependency on the government (Hitchcock and Holm 1993; Saugestad 2001). Government legislation and policies have severely affected the ability of ethnic minorities to sustain themselves, but criticism of those policies and legislation has only resulted in the government's blaming ethnic minorities for not assimilating well enough (see Saugestad 2005). In fact, the government typically relies upon a primitivist rationality for pursuing such policies (i.e., that ethnic minorities, such as the San, are too "primitive" to care for themselves and must be looked after by the government) in spite of national and international criticism that those policies further marginalize ethnic minorities.

Botswana's official promotion of an undifferentiated citizenship throws into high relief its hypocrisy with regard to government officials' deep-seated prejudices regarding the San and the injustices it imposes upon San peoples in the country, who remain on the lowest rung of Botswana's ethno-class hierarchy. For example, Festus Mogae, the former president of Botswana, infamously called the San "Stone Age creatures" (Daley 1996), and other government officials have also used this rhetoric of primitivism as a rationale for assimilating San peoples. Despite Botswana's historical stance on avoiding racial and ethnic discrimination in its government policies, it has clearly enabled an ethno-class hierarchy to persist for fifty years since Independence. The government's reluctance to redress the resulting issues of inequality has made possible an international presence through interventions by indigenous and minority rights activists, NGOs, and the global diplomatic community on behalf of the San and other minority groups in the country.

International and African Discourses of Indigeneity

International conceptions of indigeneity do not translate well in postcolonial Africa, where nascent states have established and now maintain diverse citizenries. One reason is that the movement for indigenous rights has been expressed most powerfully in settler colonial contexts, such as in the Americas and Oceania, where an indigenous identity is framed in opposition to that of a settler. However, while European colonization left the most long-lasting cultural ruptures in Africa, the continent also underwent internal migrations and colonizations before and after European arrival. Another reason is an anxiety about indigenous discourses applied in Africa, as they are thought to reflect the divisive racial legacy of European colonization. Even the idea of African ethnicities is argued to be part of European colonizing efforts (Mamdani 1996, 2002). The default position of new nation-states of the continent, therefore, is to promote their autochthonous position to outsiders and to resist further division, which is done by disregarding international pressure to conform to Western ideals.

Transnational indigenous politics (see Niezen 2003) disrupt Botswana's nationalism by articulating a global indigeneity in which San peoples are clearly included but Bantu peoples do not necessarily fit.

Regional and international agencies do not disagree that Bantu peoples are indigenous to Africa, but point to the San as being the most indigenous peoples of all southern Africa. Indeed, the multivalence of the concept of "indigenous" has led to some confusion. One notion evokes cultural traits of the egalitarian forager in cultural ecology, and it is this essentialized view that is simultaneously criticized by scholars yet used by many indigenous advocates (see Barnard 2006, 2010; Guenther et al. 2006) it is also often what the public have in mind when thinking of indigenous peoples. "Indigenous" can also be applied with socio-political and legal connotations that refer to the processes of encapsulation and marginalization by a dominant society (Gausset, Kenrick, and Gibb 2011). A somewhat similar idea is "autochthony," which refers to (legal) rights to territory by those "native" to it (Gausset, Kenrick, and Gibb 2011). The concept of autochthony is less at odds with nationalist state powers that seek to protect their sovereign rights from potential encroachment. In Botswana, the government rejects the use of indigeneity in either its essentialized cultural or socio-political and legal variants, but does support the concept of autochthony, which it refers to as indigeneity. This linguistic slippage therefore confounds communication between activists and the government.

Moving beyond the above uses of "indigeneity" and "autochthony," anthropologists now discuss "indigenous" as a subjectivity with which people can self-identify or that they can articulate (Tsing 2007). For example, Dorothy Hodgson (2009, 2011) chronicles how Maasai pastoralists of Eastern Africa *became* indigenous by embracing an indigenous subjectivity through participation in local NGOs and transnational indigenous networks. This idea of "indigenous" means that there is no clear way to define who is or is not indigenous because it is a relational, historical process of marginalization by states and other imperial powers (see de la Cadena and Starn 2007; Hodgson 2011), and it is this more conceptual way of comprehending indigeneity, rather than any official use, that is most helpful in understanding indigenous issues and indigenous agency.

Botswana is effectively a culturally hegemonic state that supports the ongoing cultural assimilation of non-Tswana ethnic groups in the country, and its promotion of undifferentiated citizenship serves to conceal ethnic inequalities. The government declares all citizens indigenous, which was originally meant to differentiate Africans from non-African settlers, and denies that its legislation and policies dispossess San peoples of rights. The government uses the concept of "autochthony" in political rhetoric, and not the notion of "indigenous," as a process of marginalization. Despite the international community's praise of Botswana as a successful example of African democracy, the government also continues to be criticized by the West for its treatment of San peoples.

Historically, the Tswana considered the San to be subhuman (as did European settlers), and until at least the mid-1930s kept them as indentured serfs (Motzafi-Haller 1994). Now the San are considered backward and unwilling to assimilate and develop. San cultural distinctiveness drew scorn from the Tswana and other Bantu peoples and European settlers, but academics, NGOs, and San and non-San activists now use their cultural uniqueness, in large part, to emphasize San indigeneity. San peoples do not have the same rights as other citizens of Botswana, and they remain at the bottom of the country's ethno-class hierarchy. It is their socio-political marginalization that grants credence to the San's being declared indigenous. Whereas activists, human rights groups, and NGOs rely on the cultural distinction and socio-political connotations of indigeneity, the government of Botswana along with many other African governments utilizes indigeneity differently, as autochthony, framing the discourse between Africans and non-Africans.

Therefore, Botswana and other African states initially declined to support the UN Declaration on the Rights of Indigenous Peoples. Former president Festus Mogae commented at the 2006 African Heads of Mission:

> Our contention as Botswana is that all black Africans are of African origin. It has to be appreciated that the situation of Africa is different from that of the Americas and Australia. Unlike in both North and Latin America and countries such as Australia and New Zealand, we did not emigrate from elsewhere to Africa, we have always belonged here. However, there are some Non-Governmental Organisations and maybe even some Governments who would like to tell Africa that some Africans are less indigenous than others and that, therefore, they deserve some special dispensations. (qtd in Zips-Mairitsch 2011, 138)

Mogae was obviously hesitant about what authority the declaration could have over the power of the nation-state in shaping its own legitimacy in the postcolonial era, and relied upon the argument that to be African means to be indigenous to Africa.[4] The government also had misgivings over self-determination and rights to land and resources, a concern shared by many other states. After revisions, the government of Botswana did, however, ratify the 2007 UN Declaration on the Rights of Indigenous Peoples, but held firm on their position:

> The position of the Government of Botswana on indigenousness to this country remains. As Botswana is inhabited by many different ethnic groups that occupied the geographical areas of present-day Botswana at different times in history, *historical developments have led these ethnic groups to develop as one and a united nation of Batswana*. All citizens of Botswana are therefore indigenous to the country with the exception of some naturalized citizens. No tribe or ethnic group is in this regard considered more indigenous than the others in the country. Government rejects outright, attempts by certain quarters to impose on Botswana, a definition of indigenous people that suits only the narrow and ill-informed agendas and interests of certain advocacy groups. (*Moemedi: The Envoy* 2007, 12, emphasis added)

Botswana held firm on its own notion of "indigenous," one more akin to autochthony. The government's position in defining how it conceives of "indigenous," however, omits the discourse of indigeneity as processual and relational. The government completely avoids acknowledging the marginalization that certain indigeneity discourses reveal. In fact, Botswana is unyielding in its presentation of its citizens as undifferentiated (i.e., diverse peoples became *Batswana*, which is the plural of Tswana).

While the government of Botswana chooses not to acknowledge either the San as the more indigenous peoples of the region, including the territory now known as Botswana, or their extreme marginalized status, other institutions, actors, and venues, such as international human rights groups, local media, and tour operators, are proving to be the right outlets for substantiating various indigeneity claims. Cultural tourism, however, repositions San ethnicity and their perceived indigeneity as a desirable commodity. Now that the government of Botswana is eager to both diversify its national economy and expand the tourism sector of its economy, cultural tourism is an important niche market, and one that thrives on the packaging of ethnic and historical difference. It may also be the vessel via which a message of San indigeneity is finally more fully accepted by the government. As tourism encounters and imaginaries are some of the "sites" where San indigeneity is re-articulated via San agency, it is worth examining cultural tourism in order to comprehend indigenous identity politics beyond state and international proclamations.

Cultural Tourism and Botswana's Political Economy

Interest in community-based tourism arose in response to Botswana's expanding tourism economy. The tourism industry is currently the second highest contributor to the country's GDP, behind the mining industry (World Travel & Tourism Council [WTTC] 2007), and the industry is expected to play a major role in economic diversification for the country. The government of Botswana rather optimistically hopes that diverse tourism ventures will also help to reduce poverty, especially in rural areas. Botswana's tourism industry employs 9.9 per cent (and rising) of the country's total workforce (WTTC 2014), including those in the category of unskilled labour, such as disadvantaged ethnic minorities who generally lack access to secondary education.

Although the majority of tourism to Botswana is wildlife- and nature-based, there is also a significant proportion of tourists who are interested in the cultural heritage of the country.[5] Due to the pervasive representation of San peoples as exemplary nomads, many international tourists visiting Botswana consider the San to be *the* first peoples of southern Africa and are nostalgic for their perceived "primitive" culture (domestic tourists are also curious). They desire and pay for cultural experiences with the indigenous San. Through such tourism encounters, tourists, tourism operators, and San peoples are involved in a discourse centring on southern African indigeneity. Tourism is therefore another type of public sphere, the "tourist sphere."

With the initial supervision of NGOs (i.e., the Kuru Family of Organisations and the Netherlands Development Organisation), community-based cultural tourism projects started in Botswana in the 1990s and are expected to help San people's transition to a cash economy. Modelled on the community-based natural resource management (CBNRM) process (see Rozemeijer 2009), community-based cultural tourism projects attempt to provide sustainable development opportunities for the San and other ethnic minorities through the self-commodification of their cultures (see Bunten 2008). For instance, a community trust is established to govern the community's commercial and political interests as the community receives funds from NGOs or enters into joint ventures with the private sector. Through the trust, community members learn how to utilize their resources for profit and how to manage their earnings through capacity-building programs offered by NGOs and the government.

San cultural tourism continues to gain stride in Botswana as the government encourages its rural poor to be less dependent on state welfare (albeit that dependency was in large part created by government legislation and policies). Examples of community-based projects with the San include cultural tourism with the Ju | 'hoansi at | Xai- | Xai in western Ngamiland (Rozemeijer 2001), cultural tourism at the Dqãe Qare San Lodge near Ghanzi (Rozemeijer 2001) and the Nharo settlements in D'Kar, cultural tourism with the !Xoo in the southern Botswana–controlled hunting area Kalagadi District 1 (Rozemeijer 2001), cultural and archaeological tourism with the Ju | 'hoansi at the Tsodilo World Heritage Site (Giraudo 2011), and cultural tourism with Khwe speakers around the Okavango Panhandle (Haug 2007). These community-based cultural tourism projects, which entail guided nature and cultural walks, traditional dance and music demonstrations, cultural photography, and the production and sale of San crafts, such as ostrich-eggshell jewellery and bow-and-arrow sets, are even advertised by the Botswana Tourism Board.

In addition to these community-based cultural tourism projects, there are a number of independent tourism operators that work with San peoples: Grasslands Safari Lodge, Ghanzi Trail Blazers, Uncharted Africa Safari Co., and many others. Private tourism operators tend to stage cultural encounters with San peoples in order to meet tourists' expectations of a nostalgic idea of hunter-gatherers or spiritual shamans. For instance, rather than taking tourists to the impoverished camps of the San where people rarely still live in grass huts or wear traditional leather clothing, tourism operators create or encourage cultural villages (see Smith 1977), where the San dress in traditional leather skins, perform games and (healing) dances, and teach tourists about local flora and fauna, part of what Bunten (2010) calls the "cultural tourism formula." This also happens in community-based tourism, but not always as deliberately. For example, at Grasslands Safaris, the lodge managers bring tourists on outings for cultural activities with nearby San – who are now landless, encroached upon by white (Afrikaner) farmers and displaced by the recently depopulated Central Kalahari Game Reserve (CKGR) – where San men, women, and children don traditional leather skins and share traditional games and foods, and of course spare time for photographs. Ghanzi Trail Blazers utilizes the services of San from CKGR resettlement camps on their private property for their niche market of overland bus tourists, who stop overnight to take a guided walk followed by an evening of traditional dance around the fire. Uncharted Africa Safari Co. even relocated Ju | 'hoansi from the | Xai- | Xai/Dobe area of northwestern Botswana to the Makgadikgadi Pans of central Botswana (tour operators do not consider the local Sokwe "traditional" enough to work in cultural tourism), where they make some money by performing dances at remote luxury camps. Whereas community-based projects conceivably position the San with authority over their cultural tourism (though in practice this is not always the case), when the private sector is involved there is perhaps a greater chance that the San will be exploited.

Prior to CBNRM cultural tourism projects, non-San, especially whites, controlled much of the cultural tourism operations in the region and profited by selling a stereotypical imaginary of the San that typically avoided any complex demonstration of the political and social marginalization they face (Garland and Gordon 1999; Guenther 2002). Thus, cultural tourism of San peoples often incited racism, one reason why the government of Botswana was formally opposed to it, since the government was concerned about the San's objectification (Hitchcock 2001). As the Botswana tourism industry evolved over the past few decades, cultural tourism appeared to offer more opportunities to empower San peoples (Hitchcock 1997, 2001). Even though the San are more in control of how they present their cultural heritage to tourists in CBNRM projects, it is challenging to decipher whether they actually control their own image by managing their own cultural tourism because the industry is vast and nebulous. NGOs and other external agencies, such as philanthropic donors and foreign government donors, also have significant influence over CBNRM projects and communities hoping to get sponsored for one. Therefore it is still unclear whether this type of cultural tourism can be less essentialist, relying on simple stereotypes of the San, or if it has the potential to reveal a more complicated narrative of San identity politics.

The San are generally caught in a double bind, as their stereotypical image as "primitive" hunter-gatherers can work against them and for them, often at the same time (see Robins 2001). In Botswana, this results in their clichéd image being used against them by a government wanting to assimilate them into Tswana society, and working for them in maintaining a niche market for tourists. Yet many tourists see beyond the façade of cultural villages and desire a more candid understanding of San culture in the present day. At the Tsodilo World Heritage

Figure 6.2 San women and a man demonstrate a melon-tossing game at the Grasslands Safari Lodge. (Copyright: Rachel F. Giraudo)

Site, Ju | 'hoan guides educate curious tourists about the hardships their community faces. Likewise, when asked about San cultural tourism, Nharo guides at Dqāe Qare share their frustration that most of the San cultural tourism industry in Botswana is owned and controlled by non-San. These encounters within the tourist sphere provide San peoples with opportunity to demonstrate their own agency in the struggles for their indigenous rights.

The Significance of a Tourism Boycott

Botswana's tourism industry is so important to the country's goal of economic diversification that it also creates space for protest. In a 2010 editorial Stephen Corry, the director of Survival International (SI), a human rights organization based in London, England, that lobbies on behalf of tribal and indigenous societies, explained why SI was calling for a tourism boycott of Botswana (Corry 2010). For over a decade, SI has seized international news headlines with articles about the Botswana government's evictions of the G | wi and G | | ana from the

CKGR, accusing the government of evicting them in order to pursue diamond prospecting and mining on that land (SI 2006). During this time, SI has called for a boycott of Botswana's diamonds, which are held in very high esteem by the government and citizens and are perceived as a national resource. Via this act, coupled with their scathing editorials regarding the treatment of the San, the human rights organization became a major nuisance to the government as well as affecting relations between the San and the government (Hitchcock 2002; Solway 2009; Suzman 2002); the government subsequently became increasingly adamant about pursuing its agenda without foreign interference (Botswana views indigenous rights as foreign ideology).

Botswana wants to maintain its sovereignty, yet government officials continue to make revealing comments about their views of the San that undermine their political integrity on the issue of non-discrimination. During SI's 2010 call for a tourism boycott of Botswana Kitso Mokaila, then minister of the environment, wildlife and tourism, angrily responded, "I don't believe you would want to see your own kind living in the dark ages in the middle of nowhere as a choice, when you know that the world has moved forward and has become so technological" (BBC News 2010). Mokaila's words expose, as did Mogae's in his infamous revelation, that the government considers San peoples culturally inferior and is frustrated by their lack of assimilation. The government has actually already differentiated its citizens, though this is kept hidden within most official rhetoric.

While the G|wi and G||ana were victorious in their 2006 court case against the government over illegalities in their relocation (Solway 2009; Taylor 2007), by late 2010 they had still not been able to return to the CKGR because the government denied them the right to access water through a drilled borehole. The government argued that if the San wanted to live in nature then they should have no modern conveniences (SI 2010).[6] In the meantime, however, the government had boreholes drilled for wildlife – paid for by Tiffany & Co. – and allowed for the building of a tourism lodge in the CKGR complete with full water facilities (SI 2010) to better stage its nature for tourists. Thus, in his editorial, Corry (2010) writes that "a so-called 'ethical' tourist company, Wilderness Safaris, has established a luxury lodge, complete with swimming pool, on Bushman land" in the CKGR, demonstrating that tourism development can lead to dispossession like diamond prospecting and mining. He argues that the new tourism boycott is a way of making international tourists "aware that they are supporting a government which profits from destroying the last hunting Bushmen in the world" (Corry 2010).

Corry clearly relies on an essentialist understanding of San as nomadic hunter-gatherers in making his case, but also returns to the debate between nature and culture as resources in Botswana's interest. SI's 2010 call for a tourism boycott of Botswana is curious because most of its previous criticism of the government focused on diamonds, which are Botswana's primary source of revenue, deeply protected by the government and part of national culture.[7] Tourism had finally become a relevant, though surprising, political tool in the country (see also Graburn 2004). Political parties within Botswana even weighed in on this boycott, often voicing contempt over the government's handling of CKGR matters. In January 2011, the G|wi and G||ana were finally allowed to use the boreholes in the CKGR, and SI's media campaign, along with the legal claims made by the G|wi and G||ana and various NGOs and lawyers assisting them, probably helped in obtaining this decision. At the very least, though, SI's campaign and the legal claims prompted a dialogue – a very political dialogue – both within Botswana and internationally about indigenous rights.

For example, in an opinion piece in the *Mmegi* newspaper a journalist writes, "the dismissive and often insulting manner in which our governments regard the demands of the Bushmen for recognition, respect and assistance as *indigenous peoples with inalienable rights to their ancestral lands and ways of life* has been unfortunate over the years" (Moabi 2010, emphasis added). There are several examples of indigeneity and indigenous rights discourses appearing in Botswana newspapers, such as *Mmegi*, the *Botswana Gazette*, and *Botswana Guardian*, wherein journalists, politicians, and other citizens argue for and against the rights of the San as indigenous peoples and the government's assimilationist position (the comment sections of the online versions of these news stories allow for further public debate).

Although conservation for wildlife- and nature-based tourism was one of the reasons that the government of Botswana evicted many San from the CKGR and their other home territories, cultural tourism potentially affords them greater visibility with which to exert their political agency. The tension between nature and culture, though, still leans in favour of nature as a more valuable economic resource. The power of culture as a symbolic, political resource may never trump nature in Botswana's tourism coffers. However, that indigeneity and San rights are becoming a greater part of national politics in Botswana through the medium of local media due to the country's motivation to diversify its economy and tourism industry means that this is a significant arena in which to behold another dynamic form of indigenous agency.

Mobilizing Indigenous Agency through Cultural Tourism

Cultural tourism is proving to be an important, though sometimes overlooked, "site" within which to observe indigenous agency. This is the case in Botswana, and the southern African region more generally, where participation in NGOs and transnational networking are studied as significant sites of indigenous politics, or where court cases against state governments are understood to be the most direct actions indigenous groups might take against an oppressive state apparatus. Each provides a particular scale by which to better analyse the web of political strategies and actions used to achieve recognition and rights.

Even though the government of Botswana ratified the UN Declaration on the Rights of Indigenous Peoples in September 2007, thereby officially accepting a notion of indigeneity and pledging to uphold the rights of indigenous peoples, this act has had little effect on the government's ill treatment of the San because of its understanding of indigeneity as autochthony. Attempts by NGOs and human rights groups to persuade the government to reconsider its staunch refusal to acknowledge San peoples as indigenous have had mixed success and are viewed with suspicion by the government. Cultural tourism, though, may be a way forward in garnering the attention of the government about the value of San cultural survival. It enables dialogue about the notion of indigeneity and the ideas of indigenous rights in tourist encounters and the news media. These venues help to shift the focus of the debate away from the meaning of the term (i.e., from its interpretation as autochthony) and towards a socio-political understanding. San-run cultural tourism is perhaps the greatest chance the San themselves have in re-conceptualizing how to use their imaginary for economic and political gain.

There are, however, signs of the government limiting or controlling cultural tourism. To begin with, community-based tourism projects were dealt a blow by the Office of the President in 2007 with the passing of the National Environment Fund, which mandates that 65 per cent of trust proceeds be returned to the central government (see Republic of Botswana 2007). CBNRM projects are thus under threat, since the appeal to local community members to manage and promote their local resources, including their cultural heritage, is lessened as proceeds are siphoned back to the central government. Furthermore, the country, having ratified the 2003 UNESCO Convention for the Safeguarding of Intangible Heritage in 2010, is in the process of inventorying the cultural heritage of the country. In essence, the government is nationalizing diverse forms and examples of cultural heritage so that nobody else – perhaps not even the ethnic groups to whom the intangible cultural heritage belongs – can profit without oversight from the government.

Another problem is that NGOs and the government impose the structure of a community trust on the operations of community-based cultural tourism projects. However, the government of Botswana recognizes "local communities" based on defined geographic areas, so many community trusts are comprised of members of more than one ethnic group. Since Bantu peoples and whites now live close to San peoples, the structure of a community trust becomes another way for them to assert control over and patronize the San. Members of more dominant ethnic groups may therefore control a trust's funding and utilize their positions on a trust board to further opportunities for themselves and their family and friends. Jealousies inevitably arise over the potential success of tourism ventures and occasionally result in non-San suppressing the San's ability to benefit from CBNRM projects.

In addition, though aimed at the higher-stakes revenue of wildlife- and nature-based tourism, a new liberalization regulation in Botswana affects cultural tourism businesses in the private sector because it restricts tourism services provided by non-citizens (Republic of Botswana 2006). Foreign tourism operators, such as those from South Africa where human rights-based political discourses are very strong in the post-apartheid era, might be more sympathetic towards the political plight of the San, though this sympathy can also perpetuate romanticized or derogatory views of the San. As this regulation is enforced, citizen-owned tourism operators in Botswana may be less willing to support the claim of San indigeneity to avoid upsetting the government.

San cultural tourism exemplifies mobility in an increasingly global era: mobile tourists, mobile capital (tourist dollars), mobile media of the San, and mobile ideologies of indigeneity. Cultural tourism and San agency through the re-articulation of an indigenous identity as a means to claim rights and resources is a local project that relies on the global. There are multiple discourses of indigeneity intersecting and being re-embedded in Botswana through San cultural tourism: that of an essentialized identity, a marginalized status, and a political stance. The need for economic diversification and more employment opportunities in a developing cash economy is softening the government of Botswana's resistance to acknowledging ethnic difference, allowing new ideas and new subjectivities to permeate national discourse. These changes can be studied through the perspective of tourism encounters and ensuing media discussions of indigenous rights. There may be challenges confronting San cultural tourism, but its potential as a growing area of indigenous agency in Botswana is important to acknowledge.

NOTES

1 I do not capitalize "indigenous" in this chapter to acknowledge its status as a contested concept in Africa.
2 There are several different ways in which San peoples are referred to today. "San" is a shortening of the linguistic family "Khoisan" (or "Khoesaan"), and is how many researchers and NGOs refer to them. "Bushmen" is a Westernized reference (*Boesman* in Afrikaans) and one often touted in popular culture and in tourism brochures. In Botswana, San peoples are now referred to as "Basarwa" (the earlier prefix "ma-" in "Masarwa," not being a prefix that referred to humans, was updated to the human prefix "ba-" after Independence) (see Motzafi-Haller 1994, 557). What all of these referents have in common is the essentializing of numerous ethnic groups from a language family based on common linguistic (i.e., click-consonants) and cultural attributes.
3 Anthropologists and archaeologists who study the prehistory of this region contentiously disagree with one another about whether the San maintained a hunter-gatherer and herding lifestyle with all of its attributes (e.g., egalitarianism and nomadism) until European colonialism and the ensuing increase of regional culture contact (for an overview of the "Kalahari Debate" see Sadr 1997).
4 Although Mogae argues that all black Africans (Bantu peoples) are indigenous to Africa, it is important to note that the San do not consider themselves racially black: they refer to themselves as red, orange, or even white.
5 More than two million foreign tourists are estimated to have visited Botswana in 2010, just under 20 per cent of whom were likely leisure tourists. Of over one million domestic tourist trips in Botswana in 2010, an estimated 15.9 per cent were for leisure (Department of Tourism n.d.). Although official statistics are not kept concerning what, exactly, leisure tourists come to Botswana to see and do, the number of operators for

wildlife/nature versus cultural tourism makes it clear that leisure tourists are primarily coming for the former.

6 See also Sesana, Seitlhobogwa, and others vs. Attorney General, MISCA No. 52–2002 (2006).

7 SI (2013) called for another boycott of Botswana's tourism industry on 26 September 2013, World Tourism Day.

REFERENCES

Barnard, Alan. 2006. "Kalahari Revisionism, Vienna and the 'Indigenous Peoples' Debate." *Social Anthropology* 14 (1): 1–16. http://dx.doi. org/10.1111/j.1469-8676.2006.tb00020.x.

Barnard, Alan. 2010. "Culture: The Indigenous Account." In *Culture Wars: Context, Models and Anthropologists' Accounts*, edited by Deborah James, Evie Plaice, and Christina Toren, 73–85. New York: Berghahn.

BBC News. 2010. "Botswana Anger at Diamond Boycott over Bushmen Rights." 3 November. http://www.bbc.co.uk/news/world-africa-11685932.

Bunten, Alexis Celeste. 2008. "Sharing Culture or Selling Out? Developing the Commodified Persona in the Heritage Industry." *American Ethnologist* 35 (3): 380–95. http://dx.doi.org/10.1111/j.1548-1425.2008.00041.x.

Bunten, Alexis Celeste. 2010. "More Like Ourselves: Indigenous Capitalism through Tourism." *American Indian Quarterly* 34 (3): 285–311. http://dx.doi. org/10.5250/amerindiquar.34.3.285.

Corry, Stephen. 2010. "Why Is Survival Calling for a Diamonds and Tourism Boycott?" *Mmegi*, 24 October. http://www.mmegi.bw/index. php?sid=2&aid=5828&dir=2010/October/Friday22.

Daley, Suzanne. 1996. "Botswana Is Pressing Bushmen to Leave Reserve." *New York Times*, 14 July. http://www.nytimes.com/1996/07/14/world/ botswana-is-pressing-bushmen-to-leave-reserve.html.

de la Cadena, Marisol, and Orin Starn. 2007. Introduction to *Indigenous Experience Today*, edited by Marisol de la Cadena and Orin Starn, 1–30. Oxford: Berg.

Department of Tourism. n.d. *Tourism Statistics 2006–2010*. Gaborone: Department of Tourism Research & Statistics Unit.

Garland, Elizabeth, and Robert J. Gordon. 1999. "The Authentic (In)Authentic: Bushman Anthro-Tourism." *Visual Anthropology* 12 (2–3): 267–87. http:// dx.doi.org/10.1080/08949468.1999.9966777.

Gausset, Quentin, Justin Kenrick, and Robert Gibb. 2011. "Indigeneity and Autochthony: A Couple of False Twins?" *Social Anthropology* 19 (2): 135–42. http://dx.doi.org/10.1111/j.1469-8676.2011.00144.x.

Giraudo, Rachel Faye. 2011. "Intangible Heritage and Tourism Development at the Tsodilo World Heritage Site." PhD diss., University of California, Berkeley.

Graburn, Nelson H.H. 2004. "The Kyoto Temple Tax Strike: Buddhism, Shinto, and Tourism in Japan." In *Intersecting Journeys: The Anthropology of Pilgrimage and Tourism*, edited by Ellen Badone and Sharon R. Roseman, 125–39. Urbana: University of Illinois Press.

Guenther, Mathias. 2002. "Ethno-tourism and the Bushmen." In *Self- and Other-Images of Hunter-Gatherers: Papers Presented at the Eighth International Conference on Hunting and Gathering Societies (CHAGS 8)*, edited by Henry Stewart, Alan Barnard, and Keiichi Omura, 47–54. Osaka: National Museum of Ethnology.

Guenther, Mathias, Justin Kenrick, Adam Kuper, Evie Plaice, Trond Thuen, Patrick Wolfe, Werner Zips, and Alan Barnard. 2006. "Discussion: The Concept of Indigeneity." *Social Anthropology* 14 (1): 17–32.

Güldemann, Tom, and Mark Stoneking. 2008. "A Historical Appraisal of Clicks: A Linguistic and Genetic Population Perspective." *Annual Review of Anthropology* 37 (1): 93–109. http://dx.doi.org/10.1146/annurev.anthro.37.081407.085109.

Haug, Margrethe. 2007. "Indigenous People, Tourism and Development?: The San People's Involvement in Community-Based Tourism." Master's thesis, University of Tromsø.

Hitchcock, Robert K. 1997. "Cultural, Environmental, and Economic Impacts of Tourism among Kalahari Bushmen." In *Tourism and Culture: An Applied Perspective*, edited by Erve Chambers, 93–128. Albany: State University of New York Press.

Hitchcock, Robert K. 2001. "'Hunting Is Our Heritage': The Struggle for Hunting and Gathering Rights among the San of Southern Africa." In *Parks, Property and Power: Managing Hunting Practice and Identity within State Policy Regimes: Papers Presented at the Eighth International Conference on Hunting and Gathering Societies (CHAGS 8)*, edited by David G. Anderson and Kazunobu Ikeya, 139–56. Osaka: National Museum of Ethnology.

Hitchcock, Robert K. 2002. "'We Are the First People': Land, Natural Resources and Identity in the Central Kalahari, Botswana." *Journal of Southern African Studies* (special issue, "Minorities and Citizenship in Botswana") 28 (4): 797–824. http://dx.doi.org/10.1080/0305707022000043520.

Hitchcock, Robert K., and John D. Holm. 1993. "Bureaucratic Domination of Hunter-Gatherer Societies: A Study of the San in Botswana." *Development and Change* 24 (2): 305–38. http://dx.doi.org/10.1111/j.1467-7660.1993.tb00487.x.

Hodgson, Dorothy L. 2009. "Becoming Indigenous in Africa." *African Studies Review* 52 (3): 1–32. http://dx.doi.org/10.1353/arw.0.0302.

Hodgson, Dorothy L. 2011. *Being Maasai, Becoming Indigenous: Postcolonial Politics in a Neoliberal World*. Bloomington: Indiana University Press.

Mamdani, Mahmood. 1996. *Citizen and Subject: Contemporary Africa and the Legacy of Late Colonialism*. Princeton: Princeton University Press.

Mamdani, Mahmood. 2002. *When Victims Become Killers: Colonialism, Nativism, and the Genocide in Rwanda*. Princeton: Princeton University Press.

Mitchell, Peter. 2002. *The Archaeology of Southern Africa*. Cambridge: Cambridge University Press.

Mitchell, Peter. 2010. "Genetics and Southern African Prehistory: An Archaeological View." *Journal of Anthropological Sciences* 88: 73–92.

Moabi, Dan. 2010. "Wither Botswana – Bushmen Less Insulting than Basarwa – Corry." *Mmegi*, 26 November. http://www.mmegi.bw/index. php?sid=2&aid=6841&dir=2010/November/Friday26.

Moemedi: The Envoy (quarterly newspaper of the Botswana Ministry of Foreign Affairs and International Cooperation). 2007. "Botswana Votes for Revised UN Declaration." 10 (July–September): 12.

Motzafi-Haller, Pnina. 1994. "When Bushmen Are Known as Basarwa: Gender, Ethnicity, and Differentiation in Rural Botswana." *American Ethnologist* 21 (3): 539–63. http://dx.doi.org/10.1525/ae.1994.21.3. 02a00050.

Niezen, Ronald. 2003. *The Origins of Indigenism: Human Rights and the Politics of Identity*. Berkeley: University of California Press. http://dx.doi. org/10.1525/california/9780520235540.001.0001.

Nyati-Ramahobo, Lydia. 2008. *Minority Tribes in Botswana: The Politics of Representation*. London: Minority Rights Group International.

Republic of Botswana. 2006. *Tourism (Reservation of Tourist Enterprises for Citizens) Regulations, S.I. 54 of 2006*. Gaborone: Government Printer.

Republic of Botswana. 2007. *Community Based Natural Resources Management Policy, Government Paper No. 2 of 2007*. Gaborone: Government Printer.

Robins, Steven. 2001. "NGOs, 'Bushmen' and Double Vision: The ‡Khomani San Land Claim and the Cultural Politics of 'Community' and 'Development' in the Kalahari." *Journal of Southern African Studies* 27 (4): 833–53. http://dx.doi.org/10.1080/03057070120090763.

Rozemeijer, Nico, ed. 2001. *Community-Based Tourism in Botswana: The SNV Experience in Three Community-Tourism Projects*. Den Haag: SNV Netherlands Development Organisation.

Rozemeijer, Nico. 2009. "CBNRM in Botswana." In *Evolution and Innovation in Wildlife Conservation: Parks and Game Ranches to Transfrontier Conservation*

Areas, edited by Helen Suich, Brian Child, and Anna Spenceley, 243–56. London: Earthscan.

Sadr, Karim. 1997. "Kalahari Archaeology and the Bushman Debate." *Current Anthropology* 38 (1): 104–12. http://dx.doi.org/10.1086/204590.

Saugestad, Sidsel. 2001. *The Inconvenient Indigenous: Remote Area Development in Botswana, Donor Assistance, and the First People of the Kalahari*. Uppsala: Nordic Africa Institute.

Saugestad, Sidsel. 2005. "'Improving their Lives': State Policies and San Resistance in Botswana." *Before Farming* 4: 1–9. http://dx.doi.org/10.3828/bfarm.2005.4.1.

Schuster, Stephan C., Webb Miller, Aakrosh Ratan, Lynn P. Tomsho, Belinda Giardine, Lindsay R. Kasson, Robert S. Harris et al. 2010. "Complete Khoisan and Bantu Genomes from Southern Africa." *Nature* 463 (7283): 943–47. http://dx.doi.org/10.1038/nature08795.

Smith, Valene L. 1977. "Eskimo Tourism: Micro-Models and Marginal Men." In *Hosts and Guests: The Anthropology of Tourism*, edited by Valene L. Smith, 51–70. Philadelphia: University of Pennsylvania Press.

Solway, Jacqueline S. 2002. "Navigating the 'Neutral' State: 'Minority' Rights in Botswana." *Journal of Southern African Studies* (special issue, "Minorities and Citizenship in Botswana") 28 (4): 711–29. http://dx.doi.org/10.1080/0305707022000043485.

Solway, Jacqueline. 2009. "Human Rights and NGO 'Wrongs': Conflict Diamonds, Culture Wars and the 'Bushman Question.'" *Africa: Journal of the International Africa Institute* 79 (3): 321–46. http://dx.doi.org/10.3366/E0001972009000849.

Survival International (SI). 2006. "Bushmen Aren't Forever – Botswana: Diamonds in the Central Kalahari Game Reserve and the Eviction of Bushmen." http://www.survivalinternational.org/files/related_material/11_513_969_diamonds_facts.pdf.

Survival International. 2010. "Outrage as Botswana Bushmen Denied Access to Water." http://www.survivalinternational.org/news/6257.

Survival International. 2013. "Tourists: Boycott Botswana over Treatment of Bushmen." http://www.survivalinternational.org/news/9586.

Suzman, James. 2001. *The Regional Assessment of the Status of the San in Southern Africa: An Introduction*. Windhoek: Legal Assistance Centre.

Suzman, James. 2002. "Kalahari Conundrums: Relocation, Resistance and International Support in the Central Kalahari Botswana." *Before Farming* 3–4: 1–10.

Taylor, Julie J. 2007. "Celebrating the San Victory Too Soon? Reflections on the Outcome of the Central Kalahari Game Reserve Case." *Anthropology Today* 23 (5): 3–5. http://dx.doi.org/10.1111/j.1467-8322.2007.00534.x.

Tlou, Thomas, and Alec Campbell. 1997. *History of Botswana*. 2nd ed. Gaborone: Macmillan Botswana.

Tsing, Anna. 2007. "Indigenous Voice." In *Indigenous Experience Today*, edited by Marisol de la Cadena and Orin Starn, 33–68. Oxford: Berg.

World Travel & Tourism Council (WTTC). 2007. *Botswana: The Impact of Travel & Tourism on Jobs and the Economy*. London: World Travel & Tourism Council.

World Travel & Tourism Council. 2014. *Travel & Tourism Economic Impact 2014: Botswana*. London: World Travel & Tourism Council.

Zips-Mairitsch, Manuela. 2011. "Kalahari Struggles: Indigeneity, Internal Displacement and Nature Conservation in Botswana – Interviews with Mathambo Ngakaeaja." In *The Governance of Legal Pluralism: Empirical Studies from Africa and Beyond*, edited by Werner Zips and Markus Weilenmann, 137–62. Vienna: Lit Verlag.

7 The Commodification of Authenticity: Performing and Displaying Dogon Material Identity

LAURENCE DOUNY

The Dogon region of Mali in West Africa is well known for its unique cultural and natural landscapes. They are characterized by the stunning vistas of the Bandiagara cliffs, which host remarkable earth architecture and necropolises of the Dogon and cave-dwelling populations known as Tellem (Bedaux 1972). In 1989, the escarpment was proclaimed a UNESCO World Heritage site (Cissé 2003). The aesthetic appeal of Dogon material culture also lies in its masks and indigo and bogolan textiles, as well as wood carvings and metal works that will be discussed below within the context of heritage tourism of the pre-Malian political crisis. Before 2012, the Dogon region represented a headline attraction for worldwide visitors, and it was certainly one of the most researched places in West Africa. The aesthetics of the location obscured an environment of scarcity and food crisis of which visitors were not always fully aware.[1]

The Dogon region, covering some 55,000 square kilometres, is located in the south area of the Niger River bend, where Dogon settlements are found alongside the Bandiagara escarpment as well as on the Bandiagara plateau and in the Seno Gondo plain. The Dogon communities that form around 700 patrilineal villages offer great cultural diversity, consisting linguistically of about 86 dialects and a pluralism of religions such as Protestantism, Catholicism, and Islam that coexist with animism, the Dogon's original system of belief. Dogon people rely on a self-subsistence economy based on the cultivation of millet, a staple crop; subsidiary cereals such as sorghum; and beans and ground nuts. They also grow onions, a cash crop, near water points. Since French colonial rule (1895–1960), Dogon culture has been nurtured by the outside world as much as by the Dogon people themselves – making the region a highly touristic spot. In the 1990s, tourism facilities,[2] guided tours, and local attractions such as the famous Dogon masquerades organized by the villagers were developed. Hotels started to burgeon in the villages, although today they are in ruins because of the destabilization of the Sahel by various armed groups, which led to the collapse of the Dogon tourism economy.

In this chapter, I concentrate on aspects of the commodification of Dogon authenticity through an examination of Indigenous development of cultural strategies on individual, community, and national levels before the beginning of the political crisis in 2012. I explore the role of Dogon commodified authenticity in, first, sustaining a local economy through heritage and tourism (Bunten 2005; Ryan & Aicken 2005) and, second, in forming a Dogon material identity (Douny 2014; Sofaer 2007). In other words, I suggest that the Dogon's authenticity, signified by the term *atem*, which refers to ancestors' traditions and thus heritage, serves to consolidate Dogon tourism economies and identity. I propose that the commodification of the Dogon's heritage and thus authenticity is grounded in complex political, economic, and social relations. Yet, following Bunten's argument, I suggest that the Dogon's heritage is shared with the outside world without "selling out" (Bunten 2008, 381).

Employing a material culture approach, I emphasize the processes by which multiple aspects of Dogon authenticity are created, recreated, and integrated over time through social interactions. Thus, a sense of "Dogon-ness" is strengthened through relations and is expressed in an authenticity term via which the Dogon introduce themselves to the outside world through material and (self)-display, with shifting values. Following Rowlands' definition, I consider the notion of display as

> the visual and material categories by which "Africa" is both imagined and made "real." Artworks, or objects that can be defined as such from particular perspectives, are an integral part of the processes that socialize people into ways of seeing things that inculcate beliefs and create meanings and understandings about the world ... objects are displayed (or not) because of the inherent power of their possession, not because of their representational qualities." (Rowlands 2009, 149–50)

By drawing upon the relationships between Dogon producers of spectacle and material culture and tourists, I show that "authenticity" takes on different meanings as it moves back and forth between heritage, political, spiritual, and economic values, which are locally appropriated or produced, negotiated and transformed through the mediation of objects. The Dogon's authenticity is therefore a means by which people express, display, and overarchingly materialize their identity (Douny 2014; Gosselain 2000) or sense of Dogon-ness. Consequently, the Dogon's commodification of authenticity as an Indigenous process of self-making through relations forms a "social movement" that goes beyond national and Western cultural heritage tourism politics and concepts of authenticity, which are, however, locally incorporated within Indigenous self-definition.

Colonial and Ethnographic Construction of Dogon Authenticity

"Authenticity" in academic debates is a complex and somewhat ambivalent concept that possesses a wide range of meanings (see, e.g., Reisinger and Steiner 2006). Broadly speaking, "authenticity" attributes a quality of being "unspoiled, pristine, genuine, untouched and traditional" to "something" (an object, a location, a performance) related to an individual or group (Handler 1986, 2).

Ideas of Dogon authenticity have their roots at colonial times. In 1931, French ethnologist Marcel Griaule led an ambitious colonial expedition called the Dakar-Djibouti Mission that aimed to collect ethnographic data across West and East Africa, including some three thousand objects that would comprise the ethnographic collections of the Trocadero Museum or Musée de l'Homme in Paris, now incorporated into the Musée du Quai Branly. Dogon culture, which Griaule encountered during this trip, immediately sparks in him a strong scientific curiosity that will eventually become a lifelong fascination with the material, religious, and symbolic dimensions of Dogon society. The aspects of Dogon ritual life and knowledge that obsessed Griaule and that he investigated with colleagues like Germaine Dieterlen produced an extensive number of publications about Dogon cosmogony. This theme, the Dogon account of the origin of the universe and of humankind, is depicted in a mythico-poetic style in Griaule's and Dieterlen's volume entitled *Le Renard pâle* (Griaule and Dieterlen 1965). As I observed during my fieldwork, the discourse some villagers engaged in concerning their culture stems from Griaule's ethnographies, copies of which can be found in popular Dogon villages.[3] Griaule's Dogon cosmogony, which has been described as an "ethnological myth" (Ciarcia 2003), has created the idea of Dogon culture as a unique model of authenticity, purity, and wisdom (Doquet 2002). Griaule's work remains today a historical, cultural heritage that has, however, been appropriated over time and used by Dogon people as a means to promote and legitimize their cultural identity in the context of tourism. Hence, the ethnographic enterprise lead by Griaule has largely contributed to the foundation of an economic basis for development of a tourist industry in the Dogon region that really started after the Second World War as a quest for exoticism and overall as a response to a Western social "malaise" (Doquet 2002, 122).

Dogon myth materializes in the landscape, masquerades and drawing-based divinations, sacred sites and remains of hunting and sacrificial practice stemming from animistic thought, the images of which dwell in the tourist's imagination. All reflect the cultural archetypes of an ancestral and authentic yet immutable traditional culture as it is labelled in many websites, tourism guidebooks, exhibitions, museum displays, documentaries, and television programs. The same clichés are used over time by Dogon entrepreneurs, performed and sold to the West, and paradoxically reinforce a sense of Dogon-ness. In this context, the "mise-en-scène" of authenticity (Doquet 2002, 117) provides a highly profitable tourist and art market for Dogon people that today extends worldwide and that appears as a "commercialization of the past and of the present" (Cissé 2007, 46). In fact, what is shown to the tourists is simply the result of the Dogon's self-awareness of their cultural significance and their experience of being observed, filmed, photographed, and interviewed through constant exposure to media and research. In the Dogon region, everything has a price, for instance, the taking of pictures. One of the villagers of Tiréli explains that "The *toubab(ou)* (white person/foreigner) has made Dogon people used to money. Here, the white is commerical. Everybody wants to have a white friend, because they bring money."[4] By bringing cash and gifts, tourists and researchers have created a situation in which Dogon villagers are used to systematically receiving things, ranging from pens to money, from visitors seen as "walking wallets" (van Beek 2005). Another result of Dogon people's awareness of the economic benefits of tourism concerns the selling of antiquities, in spite of actions taken by the Cultural Mission of Bandiagara (MCB) supported by UNESCO to increase the Dogon's' awareness of the cultural significance of their material patrimony, as we shall see below.

Dogon Authenticity as Heritage in Authentic Dogon Terms

In the Dogon area, "authenticity" is expressed in French by villagers involved in local tourism industries as *"l'authenticité Dogon."* The term has become a brand and a successful marketing technique used during cultural exchanges with tourists. In fact, it strengthens the Dogon's discourse about their culture, which is treated as a commodity. The plethora of reportage, websites, and prolific literature dedicated to Dogon culture that are produced by Western academics and non-academics as well as by Dogon intellectuals (Guindo and Kansaye 2000) are many media by which Dogon people identify themselves in terms of authenticity. The local word *atem* ("tradition" and its corollary term "heritage") is another term Dogon people commonly use to express the authenticity of their culture. As one of my informants explains: "*Atem* means 'what we have found.' That is the culture that we, Dogon people of today, have inherited from our ancestors and which we maintain through our ceremonies as well as in the course of our everyday life. *Atem* encompasses our ancestral customs or traditions." The term *atem* is also central to the discourses of Dogon intellectuals, who called themselves "traditionalists" and who are assigned the ultimate mission of preserving and promoting of Dogon culture in West Africa and beyond. One of them explains that "*atem* is the usages and customs that constitute our heritage. These traditions are passed on through generations and it is imperative that Dogon practices are perpetuated, because you know our gestures, activities, ways of living, of speaking, all of that make sense to us. It is our identity. So, *atem* is our way of behaving and our way of being Dogon. This is what you Westerners would call a 'culture.'" While *atem* refers to the Dogon's own expression of their culture and identity, the notion of *authenticity* as shaped by a tourism context reveals through, notably, performance and display of aspects of Dogon atem without disclosing Dogon's spiritual values to the outside world. Hence, Indigenous ideas have to be considered vis-à-vis Western ideas about the multifaceted notion of authenticity and its political construction. Dogon authenticity (*atem* or *authenticité*) appears in many Indigenous, colonial/ethnographic, UNESCO, government and traditionalists' discourses in the contexts of tourism performances and craft production. In other words, authenticity, which I see as primarily relational – that is, it emerges from shared experiences and through negotiation between outsiders and Dogon people – is understood here as an emic category that also integrates a Western shifting paradigm of authenticity shaped by moral and economic values.

The Consolidation of Dogon Authenticity within a Malian Political Agenda

In addition to the West's shaping of Dogon cultural authenticity, another determining factor in the consolidation of Dogon cultural identity lies in the political agenda of Mali's former president Alpha Oumar Konaré's (1992–2002), which promoted Mali's cultural richness and diversity. President Konaré supported and managed Mali's cultural resources as a catalyst for development of the national economy (Rowlands 2007, 127). Many enterprises of valorization of authentic Malian cultural diversity broadcast by media and including performing arts, architecture, and the construction of the National Museum of Mali in Bamako stand, according to Arnoldi, as "the revalorization of pre-colonial past through performance and material culture" (2006, 56). Since then, many nationally and internationally celebrated cultural events – youth festivals, the Biennale des Arts, the Cattle Crossing festival (a Fulani competition involving taking cattle across the Niger river), music festivals such as the Festival of the Desert in Timbuktu, which welcomes international Malian and Western figures, and a Dogon cultural festival – are means by which Mali as a culture is "on" display and "of" display (Rowlands 2007). One can add to this long list of performing events many material representations of Malian cultures and thus Dogon culture, such as the model of a *ginna* or family house at the National Museum where items of Dogon material culture, such as indigo textiles, masks, and ancient statuary, are displayed in the main gallery, labelled as "masterpieces of ritual art." Another initiative launched under Konaré's regime and aimed at highlighting regional culture and heritage diversity was the creation of cultural missions in culturally significant parts of Mali such as in Djenne, Timbuktu, and Bandiagara, which have since 1993 worked to protect Dogon cultural patrimony from plundering, to preserve and restore habitat, and to promote and control "eco-tourism and cultural tourism" in the Dogon region (Cissé 2003).

Konaré's political achievements in the domain of culture aimed to create national unity in a country of great cultural diversity and inherent political tensions. Probably one of the most symbolic posters designed by the Ministry of Culture and Tourism to promote tourism in Mali, which can still be seen today on the walls of some bus stations and tourism agencies across the country, depicts the face of a Fulani woman accompanied by the slogan "Tourism has a human face" (p. 7.1). This poster not only illustrates the Malian government's policy of representation and display of Mali cultural and ethnic diversity, but also, as Doquet (2002, 116) notes, embodies two essential Malian cultural values that are expressed in Bambara as *jatiguiya* (hospitality) and *maaya* (humanism). The poster promotes a form of "cultural tourism" or "ethno-tourism" grounded in cultural exchanges or a face-to-face "dialogue" between local "authentic" cultures and the tourists (Michel 2000, 201–2, cited in Doquet 2002, 115–16).

The Salvage of Authentic Indigenous Culture: A Dogon Traditionalist's Perspective

In the early 1990s Ginna Dogon, the Malian association for the promotion and protection of Dogon culture, came into being in reaction to a series of cultural events that took place in Bamako, the capital city of Mali, under the patronage of the Ministry of Sports, Arts and Culture and during which, according one of the association's co-founders, Dogon culture was totally misrepresented. By referencing the image of a Dogon big family house, a *ginna,* which symbolizes the origin, unity, and kinship structure of Dogon clans, the association decided to reintroduce Dogon culture in the light of its authentic ancestral traditions and thus heritage or *atem.* The association includes a great diversity of members who are identified by one of its co-founders as "all those who contribute to Dogon culture, ranging from 'Dogonphiles' to people of any ethnic groups who coexist with Dogon people, as such as the Fulani, Marka or the Songhay, and who all share cultural traits with Dogon because of their long-term mutual cultural influences." An unpublished association note stated: "We are … aware of the fact that today this original and authentic culture [Dogon culture] is progressively about to get dissolved by a solvent made of multiple external aggressions: Islam, Christian missions, French schooling system, communication media, economic development. Hence, it is necessary to strengthen it, to protect it so that it can resist [these aggressions] and find new directions." Likewise, as underlined by a Ginna Dogon member based in Bamako, Dogon culture is constantly threatened by the systematic plundering of Dogon villages and archaeological sites, in spite of the multiple strategies of preservation and protection of Dogon patrimony that were implemented in the early 1990s by the Cultural Mission of Bandiagara with considerable support from UNESCO. Today, Ginna Dogon activities range from the development of awareness campaigns about Dogon patrimony in rural areas to the organization of

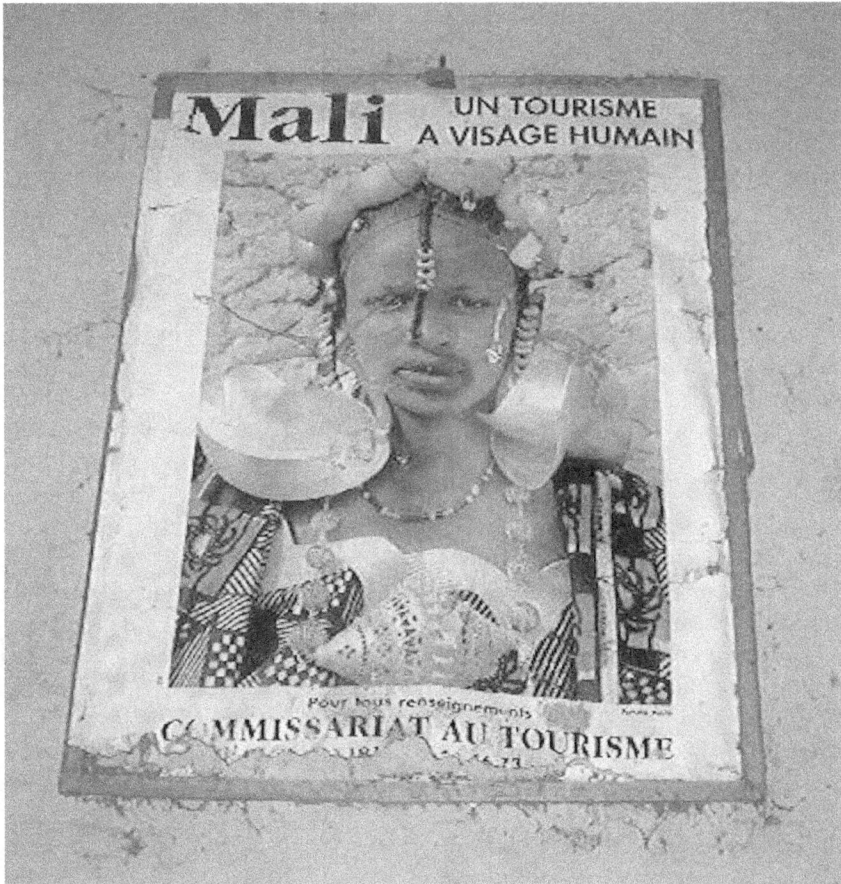

Figure 7.1 "Tourism has a human face" – poster promoting tourism in Mali that shows a Fulani woman wearing traditional gold earrings and amber beads in her hair. (Copyright: Laurence Douny)

conferences and workshops on Dogon culture and the promotion of local artists' craft. Finally, Ginna Dogon is said to contribute to local economic and social development inside and outside Mali by promoting Dogon cultural heritage.

Ginna Dogon's quest of cultural authenticity and discourse has, however, been questioned by scholars who see in this "patrimonizing enterprise," founded and lead by Bamako-based Malian administration elites, a biased economic enterprise inspired by Marcel Griaule's phantasmagoric work (Bouju 1995; Ciarcia 2003). The association's logo, as seen in Ginna Dogon's "status and rules" leaflet, depicts Dogon's *kanaga* mask, which represents the Dogon's conception of the universe as made of four cardinal points, a conception extensively reproduced and developed in Griaule's writings. A Dogon traditionalist responds: "Every people on earth possesses their own cosmogony. Why not the Dogon? Our cosmogony tells about Dogon views on the universe and on humanity. It is our ways of thinking and of doing things. That is what Dogon cosmogony is about, not Griaule's cosmogony. This is how it is still recounted today by elders in some areas of the Dogon region." One could also argue that by grounding its principles in a long-debated notion of cosmogony, the association acknowledges Griaule's ethnographic legacy, which nevertheless constitutes a historic and a heritage.

As part of Ginna Dogon's events program, a themed festival called the Ginna Dogon Festival has been organized every three years since 2005, alternating between each of the four main Dogon towns. In February 2011, the triennial festival was organized over three days in Bandiagara and based on the theme "Tradition and modernity through costumes and headdresses." Thousands of participants, including Dogon and Fulani women and hunters coming from all parts of the Dogon region, proudly paraded in front of a crowded audience composed mostly of Dogon villagers and local and national politicians, with a few tourists. Dogon traditional regalia were worn by their owners, who, according to a participant, "came all as they are." Thus, enthusiastic participants were performing "themselves" and the Dogon's *atem* by wearing garments that they still wear today at their village celebrations. People proudly represented their community and, of course, they enjoyed their brief exposure to the limelight, conscious of being filmed and watched by the entire world, which seemed to reinforce a sense of "being Dogon." In fact, as a local festival organizer said: "We want to show to people Dogon culture before it disappears, otherwise Dogon identity becomes jeopardized and then you don't know any more who is who.

So, it is essential to bring back Dogon culture to its roots." Although it may appear as a political "mise-en-scène" of authenticity elaborated by traditionalists, the festival consolidates of a sense of Dogon-ness in a spirit of national unity.

Dogon Material Authenticity in Local Museum and Village Display

In many villages, Dogon material culture is produced and sold in hotels and on the street, where new pieces can easily be confused with older ones. In an attempt to increase villagers' awareness of the traffic of art objects, the Cultural Mission of Bandiagara (CMB) built the Craft Museum of Endé (Enndé), which is overseen by a CMB-trained local management committee in charge of management of funds, maintenance of the building, and display of the objects and furniture produced by local wood carvers and blacksmiths. As in other museums set up by the CMB, in the Craft Museum of Endé the objects exhibited are selected and donated or provided by the villagers. (Some were lent by villagers, who therefore remain the owner and can retrieve them at any time.) Local material culture ranging from cooking utensils to music instruments are exhibited *in vivo* and on the basis of information provided by the objects's owner (Ermert 2003, 213). The Craft Museum of Endé is labelled a "museum for the promotion of art and craft working for local development."[5] The craft centre promotes local Dogon culture that is characterized by craft production of Endé dyers, potters, and blacksmiths and of which the cultural significance and values are grounded in the history of these families and their craft techniques that are their long-standing "savoir-faire" qualified as "traditional" and "ancestral."[6] In addition to various cultural events such as guided tours, markets, and festivals, the museum stands as another socio-cultural vector that boosts economic development. These community museums built by the villagers in traditional materials constitute, according to Ermert, "an alternative to lasting protection of patrimony and the development of sustainable tourism" (2003, 213).

From the villagers' point of view, the museum is the best means to prevent material culture from being stolen or sold to Westerners. As one villager remarked: "It is meant to prevent our precious objects from being smuggled and so to keep our history and dignity intact because we see ourselves in [these objects]." Hence, the CMB's objectives are to preserve and transmit local material and immaterial patrimony as well as to generate sustainable economic development through the

Figure 7.2 Crafts on sale in a hostel shop belonging to the chief of the village.
(Copyright: Laurence Douny)

promotion of local culture, for the Dogon as well as the outside world.
As one of my informants commented, the museum "is primarily dedicated to us. Our children need it to write their dissertations and they
need the history of these objects and of Endé. Without this, the existence of Endé doesn't make sense because a people without history is a
world without a soul." Local collections on display in the craft museum
stand as a material identity that villagers adhere to and proudly introduce to visitors.

For visitors, it is striking to see the streets of the village taking on the
aspect of an outdoor market.[7] Clothes hang on tree limbs near the place
where a tailor manufactures new pieces in front of the tourists. *Bogolan*
(mud cloths) and indigo cloths are displayed on the walls of houses and
granaries on both sides of the village main street.

This apparent abundance of various displays gives an impression of wealth that is often encountered in places attracting high numbers of tourists. The aesthetics of space makes shopping successful and easy, as tourists just have to zigzag from one side of the street to the other (Silverman 1999, 57). While a multiplicity of objects are displayed right on the ground in the alleys of the village, it is really behind the walls within the courtyard of the hostel (Figure 7.2) (belonging to the village chief) that a spectacular number of things are on chaotic view: wooden statues, clay pots, bead jewellery, ladders, hats, granary doors, carved pillars ... "Come on in, for the pleasure of the eyes" has become a slogan the shop owner uses to invite visitors to take a look at his objects. Large pieces of wooden artwork and statues are often exposed to the weather to convey an appearance of natural maturity that is a "cachet" of authenticity. The tourist just has to "excavate" mounds of objects (Lehuard 1979, 19) to find a little treasure. The objects are marketed as "traditional" and "old."

The storehouse stands as a "dumping ground" for multiple suppliers (Steiner 1994, 26), including the village's blacksmith, who produces a fair amount of objects on display in the streets of the village and in hostel shop, as we shall see. The blacksmith is considered to be the backbone of the Dogon community. Described by the villagers as a mythic and civilizing hero, he produces tools to cultivate, weapons to hunt, and cooking utensils and carved vessels among many other domestic artefacts. Along with his wives, who are potters, he is a producer of material culture. As Hoffman points out, the blacksmith has "for centuries been both artist and businessman, always exchanging services and products for goods, currency, and sometimes employing others to do his bidding" (1993, 223). While they perform distinctive functions, the community museum and the village shopping areas both define particular Indigenous cultural processes by which visitors are educated about the Dogon's culture through material display. Locally produced artefacts and their arrangement socialize foreigners into ways of seeing Dogon material authenticity and thus heritage "in-the-making" (Rowlands 2009, 149).

Commodification of Authenticity as a Domestic Spectacle

The Dogon blacksmith sculpts and assembles objects in his compound located at the foot of the escarpment at the periphery of the village, whereas his smithy was set up many generations ago on the escarpment slope. The blacksmith's house and smithy are viewed by tourists on their general guided[8] tour of the village, which operates differently according to the size of the group, the guide, and his intentions. The trip to the blacksmith's workshop is apparently intended to bring potential clients to him. As soon as tourists are reported to be heading in the village, the chief and the blacksmith among other villagers involved in the tourist industry are informed by a person or by mobile phone. The cost of the visit to the smithy and blacksmith's house is generally fixed beforehand. The daily spectacle provided by the blacksmith is performed in return for a fee that is gently expressed by the guide as intended "to give the price of kola nuts to the blacksmith."[9]

As a means of preparing the "scene", the blacksmith often takes some of his artwork from his house and begins to work on a substantial piece. And not just any piece: as one blacksmith put it, tourists are more likely to be impressed by a mask being carved in front of them than by watching him mend a spare part for a motorcycle. Like many Dogon people, the blacksmith is accustomed to performing his everyday life, here with a hint of "mise-en-scène," both elements working together to give additional value and prestige to his work. Explanations about his work as well as stories about his family and their origin are provided to the tourists in a natural way. In his compound and smithy, the blacksmith makes a great variety of objects, such as woodcarvings and metalwork, with great dexterity and strength in handling heavy materials and tools. This often creates an unexpected spectacle as he plays tricks with fire for the visitors. The tourists are delighted to meet an important Dogon figure in his everyday setting.

This spectacle constitutes a "successful technique of tourist seduction" (Hoffman 1993, 224) that is employed by the blacksmith with the connivance of the guide. Furthermore, the blacksmith's compound sets the scene for what is perceived by most tourists as an authentic interaction with local people and a "suspension of disbelief" for less credulous tourists (Hoffman 1993, 227). In addition to some mise-en-scène, the orientation of tourists within the village is well planned, for, as van Beek suggests, "the dream of meeting an unspoiled culture or a pristine environment … should not be ruptured by the presence of other tourists" (2003, 254). Performance in everyday life settings offers more "intimacy," as it enables tourists for a short while to step outside the practical reality of their trip (the hostel, the tourists they meet, their tight travel schedule) that frames their visit of the village.

The Dogon blacksmiths I worked with can replicate a broad range of material forms that they observed in various places inside and outside of Mali. During our long conversation, one young blacksmith explained that he took part in several workshops at the National Museum of Mali in Bamako, where he demonstrated his talents and where he also learned about art forms from all regions of Mali, which he can reproduce from memory but also by consulting Dogon art catalogues received from Western friends. The art books serve as an order catalogue from which potential clients can find models that he subsequently reproduces. As Hoffman notes: "Today, when the sculptor makes art for a foreign audience, he uses both his historically-based understanding of foreign perceptions of Dogon art, and the legacy of sculptural models available to him, to sculpt desirable objects and to market them under conditions that will convince a client to buy. This is not fraud but performance and theatre" (Hoffman 1993, 224). Dogon blacksmiths produce, replicate, innovate, and adapt material forms according to tourists' demands. As well, they promote a Dogon material heritage that appears as a relational ground and from which authenticity takes shape according to clients' expectations. These are grounded in their own Western definition and perception of values. As I observed, blacksmiths use particular knowledge and techniques to manipulate and alter objects and thus recreate traditional material forms (Steiner 1994, 140–5).

Therefore, the commodification of Dogon authenticity is characterized by the performance of representations of Dogon culture that have long been reproduced spontaneously here in the manner of a domestic spectacle. Tourists experience Dogon culture through self-display of embodied images of power, mysticism, and spirituality. All reinforce tourists' "authentic" and anticipated experience, which is made even more credible thanks to the mise-en-scène in domestic settings.

Material Transformation Processes: Inauthentic Object in Authentic Context

Objects of power, such as the paraphernalia of the *Hogon* (spiritual chief), are among the many traditional objects that are reproduced by Dogon blacksmiths and sold to tourists as authentic. These objects of power are artefacts whose aesthetics and materiality objectify the spiritual and political authority of the *Hogon*, on the one hand, and magical and protective powers, on the other. Thus, the ambivalent material culture of the *Hogon* reveals and at the same time conceals forms of power. Nowadays, these artefacts made for tourists represent power rather than objectifying it, since the *Hogon*'s consecration

Figure 7.3 Handmade "mass-produced" *Hogon* crowns and pendant pieces. (Copyright: Laurence Douny).

has been practically abandoned. They are made authentic on the basis of Western aesthetic appraisal but also Dogon concepts of tradition and cultural values.

A metal crown and pendants were worn together by the *Hogon*. The crown, called *hogon bamara* (hat of the *Hogon*) is today made of recycled metals. Parts of the artefact are laid out and assembled by the blacksmith in the manner of a "handmade mass production" (Figure 7.3). In his view, the metal crown, traditionally topped up with figurines and decorations (here shown in its unfinished state), is a successful visual reinforcement of the *Hogon*'s power, because of the mystic material properties of metal such as black iron or bronze that were originally used.[10] Similarly to the crown, the pendants the blacksmith produces are traditionally made to magically reinforce the political power of the *Hogon* as well as to protect him against witchcraft or malevolent spirits.

The links forming the chain of the *Hogon*'s necklaces (*hogon djigue*) contain a stone (*dugo*) that traditionally represented the power structure of the society and the *Hogon*'s connectedness to spiritual entities. As designed by the blacksmith, the necklace holds a flattened pendant that represents one of the *Hogon*'s symbols, such as a bowl, headrest, or a face representing him or a woman. According to the blacksmith who produced the object, this motif symbolizes fertility, which is one of the *Hogon*'s supernatural powers: ensuring the fertility of people and of the land. It also signifies the wealth of the *Hogon*, who could afford to marry several wives.

The *Hogon*'s paraphernalia is composed of materials that resemble the original ones. The artefacts' design is altered by the blacksmith's artistry, imagination, and overall perception of tourists' taste. Traditionally, the chain of the *Hogon*'s necklaces (and they are of course variations in style/form) were made of fewer caged beads made of bone or sacred stone (*dugo*) to which the many material symbols of the *Hogon*'s power were attached as a sign of his influence, prestige, sacredness, wealth, and worthiness. To increase the objects' value, aesthetic appeal, and authenticity, they undergo a process of aging involving short-term immersion in a bath prepared according the blacksmith's own recipe. They are then buried in earth so their surface fully corrodes, showing rust, and thus the object is disguised as an antique (Figure 7.4). As the blacksmith explains: "The 'old' is what the tourists are after: they don't really like what looks new." He counts many African tourists and art dealers among his customers.

The mask of the *Hogon*, called *lassouga guiri won* or *lassouga hogon*, is the mask that presides and guides all masks at a *Hogon*'s funeral. Placed at the head of the masquerade, the *lassouga hogon* signals the death of the *Hogon*. It not only materializes the identity of the *Hogon* but also recalls the memory and power of the late spiritual chief. In addition, its presence is said to appease the soul of the *Hogon* and to guide it in the afterlife. I was told that a blacksmith cannot carve the *lassouga hogon*, as this is seen as impure. In the past, because of its sacred dimension, the mask was carved in remote areas of the bush or in a cave sheltered from view. Access to the site was strictly forbidden to blacksmiths, *griots*,[11] women, and children. Only initiated Dogon men are involved in the process. Today, masks destined for the tourism industry (Figure 7.5) are carved in public by blacksmiths and, more generally, Dogon sculptors. Tourists are invited to watch and photograph this domestic spectacle in return for a fee that is negotiated

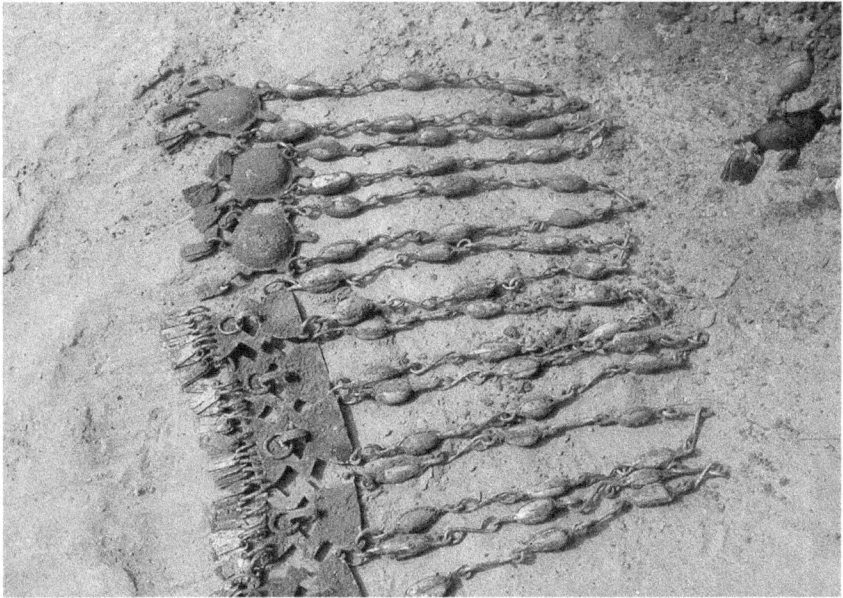

Figure 7.4 To artificially age pendants, artisans bury them in the soil for several weeks. (Copyright: Laurence Douny)

between the tourist guide and the blacksmith. In order to increase a mask's aesthetic value and therefore its price, the blacksmith added new features on the masks that materialize his own creativity and thus his signature; he always adapts to the market and tries to suit tourists' expectations, which he knows well through his experience of meeting them. Once the core of the mask is finished, the object is aged by use of a patina, well known among wood carvers. In some cases, masks and wooden statues are first smoked by being left near an indoor kitchen's stove. Then the surface is brushed off and the object is finally painted. In the past, blood sacrifices were made on the object or on a shrine to empower them.

Here, handmade material *Hogon* culture is mass produced, yet without compromising either Dogon cultural and spiritual values or the authority of the *Hogon*. The difference between an object destined specifically for the *Hogon* and one destined for a tourist lies in the fact that the first is empowered through an activation process occurring through a sacrifice and magic words.[12] This magic serves, for instance,

Figure 7.5 Mask representing the *Hogon* and worn at his funeral.
(Copyright Laurence Douny)

to protect the *Hogon* against evil things such as witchcraft, spirits, or disease. Knowledge of the activation is, of course, kept secret. Therefore, what matters for Dogon people is not the material form as such, but rather the efficacy of objects in protecting an authority figure and reinforcing a person's power. Similarly to the body ornaments I described, the mask is sold without undergoing any magical treatment that would confer power on it. Thus, the object is devoid of sacredness. In other words, the wooden piece is not made "operational" in its role of protecting and connecting with the invisible world. Here, authenticity for Dogon people lies in respect for tradition and authority figures by not selling the secrets associated with the efficacy and therefore the active principles of an object. At the same time, authenticity as perceived by tourists – aging these prestige objects in order to increase their value – creates "antiquity."[13]

Altering traditional material forms in response to a growing tourist market is certainly not a new phenomenon (Steiner 1994). Although the object is faked, it still remains authentic in a way, since its serial reproduction is "handmade" and can be labelled as "craft" or art form (Brown 1996, 33–4). The aesthetics of "old" rendered through locally made aging substances and techniques act as a marker of authenticity that aims at satisfying Westerners' obsession with antiquity (Steiner 1995). Moreover, one can argue that this practice remains authentic, in the sense of "true" to Dogon culture, by concealing ritual practice and the secret knowledge associated with it. In other words, what is sold is the material representation of culture, not the practices, the agency, ontology, and efficacy of objects that is conveyed through magic. That is to say, it is a commodification of authenticity or the selling of culture without compromising its cultural, intellectual, and spiritual values (Bunten 2008). In the tourist's view, buying the copied object at the source through no intermediaries – travelling long distances to purchase items in their context of production – constitutes another aspect of authenticity. Hence, authenticity becomes also grounded in relationships and interaction with local people, as "tourism has a human face" that is promoted by the Ministry of Culture and Tourism with its welcoming policy, as mentioned above. Relational authenticity is a form of dialogue and encounter between an "authentic" blacksmith and tourists. In other words, the tourist creates an authentic experience by visiting and potentially acquiring an artwork of the blacksmith that is handmade, even if the object is not an authentic antique.

Commodified Authenticity and Material Identity "In-the-Making"

I have focused on the transformative processes by which authenticity, locally expressed as heritage or *atem*, is altered through the commodification of Dogon cultural identities in performance, in visual and material displays, and in the context of tourism and heritage practice. I suggest that Dogon authenticity as a cultural construct and a process reveals – in the course of Western/non-Western and local negotiations – multiple forms of shifting economic, political, and cultural values. Authenticity is thus primarily relational in the sense that it is redefined across time and within complex networks of interactions between the Dogon and the outside world. I have shown that Dogon people who are conscious of the Western gaze and its search for "exoticism" have learned over time to reinvent their culture through particular forms of self-presentation, of "being Dogon" – that is, through changeable and adaptable processes of self-definition. Hence, the authentic Dogon self oscillates between the perceptions of Westerners/outsiders and local perceptions that integrate them. It materializes through domestic spectacle and material culture displays that form a Dogon material identity "in-the making." Within the context of heritage tourism, the Dogon's commodified authenticity is adapted to shifting cultural contexts, yet it remains grounded in the Dogon's cultural heritage or *atem*, the principles of which are undisclosed to the outside world. Finally, the Dogon's commodification of authenticity stands as a means by which Dogon people make themselves in the twenty-first-century world.

NOTES

1 These data are drawn from the fieldwork I conducted between 2003–4 that was sponsored by the Wenner-Gren Foundation and in 2005, 2008, and 2010–11 (therefore before the start of the Malian political crisis in 2012).
2 Issues concerning the positive and negative economic impacts of tourism on the Dogon's daily lives have been extensively addressed elsewhere (e.g., Lane 1988; van Beek 2005; Walther 2001).
3 Griaule's book *Dieu d'eau: Entretiens avec Ogotemmeli* (1966), crossed check with his entire body of work, prompted many posthumous criticisms (e.g., van Beek 1991).
4 All quotes in French are translated by the author.

5   "Musée pour la valorization de l'art et de l'artisanat au service du développement local" (leaflet published by the CMB).
6   "Musée pour la valorization de l'art."
7   The displayed objects are produced by various craftsmen from the village and from outside who place them on deposit, in return for a commission taken by the owner of the village hostel, who is the chief of the village and who manages the business.
8   Guided tours in Dogon villages are operated by professional Dogon guides who are native to a Dogon village. Sometimes, non-professional villagers act as guides. This is negotiated between the professional guide and the villagers.
9   Kola nuts were traditionally offered by visitors as a sign of respect and are today replaced by money.
10   One elder claimed that the crown is traditionally made of hard wood. According to him, the blacksmith appropriates objects of power that he alters in order to make them more meaningful and attractive.
11   *Griots* are members of a class of intellectuals and performers who act as advisors to ruling classes in stratified West African societies. With training in traditions and history, *griots* are authoritative culture bearers even in today's globalizing world.
12   It's worth noting a difference of opinion in this matter. The Endé blacksmith's practice was criticized by two elders of a neighbouring village, and he was described as corrupted, because in their view the *Hogon*'s paraphernalia should not be exposed to people's gaze out of respect for *Hogon*s, who represent society's moral and spiritual values. Yet in Endé and in places where the *Hogon* tradition has been abandoned, the replication of such objects is fully approved by the elders' council because the replicas are made differently from the original and are not magically loaded.
13   The mask would be sold for CFA 85,000 (USD $177). No price was given to me regarding the pendant and the crown.

REFERENCES

Arnoldi, Marie-Jo. 2006. "Youth Festivals and Museums: The Cultural Politics of Public Memory in Postcolonial Mali." *Africa Today* 52 (4): 55–78. http:// dx.doi.org/10.1353/at.2006.0037.
Bedaux, R.M.A. 1972. "Tellem, reconnaissance archéologique d'une culture de l'Ouest africain au Moyen Age: Recherches architectoniques." *Journal de la Société des Africanistes* 42 (2): 103–85. http://dx.doi.org/10.3406/ jafr.1972.1700.

Bouju, Jacky. 1995. "Tradition et identité: La tradition dogon entre traditionnalisme rural et néo-traditionnalisme urbain." *Enquête* 2: 95–117.

Brown, David. 1996. "Authentic Fakes: Tourism versus Pilgrimage." In *The Tourist Image: Myths and Myth Making in Tourism*, edited by Tom Selwyn, 33–47. Chichester: John Wiley & Sons.

Bunten, Alexis C. 2005. "Commodities of Authenticity: When Native People Consume Their Own Art." In *Exploring World Art*, ed. Eric Vendrux, Pamela Rosi Sheffield, and Robert L. Welsch, 317–36. Long Grove: Waveland

Bunten, Alexis C. 2008. "Sharing Culture or Selling Out? Developing the Commodified Persona in the Heritage Industry." *American Ethnologist* 35 (3): 380–95. http://dx.doi.org/10.1111/j.1548-1425.2008.00041.x.

Ciarcia, Gaetano. 2003. *De la mémoire ethnographique: Exotisme au Pays Dogon*. Paris: Editions de l'EHESS.

Cissé, Lassana. 2003. "La préservation d'un site du patrimoine mondial." In *Regards sur les Dogon du Mali*, edited by R.M.A. Bedaux and J.D. Van der Waals, 207–12. Gent: Snoeck.

Cissé, Lassana. 2007. "Tourisme et associations culturelles au Pays Dogon." In *L'Afrique des associations: Entre culture et développement*, edited by Diop Momar-Coumba and Jean Benoist, 39–49. Paris: Karthala.

Doquet, Anne. 2002. "Dans les coulisses de l'authenticité africaine." *Les Temps Modernes* 4 (620–21): 115–27. http://dx.doi.org/10.3917/ltm.620.0115.

Douny, Laurence. 2014. "Wild Silk Wrappers of Dogon: Wrapping and Unwrapping Material Identities." In *Wrapping & Unwrapping Material Culture: Archaeological and Anthropological Perspectives*, edited by Susanna Harris and Laurence Douny, 173–92. Walnut Creek: Left Coast.

Ermert, Elisabeth. 2003. "Le Musée communautaire de Nombori-Une nouvelle stratégie pour la conservation locale de la culture." In *Regards sur les Dogon du Mali*, edited by R.M.A. Bedaux and J.D. van der Waals, 213. Gent: Snoeck.

Gosselain, O., 2000. "Materializing Identities: An African Perspective." *Journal of Archaeological Method and Theory* 7 (3), 187–217.

Griaule, Marcel, and Germaine Dieterlen. 1965. *Le Renard pâle*. Book 1, fasc. 1: *Le mythe cosmogonique; La création du monde*. Paris: Institute d'Ethnologie.

Griaule, Marcel. 1966. *Dieu d'eau: Entretiens avec Ogotemmêli*. Paris: Fayard.

Guindo, I., and H. Kansaye. 2000. *Nous les Dogons*. Bamako: Le Figuier.

Handler, Richard. 1986. "Authenticity." *Anthropology Today* 2 (1): 2–4. http://dx.doi.org/10.2307/3032899.

Hoffman, Rachel. 1993. "Seduction, Surrender, and Portable Paradise: Dogon Art in Modern Mali." In *Secrecy: African Art that and Reveals and Conceals*, edited by Marie H. Nooter, 223–33. New York: Museum for African Art and Pres-tal-Verlag.

Lane, Paul J. 1988. "Tourism and Social Change among the Dogon." *African Arts* 21 (4): 66–9. http://dx.doi.org/10.2307/3336748.

Lehuard, Raoul. 1979. "Un voyage en Haute-Volta." *Arts d'Afrique Noire* 31: 11–9.

Michel, Frank. 2000. *Désirs d'ailleurs: Essai d'anthropologie des voyages*. Paris: Armand Colin.

Reisinger, Yvette, and Carol J. Steiner. 2006. "Reconceptualizing Object Authenticity." *Annals of Tourism Research* 33 (1): 65–86. http://dx.doi.org/10.1016/j.annals.2005.04.003.

Rowlands, Michael. 2007. "Entangled Memories and Parallel Heritages in Mali." In *Reclaiming Heritage: Alternative Imaginaries of Memory in West Africa*, edited by Ferdinand de Jong and Michael Rowlands, 127–45. Walnut Creek: Left Coast.

Rowlands, Michael. 2009. "Africa on Display: Curating Postcolonial Pasts in the Cameroon Grassfields." In *Postcolonial Archaeologies in Africa*, edited by Peter R. Schmidt, 149–62. Sante Fe: SAR.

Ryan, C., and M. Aicken, eds. 2005. *Indigenous Tourism: The Commodification and Management of Culture*. London: Elsevier.

Silverman, Eric. 1999. "Tourist Art in the Sepik River." In *Unpacking Culture: Art and Commodity in Colonial and Postcolonial Worlds*, edited by Ruth B. Phillips and Christopher B. Steiner, 51–66. Berkeley: University of California Press.

Sofaer, J. 2007. *Material Identities*. Oxford: Blackwell.

Steiner, Christopher. B. 1994. *African Art in Transit*. Cambridge: Cambridge University Press.

Steiner, Christopher. B. 1995. "The Art of the Trade: On the Creation of Value and Authenticity in the African Art Market." In *The Traffic in Culture: Refiguring Art and Anthropology*, edited by Georges E. Marcus and Fred, R. Myers, 151–65. Berkeley: University of California Press.

van Beek, Wouter E. 1991. "Dogon Restudied: A Field Evaluation of the Work of Marcel Griaule." *Current Anthropology* 32 (2): 139–67. http://dx.doi.org/10.1086/203932.

van Beek, Wouter E. 2003. "African Tourist Encounters: Effects of Tourism in Two West-African Societies." *Africa: Journal of the International Africa Institute* 73 (3): 251–89.

van Beek, Wouter E. 2005. "Walking Wallets: Tourists at the Dogon *Falaise*." In *Wari Matters: Ethnographic Explorations of Money in the Mande World*, edited by Stephen Wooten and Jan Jansen, 191–214. Munster: Verlag Lit.

Walther, Olivier. 2001. *Mémoire en Géographie*. Lausanne: Institut de Géographie.

PART THREE

Knowledge Movements

8 Streams of Tourists: Navigating the Tourist Tides in Late-Nineteenth-Century Southeast Alaska

KATHRYN BUNN-MARCUSE

The real entertainment of the day came after we had bought our baskets and spoons and carvings at the trader's stores, and were enjoying a few dry hours in the cabin. Then the Indian women came tapping at the windows with their bracelets, and the keen spirit of the trade having possessed us, we made wonderful bargains with the relenting savages. A tap on the window, and the one word, "Bracelet!" or the Chinook "Klickwilly," would bring all the ladies to their feet, and the mechanical "how much" that followed became so automatic during the day, that when the porter rapped at night for lights to be put out, he was greeted with a "how much" in response. (Scidmore 1885, 91–2)

In the 1880s, the advent of regular steamship service to southeast Alaska caused the tourist economy to boom in the small, coastal villages. Over the next several decades, tourism became the fastest-growing economic engine of the region. Like the yearly salmon runs so familiar to Native people, travellers from the United States arrived in waves, storing up fodder for their journals and spawning future returns of travellers that would also search out the locales, experiences, and artworks of previous summers. These were formative years for the burgeoning Native art market, with artists reaping the benefits of the new cash economy, selling the artworks to travellers, tourists, dealers, and anthropologists.[1] Travellers were anxious to buy souvenirs directly from Native venders, an activity touted in the tourist literature as an integral part of the Alaska tour. Travellers' journals and experiences – published in the popular press and periodicals of the time – showed the excitement of voyages to the wilds of Alaska, America's newest territory. Native artists skilfully negotiated the demands of tourists, who had a specific set of expectations and desires based on these published travelogues. Tlingit, Haida, and Tsimshian merchants capitalized on the structure of the steamship route, wherein tourists were delivered to scheduled ports at designated times. These salesmen and women understood tourists' expectations, created by published reviews of how best to have an "authentic" experience – buying directly from the Native vendor rather than patronizing the curio shops in their departure cities of Seattle or San Francisco. These artists worked in direct competition, or sometimes in collaboration, with the curio stores or even manufacturing operations owned by non-Native businessmen. Artists of the time built on their Indigenous identity as a key marketing technique to meet the expectations and demands of the tourist. The market for Native products provided rich opportunities to earn money in ways acceptable to officials in the colonial world of the new American territory, while still allowing carvers and weavers to set their own schedules, follow the market, or participate in customary food harvesting or potlatching.[2] As colonial policies alienated Native people from their traditional economies, the growth of the tourist trade brought new opportunities for practising and performing culture for the cash economy. Most important, being successfully self-employed brought the resources to participate in the colonial economy as well as funds to reinforce hereditary positions or increase status within Indigenous social systems without regard for – and even in contradiction to – colonial policies interdicting those systems.

This chapter considers how Native artists exploited the fertile ecosystem of the tourist trade. Native artists knew well how to tend the seasonal tourist runs, ensuring that tourists left silver dollars shimmering in their wake. By considering their commercial artworks and the circumstances of production against the journals of travellers to the region, I expose some strategies used by Native artists to efficiently harvest the seasonal bounty by marketing a rich set of creations to maximize sales to diverse tastes.

Like other essays in this volume, this chapter looks at how the interactions between tourists and Indigenous hosts revolved around cross-cultural encounters mediated by consumer demands. The examination here of an early site of cultural tourism, in late-nineteenth-century Southeast Alaska, reveals that many of the tropes employed in current cultural tourism venues were already established well over a hundred years ago and that strategic deployment of the knowledge of those tropes by Native artists and salespeople was used to advantage even in the early days of cultural tourism.[3]

In 1890, census data showed the population of Alaska was 32,052, with 4,737 Tlingit who resided mostly in the southeast region of the state (United States 2016). Within the next ten years the population of the state almost doubled; tourism and mining were major contributors to this explosion. Southeast Alaska is a region of high mountains and thick rainforest that cover an archipelago of islands, and includes deep fjords on the mainland. The Tlingit and Kaigani Haida villages in this region were organized into two exogamous clans with subclans organized by house groups. Towns with a mixed white and Indigenous populations existed on territory previously controlled by clans. The territory of Alaska had been transferred to the United States in 1867 from the Russians. Russian incursions into the region began in the early 1700s with official proclamation of possession in 1799. At the end of the nineteenth century, many Native residents were following customary resource rounds, particularly in sites away from towns; others had moved into single-family homes with Western furniture and clothing and were involved in industry, especially canning, logging, mining, and art production for the tourist trade. While cash was in circulation, there was still much trade in goods, and blankets continued to serve as a medium of currency (Scidmore 1893a, 57).

The advent of the tourist trade in Southeast Alaska is well documented both in the travel literature of the time and, in recent years, by authors who astutely analyse the social underpinnings that formed the attitudes, biases, and expectations of late-nineteenth-century travellers (Cole 1985; Campbell 2007; Lee 1999; Raibmon 2005). What is missing in this record is the Native perspective. Unlike examinations of modern Indigenous tourism practices, in this case we do not have the voices of Indigenous writers examining their own situations – we don't have enough evidence to know if there was the collective reflection on strategic actions of performance and marketing that there is now. (Some evidence does show solidarity in the pricing of goods and in certain practices of interaction.) While we may never know directly what the artists of the time were thinking, we can reread the writings of nineteenth-century travellers and look between the lines, attempting to mediate nineteenth-century attitudes and find clues revealing Indigenous social actions. We can look again at known materials and at previously unexamined materials and construct a different story than the one we know.[4] Certainly, direct information from descendants and oral histories that are carefully kept in families are a key resource, and much more work needs to be done in this area.[5]

Art historical research can add to the picture of tourism at the end of the nineteenth century in southeast Alaska. Reexamining the material productions of the time, looking at what was sold to tourists as well as identifying when, where, and how it was sold, reframes what was previously described by social historians, ethnographers, and anthropologists. We can assess what those products looked like and why certain motifs and forms were used by artists, and glean internal motivations for participation in the commercial art trade from the extant historical record.

This chapter sketches a process for understanding Indigenous strategies through reviewing some of the current literature on the period, reexamining the nineteenth-century travel writings for clues to Indigenous actions, and, most intensely, turning attention to the commercial artworks of the time. I do not presume here to speak *for* the Native artists and vendors of the time; I cannot represent the Native voice, but I hope that this research can reveal new perspectives into the production side of the tourist market as compared to the consumer and collector side (Cole 1985; Lee 1999). By examining artworks in their commercial context, it is possible to gain perspective on how artists navigated the rough waters of the new colonial economy, trading on non-Native notions of authenticity and expression, and timing their production of artworks to the seasonal cycle of tourism, to maximize their economic returns.[6] As such, this essay is also a response to Alexandra Harmon's call for investigations into the economic history of Native Americans (Harmon 2010, 8).

Mapping the Ecosystem: Studies of Tourism and Art

The ecosystem of the tourist industry in Alaska and the role of Tlingit artists and vendors have been explored and described in a number of publications, most significantly for this article Lee (1999), Raibmon (2005), and Campbell (2007).[7] Molly Lee's 1999 article "Tourism and Taste Cultures" in Southeast Alaska examines three types of collectors as well as their strategies for collecting; their interpretations of authenticity; and their display penchants for the material they accumulated. Lee observed that the "feedback process" between producers and consumers is hard to track and bases her study on the information gleaned from consumer demand (1999, 280). Jules-Rosette noted that tourist art is really a cyclical process of "communication and cultural combination" with influences, expectations, technologies, and aesthetics flowing around, back and forth. If, as she wrote, "tourist art is a microcosm of the processes of socioeconomic change" (1984, 8–9), then an investigation of tourism in Alaska from the side of both collector and producer is key to understanding the decades of momentous change in the region. Elsewhere, I have examined the role of museum collectors and their biases towards products for sale in the tourist market (Bunn-Marcuse 2015). This article mirrors Lee's investigation of buyers by examining the production side of the market, noting what was for sale, how it was sold, and how artists capitalized on buyer's expectations.

Tourist art goes by a number of different names: it has been called art-for-sale, art of acculturation, souvenir art, commodity, airport art, and commercial art (Graburn 1976). In popular literature from the eighteenth, nineteenth, and twentieth centuries, it was called curiosity, memento, bric-a-brac, curio, knickknack, geegaw, trinket, souvenir, and even kitsch (Phillips 1998, 6). These categories have been traditionally contrasted with the artefact/ethnological specimen and, as such, were frequently overlooked by scholars before the 1970s. The essentialist theories of anthropologists and art historians in the late nineteenth and early twentieth centuries demanded that objects without a place in "traditional" society be left out of examinations of those cultures. Any item made specifically for sale to outsiders was carefully excluded from their studies. Objects that reflected cross-cultural interactions complicated their attempts to reconstruct the history of "primitive" art.

When anthropologists, and later art historians, started looking at these cultures, they were working under Victorian ideas of race, in which hybridity was considered degenerative and a corruption of the "pure" forms of an imagined static, pre-contact culture (Phillips 1998, 10). Tourist art was seen as a sign of hybridity and acculturation, replacing traditional arts and crafts with "junk" (Jules-Rosette 1984, vii). Many publications from the mid-twentieth century denigrated the changing forms and aesthetics of the period and questioned the authenticity of tourist productions rather than recognizing the economic incentives and possibilities for Indigenous signification that art-for-sale might provide (Inverarity 1946, fig. 155; Kaufmann 1976; Norris 1987, 22; Wyatt 1984).

However, the examination of Indigenous artwork made for sale gained scholarly acceptance over the last forty years, beginning with Nelson H.H. Graburn's seminal 1976 volume *Ethnic and Tourist Arts: Cultural Expressions from the Fourth World*. Previous to that time, so-called tourist art was passed over by scholars. In addition, while the making of art has gone hand in hand with selling art, the economic realities of being an Indigenous artist have escaped scrutiny in the literature about the Northwest Coast, perhaps due to the Western distaste for linking art and money, for casting art into a commodity framework (Myers 2001, 54), or because the study of economic activity has fallen outside the spheres of anthropological and art historical academic interest (Harmon 2010, 11; Keane 2001, 66).

Recent studies of commoditized art forms refocus some of the emphasis away from the evaluation of changing aesthetics to strategic awareness of market forces by Native artists (Phillips and Steiner 1999). And while the binary categories of "for use" and "for sale" have long been reified in anthropological literature, recent studies and research show that those categories are often entirely fictitious or exist only at the moment of exchange rather than being inherent to the object (Appadurai 1986; Bunn-Marcuse 2015; Bunten 2006; Glass 2011; Kopytoff 1986).

It is critical to ask, what can we learn about the making of art at the turn of the century in Southeast Alaska from examining these previously discounted artworks in conjunction with the written record? By looking at examples of specific works, we can perceive both what was being produced and sold and, in conjunction with traveller's journals, get a glimpse of the interactions between artist or seller and consumer. Streams of income, iconography, and influence flowed through the tourist industry and the art market, creating a fertile and dynamic environment encompassing visitors, businesses, consumers, artists, and vendors.

Spawning a New Economy – The Growing Tourist Season in Alaska

While the real tourist boom did not hit southeast Alaska until the Pacific Coast Steamship Company began passenger cruise service in 1884, the freight and mail runs that served the coast had been bringing tourists in smaller numbers for decades. Emil Teichman's journal of his visit to Sitka in the 1860s shows that Tlingit merchants were already marketing their souvenirs as well as meat and fish to visitors and residents of the American settlement there (Teichmann 1963, 214). By the 1870s and early 1880s, the economic incentives for being a part of the cash economy were well in place in southeast Alaska. When Sophia Cracroft visited Wrangell in 1870, she described the Tlingit people there as ready to sell, inviting her into their houses, arranging seating for her and her fellow travellers and bringing out their wares (Cracroft and Smith 1974, 132). In 1880, Daniel Gordon visited with William Duncan at New Metlakatla and found carvers working on a variety of items, including silver bracelets decorated with Tsimshian beaver designs and American eagle designs that he noted were "frequently purchased and worn as curios by white visitors" (Gordon 1880, 45–6). Already, artists were actively involved in shaping the market for their goods. Eliza R. Scidmore, who wrote extensively on travel in Alaska, noted in the 1890 census report that the Tlingits "have been keener than the whites in seeing the possibilities of the tourist trade" (1893b, 44).[8]

The popularity of the cruises grew quickly once regular steamship service began in 1884.[9] The 1890 Census report lists 25,048 tickets sold by the Pacific Coast Steamship Company between 1884 and 1890, with the numbers growing from 1,600 the first season to over 5,000 in the last two years. It was estimated that each tourist spent between fifty and one hundred dollars on curios (United States 1893, 250–1). In Native communities, supplies and goods for everyday life were purchased with money earned through the tourist trade; this money was also used for potlatching. Tlingit and Haida potlatches of the 1880s and 1890s often featured gifts of money as well as purchased and locally produced goods and food (Boursin 1893b, 54; Scidmore 1885, 58). A Fourth of July potlatch at Klawock – held under cover of colonially sanctioned festivities[10] – was an occasion when "the clerks at the store were taxed to their utmost to wait upon the Natives, who brought in their furs and dug out from their pockets many a silver and gold piece, for the purchase of some article of clothing, blankets, or groceries, which were to be distributed among their friends as an evidence of good will and friendship" (United States 1893, 33). Cash, used to purchase manufactured goods or for distribution or display itself, was critical to the honouring of high-ranking chiefs who by the late nineteenth century might be memorialized under "a mountain of cloth" or with "wash-basins full of silver currency" (Collison 1915, 278; United States 1893, 33). Some Tlingit individuals reportedly kept large quantities of cash ("silver in sums ranging from $8,000 to $10,000") out of circulation and in reserve for display at the potlatch (Scidmore 1893b, 44).

In fact, the Alaskan economy as a whole depended heavily on tourism and especially on the production of Alaska Native curios. The 1890 census reported that Sitka "is supported chiefly by the trade of the Sitka and Yakutat Natives, who sell their furs, baskets, carvings, spoons, bracelets, beadwork, etc., and purchase all their clothing and a constantly increasing proportion of food and utensils" (Boursin 1893a).[11] This was a reliable, profitable trade and one in which the Native vendors, non-Native businesses, and steamship companies depended on each other for success.

Fishing for Buyers

In Alaska, like other travel locales, the "buying experience" was a key part of the tourist adventure touted in the tourist literature as an integral part one's trip (MacDowell 1905). There were a variety of "buying experiences" to choose from, each with its own appeal, ranging from familiar interactions of the trading store to the more "exotic" adventure within the Tlingit and Kaigani Haida villages. Native artists and traders took advantage of all of these venues by selling directly to travellers, supplying the mainly white-owned stores, and taking commissions from Indigenous patrons. Native designs were also used by commercial manufacturers outside of Alaska and in cottage industries within the territory (Bunn-Marcuse 2015).

Tourist literature of the time advertised Alaska's Native population as part of the landscape, a key element in experiencing the wildness of America's newest acquisition, the "Land of the Midnight Sun." Native people and artwork were an iconic part of the expected experience for the tourist in late-nineteenth-century Alaska; images of poles, baskets, and people were ubiquitous in the travel brochures and promotional material (Figure 8.1). Many of the early guidebooks gave titillating accounts of visiting with Alaska's original residents in their homes, daring the tourist to enter into dwellings that might challenge the sensibilities of the Victorian traveller. Writers emphasized the smells of blankets, fish, and smoke that might be encountered as well as the exotic dress: labrets[12] were frequently mentioned even though their use was being abandoned by the end of the nineteenth century (Lukens 1889: 54; Union Pacific Railway Company c. 1890, 54). However, the travel writers also noted Native vendors' keen business acumen and challenged the tourist to try their skills in bargaining (Ballou 1889, 269–70; Scidmore 1885, 117; Stoddard 1899, 101).

Artists seemed to understand what tourists were looking for, when they were buying, and what they were willing to pay. This understanding of market demands was balanced against what artists were – and were not – willing to do and by internal motivations affecting what was produced and how it was sold.[13] Market demand was so strong that many travel writers noted that the Tlingit and Haida were skilled salesmen and women, getting their desired price through a strategic lack of

FEBRUARY to MAY 1896, Inc.

FEBRUARY to MAY 1896, Inc.

Pacific Coast Steamship Co.

Pacific Coast Steamship Co.

TOTEM POLES
KASA-AN VILLAGE
·ALASKA·

GOODALL PERKINS & CO.

TICKET OFFICE
PALACE HOTEL
4 NEW MONTGOMERY ST.
SAN FRANCISCO, CAL.

GENERAL AGENTS
10 MARKET STREET,
SAN FRANCISCO,
CAL.

POINT BONITA,
ENTRANCE TO GOLDEN GATE

·GOODALL·PERKINS·
·& CO.·

GENERAL AGENTS·
10 MARKET STREET,
SAN FRANCISCO, CAL.

TICKET OFFICE
4 NEW MONTGOMERY ST.
PALACE HOTEL,
SAN FRANCISCO, CAL.

© Cartography Associates, David Rumsey Collection

Figure 8.1 Pacific Coast Steamship Company timetable cover, 1906, showing Kasaan village with houses and totem poles. Courtesy David Rumsey Map Collection, David Rumsey Center, Stanford Libraries.

price bargaining (Lukens 1889, 64). In the village of Kasaan, Stoddard recorded, "There is much haggling over the price of a curio, and but little chance of a bargain. If one has his eye upon some coveted object, he had best purchase it at once at the first figure; for the Indian is not likely to drop a farthing, and there are others who will gladly outbid the hesitating shopper" (Stoddard 1899, 101–2). The silversmith Sitka Jack was known to have actively urged other sellers to ask more for their wares (Scidmore 1885, 105).

No written records reveal whether Tlingit women set their sales prices at collective meetings, but it seems certain that there was community knowledge of the going rates for certain objects. Many travellers were amazed at the uniformity of prices: "We came to the conclusion that there must be a Trades Union here, for the uniformity of prices was remarkable, and there was a positive firmness about the market" (Lukens 1889, 54; Smetzer 2014, 68). As well, there came to be other understandings of commercial interactions. The practice of being paid to have a photo taken was widespread, and a number of photos showing Tlingit women with their faces averted illustrate a solidarity that arose even when group shots were taken without fair compensation (Campbell 2007, 165–6; Collis 1890, 99–100; Raibmon 2005, 145–46; Scidmore 1885, 28).[14] Guidebooks and published travel reports not only set the expectation that travellers would buy artworks from and interact with the Tlingit and Haida people, but they also warned travellers of these reciprocal terms of expected compensation established by the artists and saleswomen.

Tlingit salespeople – male artists selling their carvings and jewellery as well as women selling their basketry, moccasins, dolls, and other pieces made by family members – capitalized on the consumers that the steamships delivered on schedule and en masse. Like the annual salmon runs, the steamship schedules allowed the artists (both men and women) to bank on a certain amount of economic activity on given days and throughout the summer. According to Scidmore, two of the silversmiths in Sitka, Kooska and Sitka Jack, "work night and day on special orders while the vessel is at the wharf. If you give them the order in the morning the bracelets are ready in the afternoon, as carefully finished and engraved as any of the others of their make" (1885, 179). Artists and sellers worked when the market was "on," no matter the hour. The arrival of a steamship into ports of call such as Sitka was announced with a cannon shot (Knapp and Childe 1896, 11). Septima Collis wrote in 1890 that everyone – Indians and whites alike – would

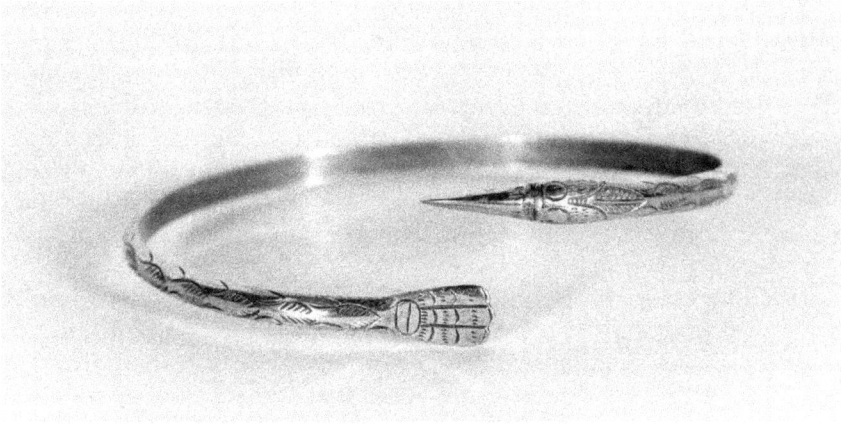

Figure 8.2 Silver bracelet attributed to Billy Wilson, Tlingit, n.d. Denver Art Museum Collection: purchase from G. T. Emmons, 1942.169. Photo courtesy of Nancy Harris.

turn out to greet the ship, no matter how late the hour of arrival; on her arrival in Sitka at midnight, all the Indians turned out with their wares (and all the whites turned out in anticipation of the latest newspaper) (Collis 1890, 87–8).[15]

Setting the Hook: Tourist Perceptions of the Personalized and Localized

Some of the most popular items, especially for female travellers, were silver and gold bracelets. On the Northwest Coast, these were made from currency (most often American silver coins) starting in the 1830s and 1840s, and by the 1860s were a regular part of both Indigenous adornment and the art market. They were decorated with crest designs as well as Victorian-inspired floral and foliate motifs (Bunn-Marcuse 2000). Scidmore's description of bracelets made to order on the day of commission confirms Emmons's assertions that a new, narrow bracelet design was invented specifically to meet the demand of the tourists. He identified several bracelets as being "of the very narrow type made first about 1880 for the newly developing tourist trade" (Figure 8.2), noting that "the wider native types took too long to make to keep the trade supplied" (Emmons 1932–44, 11 May 1941).

The invention of this new, narrower bracelet would have accomplished a number of goals for the artist, all of which would raise productivity and increase profit: they could be made more quickly, thus replenishing supplies;[16] they required less source material, and were thus cheaper to produce; and they could be executed "on commission," giving buyers the impression of a one-of-a-kind souvenir made specifically for them. This personalized service was more fiction than reality: museum collections show that artists executed certain designs repeatedly.

Taken together, these strategies suggest that Native artists carefully structured their industry and efforts to maximize their economic return during the brief but intense tourist season. Sheldon Jackson, the head of the Presbyterian mission in Sitka, noted that stores in many southeast towns were empty by the end of summer in 1885, and he advised that the only time to collect material was in spring before the summer rush (quoted in Cole 1985, 99). Maturin Ballou also noted that once every fortnight the steamer cleaned out the wares of artists, including silver bracelets, rattle, spoons, miniature poles, and canoes. He wrote, "The natives, as a rule, are completely cleaned out of their stock of these productions, and they do not fail to realize fair prices, enabling them to live very comfortably" (Ballou 1889, 261).

A similar situation existed for model totem poles. Poles were an iconic symbol of Alaska's Native residents, signifying what tourists then perceived as the old, soon-to-be-extinct practices of a dying culture (Jonaitis 1999, 109). Scidmore wrote of visiting "Indian villages with traditions and totem poles centuries old" and revelled in her visit to Howkan as the spot with more poles than any other and thus one of the "most interesting" stops on the whole voyage (1885, 269).[17] The link between ancient cultures and what tourists (incorrectly) assumed was their imminent demise made miniature poles one of the most desirable souvenirs of this romantic past (Jonaitis and Glass 2010, 103).

Curio stores in Alaska and all along the coast, especially in Seattle and Victoria, offered a dizzying array of model poles, many of them duplicates of a single design (Duncan 2000, 180–6; Scidmore 1885, 284). One of the most often reproduced poles was the Chief Shakes Raven pole from Wrangell, Alaska (Figures 8.3 and 8.4). Model poles, while not personalized for the individual like bracelets, often were "localized," allowing tourists to purchase a diminutive replica of the poles they had just seen in the village and providing them with a representative symbol of Alaska as well as a memento of having seen the full-size

Figure 8.3 Postcard of Chief Shakes' Raven Totem pole, Wrangell, c. 1901. Photo by Winter & Pond. University of Washington Libraries, Special Collections, UW37691.

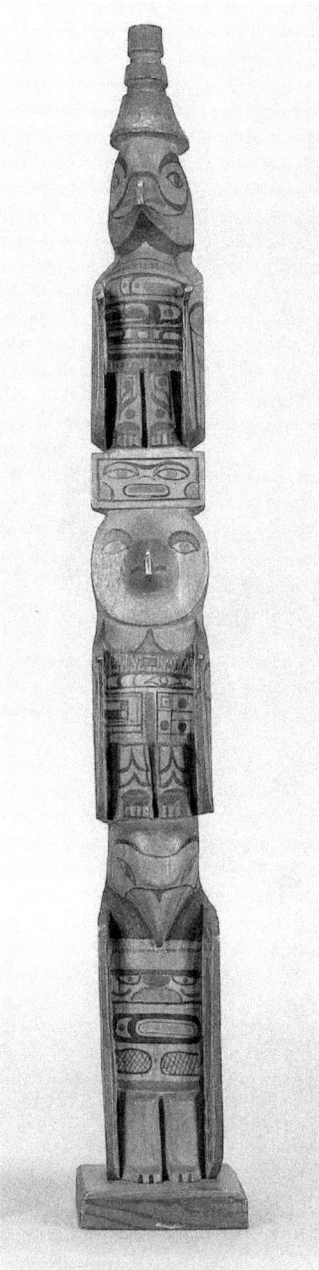

Figure 8.4 Model of Wrangell Raven pole, made by Frederick Alexcee (Tsimshian). University of British Columbia, Museum of Anthropology catalogue number A2206. Photograph by Derek Tan, courtesy UBC Museum of Anthropology, Vancouver, Canada.

pole in situ.[18] After admiring the poles in Tongass, Sophia Cracroft found three-foot models of the village poles for sale at the Waldron's trading post (Cracroft and Smith 1974, 132).

Souvenir spoons were another item commonly marked with the names of villages and other ports of call (such as glaciers or mining operations). Souvenir spoons were a tourist phenomenon for travellers throughout North America and Europe. Native silversmiths competed directly with commercially manufactured spoons stamped with scenes of local interest – log cabins, glaciers, salmon, bears, steamships, miners, and of course Native motifs such as totem poles, shamans or witches, and even local individuals (Chief Kasko appears on one spoon by Mayer Bros) (Hall 2004, fig. 3.8)[19] Competing with these commercial vendors meant that Indigenous artists had to capitalize on tourists' desire for authenticity[20] by selling their works directly to visitors or allowing tourists to watch them at work. Kasaan (aka Haida) John and Rudolph Walton were two artists that travellers' mentioned by name as demonstrating their artistic process. The Tlingit artist Johnny Kasank was even featured on a postcard labelled "Native Jeweller making Bracelets, Wrangell, Alaska," so that customers might document the direct relationship with an Indian artist. None of this prevented artists from supplying the traders' stores to take advantage of that source of income as well.

Stores commissioned works from artists over the winter to stock through the summer months. Some store owners provided sheet silver or stock spoon blanks for artists to engrave (Scidmore 1893b, 43). The curio store in Kasaan hired Chief Sonihat to produce silver rings. One writer recounted that

> after Chief Son-i-yat got so he could make round rings to size the fellows at Kasaan kept him so busy filling their orders he never had much left over to sell to the tourists when they come in on the boat. He hammered out a few extra-fancy rings, to order, from $20-gold pieces, but they was too rich for my blood. (McKeown 1951, 225)

Edward Mather worked for the Bethelsen and Pruell store in Ketchikan, which advertised "genuine Indian Silver Bracelets and spoons made by Mr. Mather, a Metlakatla Indian who was with Father Duncan when he first brought his Indians to Alaska" (Hall 2004, 44). While these artists worked for the white-owned stores, a few artists were able to open their own stores, including Rudolph Walton and, later,

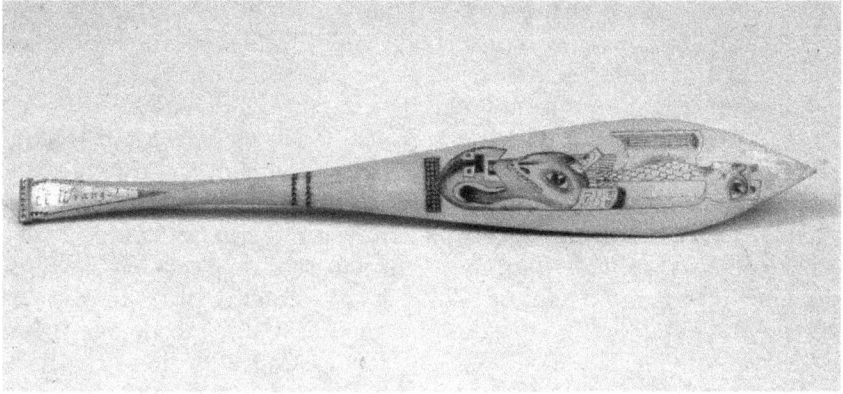

Figure 8.5 Model paddle, marked "Fort Wrangell" and decorated with a conglomerate design of the Howkan Eagle and a whale. Courtesy of the Burke Museum of Natural History and Culture, catalogue number 2.5E-1664.

Jim Williams. Stores owned by Native artists competed directly with white-owned stores and had an edge over them by having the artist at hand. The Tlingit silversmith Jim Williams and his wife owned their own store, the Native Curio Shop, in Skagway after the turn of the century (Hall 2004, 43).

Other "localized" items included spoons, baskets, moccasins, and wall-pockets decorated with the name of individual ports of call (Figure 8.5). All of these souvenirs were graphic markers of an imagined Alaska (Figure 8.6), as understood by tourists and promoted by Alaskan steamship companies; the tourists' own experiential encounter with Indigenous artworks layered their expectations and experience onto the iconographic souvenir.

Reeling Them In: Encountering Authenticity

Like the interest in model poles that signified to tourists the vanishing beliefs of local Indians, travellers were drawn to other products and materials that symbolized "ancient practices." Copper was understood to be an archaic material associated with pre-contact productions. One tourist was thrilled at being shown a chunk of copper ore in excess of sixty pounds, demonstrating the mineral riches of the region (Ballou 1889, 289).[21] Scidmore noted that copper products were especially

Figure 8.6 Tsimshian basketry purse (Metlakatla?), with "ALASKA" in red false embroidery. Courtesy of the Burke Museum of Natural History and Culture, catalogue number 25.0/378.

available among the Chilkat, "as the art of forging copper was long ago a secret of theirs" (1885). The most thrilling products in copper were daggers, made for sale to tourists and incorporating copper blades (some of which were commercially forged) with Tlingit imagery on their wooden pommels. Although many of the fighting daggers of the Tlingit had been made out of iron, a copper blade fit tourists' expectations of pre-contact warfare (Verplank 2009). The sale of daggers built on the fierce reputation of the northern Tlingit ("the very name Chilkat has become synonymous with bloodshed" [Lukens 1889, 68] was a typical description). Imagery as well as materials were popular in reinforcing the ferocity of the Chilkat Tlingits.

In her study of Tlingit daggers, Ashley Verplank noted that the majority of daggers from the time were embellished with grizzly (or brown)

Figure 8.7 Made-for-sale Tlingit dagger with copper bear pommel. National Museum of the American Indian, Smithsonian Institution (15/4536).

bear imagery. She writes, "What animal is more closely associated with the last frontier than this fierce creature? The implied savagery of this beast was directly linked to the untamed wilderness of Alaska and most likely contributed to its artistic success. Numerous bear pommel daggers were carved from sheep horn and covered with real fur. Their features were given an extra dazzle with abalone inlay and riveted copper highlights" (Verplank 2009, 123) (Figure 8.7). These new copper daggers, while imitating the older forms, were no longer functional: the beautifully crafted raised medians were riveted on rather than forged in, undermining the blade strength. Scidmore happily reported that this "warlike and aggressive people" now practiced "the arts of peace" and that they had miniature totem poles and canoes, pipes, masks, and spoons as well as the copper knives and arrow tips that were "distinctly Chilkat work." On Scidmore's visit to the village in Lynn Canal, her group was thrilled to have the rare "relics of the stone age ... brought forth" (1885, 105).

"Ancient" relics proved so popular that a number of artists developed expertise in the creation of new antiques: "several individuals make a specialty of producing specimens of any degree of antiquity desired" (United States 1893, 250). In fact, one trader was so anxious to fill the orders from scientists of eastern museums that he was going to bring in a skilled stone carver to fill orders for "stone age implements" (Scidmore 1885, 106). While the secret of artificial aging was known to museum collectors – Emmons noted that expert Chilkat metal workers were aging their products to a "dull, dark green" (1991, 397) – tourists provided enough of a market for a thriving small-scale industry. At the P.E. Kern Native Curio Workshop in Skagway, Peter Kern hired Tlingit artists to make souvenirs, specializing in metal products. Kern marketed the authenticity of his products as their key selling point, even picturing one of his workers, John Kasko, in his advertisements in the *Daily Alaskan* and inventing legends to promote the Alaskan origin of the swastika motif that appeared on many of the products in his shop's Indian Department (Lenz 2004, 90; Verplank 2009, 117). Kern's store provided employment for eighteen Chilkat Tlingits. These "artists and artificers" as he called them worked at the store and were provided with the raw materials of abalone and copper, ordered wholesale from California suppliers (Emmons 1991, 380; Hall 2004, 62).

Other Tourist "Traps"

The Tlingit were great entrepreneurs and found additional ways to tap the tourist market. A least one group were involved in dance performances, one of the earliest instances of heritage performance for tourists in Alaska.[22] Septima Collis described a dance troupe based in Juneau but advertised in printed circulars as far south as Tacoma:

> Native dance, by the renowned dancers of the Thlinkit tribe of Alaska Indians, under the management of D. Martini, the Barnum of Alaska, and the celebrated Takou Chief, *Yash Noosh,* head chief of one of the most warlike tribes of Alaska, but have succumbed [sic] to the influences of civilization. Admission $1. Children 50 cts. The performance will commence immediately after the arrival of the excursion steamer at Juneau, Alaska. (1890, 168–9)

The program for the dances outlines the "ancient" dances, some purportedly out of practice "since the days of Baranof" and others performed "more than 200 years ago." As well, the program highlights the expertise of the manager, D. Martini, testifying to his knowledge of Indian culture as signified by collections he made for the Smithsonian and British Museum, the quality of his troupe, and the great value of "first-class attractions at popular prices."

Certainly it appears the program did deliver. Collis raves about the dancers' attire: the ermine skins, blankets, headdresses, and even the swirling eagle down. At the end of the performance, she and her fellow travellers sign the guest book, "to impress the tourists that followed us," and she went as far as to purchase the totem pole featured in the performance (Collis 1890, 174). But Collis did not enjoy all aspects of her experience. Like other Victorian writers who described the travails of searching for baskets and other curios in Native homes in Sitka's Ranche and elsewhere, Collis was discomforted at close quarters with the dance performers and others in the small tent on the waterfront. Her account, like so many others, is replete with shockingly raw contempt and disdain for the people whose practices and artefacts she so desired to witness and acquire.

It must have been an exceedingly tricky balancing act for Native vendors and artists to meet tourists' expectations for authenticity and interaction while still accommodating certain Victorian standards. There was no one successful approach – Native people were damned for not abiding by Victorian practices of dress, hygiene, and decorum but also for being uninteresting and too modern when they appeared in Western clothing and mien, as did Chief Yash Noosh, who appeared to Collis "not in the garb of a warlike Indian chief, but in that of a quiet guardian of the public peace, commonly called a policeman" (Collis 1890, 169). Perhaps the only winning strategy was to exploit all expectations and venues, to accommodate the spectrum of consumer tastes and habits (Lee 1999). Like postcard manufacturers that sold images ranging from "Yah-Yicks a civilized Alaskan belle" in Western dress, to those that pictured the Tlingit shaman Skandoo with the tools of his kit, Tlingit sellers had to accommodate many tastes; so while some travellers ignored the trader's stores in a "hasty rush for the Indian tents" (Scidmore 1885, 105), others were assured of a "courteous reception" in Walton's own store in Sitka "as Rudolph speaks English well" (Hall 2004, 41). These stark images, of the civilized and the primitive, reinforce traveller's expectations of a clear choice between the old and the new for Alaska's Native peoples. The reality was much more complicated, demanding a careful manoeuvring between colonial demands, tourist expectations,

Figure 8.8 Tsimshian basket decorated with strawberries. Courtesy of the Burke Museum of Natural History and Culture, catalogue number 1-1769.

and kinship obligations in order to navigate the colonial economy and chart a course for economic and cultural survival.

Abundant Shoals: A Wealth of Imagery

Native artists did not always ground their material productions in their own cultural aesthetics. They expanded their traditional repertoire to provide a variety of choices for tourists whose tastes ranged from a desire for the "characteristic figures of the ancient animal deities" to others who purchased the scrolls, American eagles, and other designs of "civilized fashion" (Knapp and Childe 1896, 169; Scidmore 1885, 39). Basketry and silverwork provide the best examples of the plethora of imagery being produced. A number of new creations in basketry appeared for sale, including tablemats, every possible shape of basketry-covered bottles, and even virtuoso productions like miniature basketry tea sets. None of these were traditional to the Northwest Coast, but all were perfect additions to the Victorian cozy-corner. Woven motifs included Indigenous designs in geometric pattern as well as naturalistic renditions of local plants, such as strawberries and wildflowers (Figure 8.8).

Artists adapted many Euro-American motifs to their work in silver as well (Bunn-Marcuse, 2013). The number of bracelets with these designs in museum collections attests to their popularity. They are mentioned as well in the journals of coast travellers: "The old designs are being replaced by American flags, E Pluribus Unum eagles, clasped hands, and other borrowed atrocities. They might as well come from New Jersey!" (Knapp and Childe 1896, 169). The above list of borrowed designs represents only a small portion of those found on nineteenth- and early-twentieth-century silver. Others included American eagles, hearts, Victorian foliate patterns, scrollwork, the lion and unicorn, individual names, and combinations of Victorian floral designs with Native-style animals. And while a number of writers lamented the intrusion of these non-Native designs into the repertoire, the designs were clearly popular sellers.[23] These designs were not only popular with non-Native consumers but were a large part of the Indigenous market for silverwork as well, allowing artists to produce similar designs for all of their patrons (see Bunn-Marcuse 1998, 2000, 2011, p. 64).

Art historian Ruth Phillips sheds some light on the popularity among tourists of floral engraved silver bracelets (Figure 8.9). As with the beaded whimsies of the Great Lakes region, the main consumers (or recipients) of these items were women. While twentieth-century scholars frequently consider these designs to be devoid of meaning, the flower has long been the ultimate symbol of femininity, and nineteenth-century Victorian women were very knowledgeable about species of flowers, which types were currently fashionable, and the subtleties of popular meaning attached to each kind. This enhanced reading of floral patterns is no longer a part of the twentieth-century gaze (Phillips 1998, 188).

Nancy Pagh's analysis of women's writings in Alaska notes that while women often decried the large and majestic landscape as too awesome for their powers of description, they had an impressive command of the nomenclature and botany of flowers and detailed their experiences with the wildflowers of the region, often listing many they were familiar with. In a single paragraph, one traveller, Gladys O'Kelly, celebrated poppies, daisies, painter's brush, marguerites, and forget-me-nots. Pagh notes that writers of the time contrasted the delicate and lovely nature of these small flowers to the majestic but chilly grandeur of the vast Alaskan geography (1999, 13). Silver jewellery, basketry, or moccasins decorated with floral designs (Figures 8.8 and 8.9), while seemingly copies of Victorian floral work, might also have served as mementos of Alaskan experiences in much the same way as miniature

Figure 8.9 Silver bracelet, possibly a mountain avens flower. Courtesy of the Burke Museum of Natural History and Culture, catalogue number 2011-49/1.

totem poles and canoes functioned – they were souvenirs linked to the places and people encountered on the Alaskan tour.

In addition to the simple fact that Euro-American designs seemed popular with tourists, artists may have had other inspiration for their creations. Tlingit and Haida artists might have considered them particularly appropriate for non-Native consumers. Perhaps certain Euro-North American designs appeared to be analogous to the crest figures that Native consumers wanted on commissioned bracelets. Robin Wright has pointed out that Euro-North American sailing ships had billet heads or figureheads on their bows, much as Haida canoes had crest designs on theirs (1977, 73). Perhaps these ship designs seemed to be appropriate "crests" for their white customers. Perhaps the American eagle appeared to Native artists as the quintessential American "crest," particularly suited for "Boston men" and their wives (Bunn-Marcuse 2000).[24] There is no written evidence to say for certain what the reasoning was behind these adopted images, but the simple fact of their popularity made them a smart addition to the artists' repertoire.

Sustaining the Harvest

In recent years, ecologists have quantified how salmon contribute to the sustenance of the forests and streams where they return to spawn (Gulick 2010; Helfield and Naiman 2001).[25] Perhaps the tourist trade played a similar role at the end of the nineteenth century, providing new economic possibilities for Indigenous artists of the time.

The height of tourism on the Northwest Coast coincided with the increased presence of missionaries. Tourists not only explored "prim- itive" practices but also visited the bastions of "civilization," such as the Sitka Mission's Cottages and performances by the Reverend Dun- can's Metlakatla Band. On the one hand, travel writers deplored signs of change and acculturation, lamenting the modern influences that "corrupted" ancient practices and art forms, while on the other they sang the praises of the mission schools, Christian education, and train- ing programs. Phillips points out that Native people were living with contradictory messages, one to assimilate, the other "to produce their ethnicity according to archaic stereotypes" (1998, 14). This created pain- ful confusion about identity. On the Northwest Coast, potlatches were banned by Indian agents in the US and outlawed by the Canadian gov- ernment. Traditional ceremonialism was under attack by the colonial administrators at the same time that American museums were commis- sioning traditional ceremonial artworks. Some Native people followed the church and government in their instruction to leave behind Tlingit practices of seasonal migrations, kinship obligations, and ceremonial practices, while others were strongly involved in those pursuits, and many others found a middle ground. Caught in the rip tides caused by competing forces, Alaskan Native families learned to carefully navigate these new waters. The cash economy was one of the vessels that car- ried them through.[26] In many families, women provided critical cash income through their creations. While basketry was sought out during the craft craze of the time, sewn and beaded work, including moccasins, dolls, purses, gloves, and wall pockets, was faster to produce and a large part of the income that was brought in (see Smetzer 2007, 2009, 2014). The production of Indigenous artworks as commodities was a means of cultural survival, and the objects themselves mediate intercultural relationships of trade, misunderstanding and bias, and a commercial middle ground (Glass 2011, xvii, 7). They could affirm the very identity that was being threatened and provide the financial means to support participation in either the modern or Tlingit life or more likely, both.[27]

Unlike studies of contemporary Indigenous tourism or art market economies today, there is very little direct record of the strategies and reflections of Native artists or salespeople during the early years of tourism in Alaska. By examining the kinds of items they produced, what those items looked like, and how they were marketed, and cross-referencing travellers' letters and journals, we can start to fill in a broader picture of the time. Comparisons to today's multi-million-dollar cruise ship industry in Alaska would show some of the same techniques at play (though today only a minute percentage of revenue returns to Native hands): the iconic use of Indigenous identity in advertising, the miniaturization of Indigenous symbols (totem pole, houses, dolls in Native garb), the packaging of performance, and the directed viewing of and interactions with the landscape. The tourist runs first spawned over a century ago are still recognizable today.

NOTES

1 In Alaska, the term "Native" is often used in referring to Indigenous populations. It is not considered derogatory as it is in other regions and is often used in legal and cultural descriptions (i.e., the Alaska Native Claims Settlement Act or the Alaska Native Heritage Museum). As such, I will use the term "Native" in this article. In keeping with the terminology of this volume, I will use "Indigenous" as a generalized term but "Native" where it seems most in keeping with historical description.

2 The term "potlatch" refers to a gathering at which key clan or group business is publically conducted, and at which marriages, transfers of leadership or ownership, memorials, or other markers of life-status change are celebrated and guests are paid to witness the proceedings. Potlatches were the platform for the legal and economic system on the Northwest Coast before European contact and throughout the nineteenth century, and they continue to be one of the primary vehicles for transference and demonstration of cultural knowledge and rights today. There are many types of potlatches on the Coast with terminology and practices specific to each nation. Among the Tlingit, the term *ku.eex* refers to a memorial potlatch and the English gloss, "party," is also used. In other parts of the Coast, "potlatch" is still in use. At the end of the nineteenth century and lasting through the mid-twentieth century, the potlatch became the target of colonial policies that either outlawed or actively discouraged them in Canada and the United States (Cole and Chaikin 1990, Kan 1989).

3 See in particular Bunten and Douney, this volume, for expectations of authenticity in performance, setting, and material culture souvenirs.

4 Mique'l Dangeli's (nee Askren) work on B.A. Haldane exemplifies the re-examination of historical images to find new evidence of Indigenous agency in contrast to the story of colonial acculturation that had been told for decades about the community at Metlakatla (Askren 2006).

5 Joyce Walton Shales's (1998) dissertation on the Tlingit artist and businessman Rudolph Walton brings together publicly available historical records as well as family archives.

6 A few artists, like Charles Edenshaw, were able to produce art full time, year round. Many others fit their art production into the schedule of other seasonal resource harvesting, working around the commercial and Indigenous fishing and gathering seasons.

7 Paige Raibmon and Robert Campbell discuss the cumulative effect of contemporary travel writings on travellers' expectations in late-nineteenth-century Alaska. Raibmon's examination of Tlingit reactions to tourism, and tourism's relationship to missionary activities in Sitka and Campbell's analyses of how travellers' understandings of Alaska's people and landscape were shaped through late-nineteenth-century theories on race, class, and gender, are thorough and insightful and are key reading for an understanding of the market as a whole. In this article, I agree with many of their conclusions and provide further details on the activities and, most specifically, on the artworks made for the tourist trade.

8 By the first US census of Alaska in 1880, the count of total Alaska Natives was 32,996, along with 430 white settlers who lived mostly in the southeast. The 1890 census numbers the Tlingit population in Southeast Alaska at 4,737. Massive influxes of settlers to the region due to mining interests in the years between 1880 and 1900 changed the percentage of Native to non-Native inhabitants dramatically, with the white population growing to 4,298, more than half of which were temporary cannery workers (Hunsinger and Sandberg 2013, 4–5; Sandberg 2013, 9).

9 Hawker credits the stabilization in the Alaskan economy in the 1880s to the recovery from Civil War uncertainties. This stabilization was crucial for the developing steamship tour companies (Hawker 1991, 130).

10 For a discussion of other American holidays that were used to provide a new context for potlatching, see Raibmon's discussion of the Sitka Tlingit celebrations of Thanksgiving (2005, 94, 168–9).

11 The economic importance of sales of curios from the nineteenth century through the mid-twentieth century, especially items such as beaded

moccasins, dolls, and other souvenirs produced by women, is discussed by art historian Megan Smetzer (2014, 2009).

12 Labrets (literally, lip ornaments) of bone, stone, or shell, usually inserted into holes on either side of the mouth of both men and women, as a mark of class and family membership amongst the Northwest Coast Indians of the United States and Canada and the Yukp'iit and Inupiat of Alaska.

13 Tourists and museum collectors were interested in buying what was not for sale as well, and there are a number of instances where offers were rebuffed (Cole 1985, 301; Enge 1996; Scidmore 1885, 27).

14 A photo in the University of Washington Special Collections, NA904, shows at least fourteen women in close range of the camera, all with faces averted. This photo by Frank Laroche was taken in Sitka, along Lincoln Street in 1904. Other photos from the same location show women selling their wares and all looking at the camera (UW Special Collections, NA2551).

15 This practice continued to occur into the 1930s, when Barrett Willoughby witnesses it in Sitka at 2:30 a.m. (Willoughby 1930, 11–18).

16 The wider type of bracelet was more time intensive, and Emmons noted that it was difficult for a collector to find these types once the tourists had arrived: bracelets "simply were exhausted except in outlying villages between 88 & 98 when white tourists came" (Emmons 1932–1944, 28 March 1942).

17 Scidmore found Sitka quite lacking in interest due to the absence of poles, painted house fronts, and the "Indians themselves [who] are much too given to ready-made clothes and civilized ways to be really picturesque" (1885, 175). White travellers believed poles were as old as the Tlingit and Haida cultures themselves, although the Tlingit used interior houseposts and painted housefronts to display clan affiliation; the free-standing totem pole originated with the Haida and its use did not spread to other parts of the Northwest Coast until the nineteenth and twentieth centuries.

18 In *The Totem Pole: An Intercultural History* Jonaitis and Glass examine numerous aspects of the commercialization of poles, including a discussion of model poles and Alaskan curio shops (2010, 62, 96–7, 103–4).

19 June Hall examined the history of souvenir spoons in Alaska. Her study includes both commercial manufacturers and Native artists and provides the greatest number of extant attributions of spoons to Native silversmiths (Hall 2004).

20 I use the term "authenticity" here in the full understanding of its problematic and relativist history. Rather than put it in quotations referencing current discussions of the nineteenth-century biases that

attend it, I let it stand as a term that was fully in use in the time period and trust that the reader will place it within that context. For further discussions of the term see Raibmon (2005, 3, 206).

21 Ballou's chapter "Mineral Deposits" explores the possible extraction resources in Alaska, such as copper, petroleum, and gold, that would stimulate development in Alaska and bring it into competition with other regions, a colonial strategy to advance its progress towards becoming a territory and coming under the land-use laws of the United States (Ballou 1889, 289; Raibmon 2005, 143).

22 A number of Indigenous groups from the Northwest Coast had staged performances outside of the region previous to this, including the Nuxalk men who travelled to Germany in 1885 and the Kwagiulth that performed at the Chicago World's Fair in 1893. There is one other known tourist account of a Tlingit performance circa 1890 by an anonymous writer whose account is in the archives of the Alaska State Library, Ms 4, Box 7, folder 4. 10–11 (Smetzer 2007, 230).

23 The production of indigenized Euro-American designs probably started before 1850, was well established by the 1860s, and continued into the 1930s or 1940s.

24 Americans were generally known as "Boston men" by Native groups on the Northwest Coast.

25 Salmon that swim upriver and die – whether before or after spawning – are often carried by bears and eagles into the forest. Recent studies document that trees and shrubs near spawning streams can receive almost one-quarter of certain nutrients from salmon, improving the riparian habitat that is critical to future salmon generations and the long-term productivity of the streams (Gulick 2010). I was intrigued by the synergy of this system and its possible implications for the metaphor of tourist-season-as-salmon-run.

26 A few Tlingit were renowned for making a good living off the tourist economy, including well-known individuals such as Kajiint (Princess Tom), but some reports asserted, perhaps over-optimistically, that the wealth was more wide spread. The Union Pacific guide suggested that "none of them are poor, all have some money, and some have wealth by the thousands; … many are rich, having more than $20,000 in good, hard cash" (c. 1890, 48, 54).

27 Raibmon's discussion of the Davis case involving the judicial weighing of "civilized" versus "Tlingit" lifestyles shows how, despite the court's and church's desire to draw a line between these two, many Tlingits were living a life that seamlessly incorporated both (2005, 181–97).

REFERENCES

Appadurai, Arjun, ed. 1986. *The Social Life of Things: Commodities in Cultural Perspective*. Cambridge: Cambridge University Press. http://dx.doi.org/10.1017/CBO9780511819582.

Askren, Mique'l Icesis. 2006. "From Negative to Positive: B.A. Haldane, Nineteenth Century Tsimshian Photographer." Master's thesis, University of British Columbia.

Ballou, Maturin M. 1889. *The New Eldorado: A Summer Journey to Alaska*. Boston: Houghton, Mifflin.

Boursin, Henry. 1893a. "The Mines of Alaska." In *Report on Population and Resources of Alaska at the Eleventh Census: 1890*, 229–42. Washington, DC: US Government Printing Office.

Boursin, Henry. 1893b. "The First District of Alaska from Prince Frederick Sound to Yakutat Bay." In *Report on Population and Resources of Alaska at the Eleventh Census: 1890*, 42–4. Washington, DC: US Government Printing Office.

Bunn-Marcuse, Kathryn. 1998. *Reflected Images: The Use of Euro-American Designs on Northwest Coast Bracelets*. Master's thesis, University of Washington, Seattle.

Bunn-Marcuse, Kathryn. 2000. "Northwest Coast Silver Bracelets and the Use of Euro-American Designs." *American Indian Art Magazine* 25 (4): 66–73, 84.

Bunn-Marcuse, Kathryn. 2011. "Bracelets of Exchange." In *Objects of Exchange: Transition, Transaction, and Transformation on the Late-Nineteenth Century Northwest Coast*, edited by Aaron Glass, 61–9. New York: American Museum of Natural History and Bard Graduate Center. Distributed by Yale University Press.

Bunn-Marcuse, Kathryn. 2013. "Eagles and Elephants: Cross-Cultural Influences in the Time of Charles Edenshaw." In *Charles Edenshaw*, edited by Robin Wright and Daina Augaitis, 174–87. London: Vancouver Art Gallery/Black Dog Publications.

Bunn-Marcuse, Kathryn. 2015. "Tourists and Collectors: The New Market for Tlingit and Haida Jewelry at the Turn of the Century." In *Sharing Our Knowledge: The Tlingit and Their Coastal Neighbors*, edited by Sergei Kan, 417–40. Lincoln: University of Nebraska Press.

Bunten, Alexis C. 2006. "Commodities of Authenticity: When Native People Consume Their Own Tourist Art." In *Exploring World Art*, edited by Eric Venbrux, Pamela Sheffield Rosi, and Robert L. Welsh, 317–36. Long Grove: Waveland.

Campbell, Robert. 2007. *In Darkest Alaska: Travel and Empire along the Inside Passage*. Philadelphia: University of Pennsylvania Press. http://dx.doi.org/10.9783/9780812201529.

Cole, Douglas. 1985. *Captured Heritage: The Scramble for Northwest Coast Artifacts*. Seattle: University of Washington Press.

Cole, Douglas, and Ira Chaikin. 1990. *An Iron Hand Upon the People: The Law against the Potlatch on the Northwest Coast*. Vancouver/Seattle: Douglas & McIntyre/University of Washington Press.

Collis, Septima Maria Levy. 1890. *A Woman's Trip to Alaska; Being an Account of a Voyage through the Inland Seas of the Sitkan Archipelago, in 1890*. New York: Cassell Pub. Co.

Collison, W.H. 1915. *In the Wake of the War Canoe: A Stirring Record of Forty Years' Successful Labour, Peril & Adventure Amongst the Savage Indian Tribes of the Pacific Coast, and the Piratical Head-Hunting Haidas of the Queen Charlotte Islands, B.C.* London: Seeley Service.

Cracroft, Sophia, and Dorothy Blakey Smith. 1974. *Lady Franklin Visits the Pacific Northwest: Being Extracts from the Letters of Miss Sophia Cracroft, Sir John Franklin's Niece, February to April 1861 and April to July 1870*. Provincial Archives of British Columbia Memoir, No. 11. Provincial Archives of British Columbia, Victoria, BC.

Duncan, Kate. 2000. *1001 Curious Things: Ye Olde Curiosity Shop and Native American Art*. Seattle: University of Washington Press.

Emmons, George. 1932–44. "Correspondence with Frederic Douglas." Native Arts Department correspondence files, Denver Art Museum.

Emmons, George. 1991. *The Tlingit Indians*, edited by Frederica de Laguna. Seattle: University of Washington Press.

Glass, Aaron. 2011. *Objects of Exchange: Social and Material Transformation on the Late Nineteenth-Century Northwest Coast*. New York: Bard Graduate Center. Distributed by Yale University Press.

Gordon, Daniel M. 1880. *Mountain and Prairie: A Journey from Victoria to Winnipeg Via Peace River Pass*. Montreal: Dawson Brothers.

Graburn, Nelson H.H. 1976. *Ethnic and Tourist Arts: Cultural Expressions from the Fourth World*. Berkeley: University of California Press.

Gulick, Amy. 2010. *Salmon in the Trees: Life in Alaska's Tongass Rain Forest*. Seattle: Mountaineers.

Hall, June. 2004. *Alaska Souvenir Spoons & the Early Curio Trade*. Juneau: Gastineau Channel Historical Society.

Harmon, Alexandra. 2010. *Rich Indians: Native People and the Problem of Wealth in American History*. Chapel Hill: University of North Carolina Press.

Hawker, Ronald W. 1991. "Frederick Landsberg: A Pioneer Indian Art Dealer in Victoria, Canada." *Western States Jewish History* 23 (2): 128–38.

Helfield, James M., and Robert J. Naiman. 2001. "Effects of Salmon-Derived Nitrogen on Riparian Forest Growth and Implications for Stream Productivity." *Ecology* 82 (9): 2403–9. http://dx.doi.org/10.1890/0012-9658(2001)082[2403:EOSDNO]2.0.CO;2.

Hunsinger, Eddie, and Eric Sandberg. 2013. *The Alaska Native Population.* Alaska Economic Trends.

Inverarity, Robert Bruce. 1946. *Northwest Coast Indian Art: A Brief Survey.* Museum Series no. 1. Seattle: Washington State Museum.

Jonaitis, Aldona. 1999. "Northwest Coast Totem Poles." In *Unpacking Culture: Art and Commodity in Colonial and Postcolonial Worlds*, edited by Ruth B. Phillips and Christopher Burghard Steiner, 104–21. Berkeley: University of California Press.

Jonaitis, Aldona, and Aaron Glass. 2010. *The Totem Pole: An Intercultural History.* Seattle/Vancouver: University of Washington Press/Douglas & MacIntyre.

Jules-Rosette, Bennetta. 1984. *The Messages of Tourist Art: An African Semiotic System in Comparative Perspective.* New York: Plenum. http://dx.doi.org/10.1007/978-1-4757-1827-0.

Kan, Sergei. 1989. *Symbolic Immortality: The Tlingit Potlatch of the Nineteenth Century.* Washington: Smithsonian Institution Press.

Kaufmann, Carole N. 1976. "Functional Aspects of Haida Argillite Carvings." *Ethnic and Tourist Arts: Cultural Expressions from the Fourth World*, edited by Nelson H.H. Graburn, 56–69. Berkeley: University of California Press.

Keane, Webb. 2001. "Money Is No Object: Materiality, Desire, and Modernity in an Indonesian Society." In *Empire of Things*, edited by Fred Myers, 65–90. Sante Fe: School of American Research Press.

Knapp, Frances, and Rheta Louise Childe. 1896. *The Thlinkets of Southeastern Alaska.* Chicago: Stone and Kimball.

Kopytoff, Igor. 1986. "Cultural Biography of Things: Commoditization as Process." In *The Social Life of Things: Commodities in Cultural Perspective*, ed. Arjun Appadurai, 64–91. Cambridge: Cambridge University Press. http://dx.doi.org/10.1017/CBO9780511819582.004.

Lee, Molly. 1999. "Tourism and Taste Cultures: Collecting Native Art in Alaska at the Turn of the Twentieth Century." In *Unpacking Culture: Art and Commodity in Colonial and Postcolonial Worlds*, edited by Ruth B. Phillips and Christopher Burghard Steiner, 267–81. Berkeley: University of California Press.

Lenz, Mary J. 2004. "No Tourist Material: George Heye & His Golden Rule." *American Indian Art Magazine* 29 (4): 86–95, 105.

Lukens, Matilda B. 1889. *The Inland Passage: A Journal of a Trip to Alaska.* San Francisco[?].

MacDowell, Lloyd. 1905. "Alaska Indian Basketry."

McKeown, Martha Ferguson. 1951. *Alaska Silver*. New York: Macmillan.

Myers, Fred, ed. 2001. *Empire of Things*. Sante Fe: School of American Research Press.

Norris, Frank. 1987. "Showing Off Alaska: The Northern Tourist Trade, 1878–1941." *Alaska History (Anchorage, Alaska)* 2 (2): 1–18.

Pagh, Nancy. 1999. "An Indescribable Sea: Discourse of Women Traveling the Northwest Coast by Boat." *Frontiers: A Journal of Women Studies* 20 (3): 1–26. http://dx.doi.org/10.2307/3347216.

Phillips, Ruth B. 1998. *Trading Identities: The Souvenir in Native North American Art from the Northeast, 1700–1900*. Seattle: University of Washington Press.

Phillips, Ruth B., and Christopher Burghard Steiner, eds. 1999. *Unpacking Culture: Art and Commodity in Colonial and Postcolonial Worlds*. Berkeley: University of California Press.

Raibmon, Paige. 2005. *Authentic Indians: Episodes of Encounter from the Late-Nineteenth Century Northwest Coast*. Durham: Duke University Press. http://dx.doi.org/10.1215/9780822386773.

Sandberg, Eric. 2013. *A History of Alaska Population Settlement*. Juneau: Alaska Department of Labor and Workforce Development.

Scidmore, Eliza Ruhamah. 1885. *Alaska: Its Southern Coast and the Sitkan Archipelago*. Boston: D. Lothrop.

Scidmore, Eliza Ruhamah. 1893a. "Additional to First District: The Natives." In *Report on Population and Resources of Alaska at the Eleventh Census: 1890*, 54–63. Washington, DC: US Government Printing Office.

Scidmore, Eliza Ruhamah. 1893b. "Some American Spoons." *The Jeweler's Circular and Horological Review* (September 27): 42–3.

Shales, Joyce Walton. 1998. "Rudolph Walton: One Tlingit Man's Journey through Stormy Seas, 1867–1951." PhD diss., University of British Columbia, Vancouver.

Smetzer, Megan A. 2007. "Assimilation or Resistance? The Production and Consumption of Tlingit Beadwork." PhD diss., University of British Columbia, Vancouver.

Smetzer, M.A. 2009. "From Ruffs to Regalia: Tlingit Dolls and the Embodiment of Identity." In *Women and Things: Gendered Material Practices, 1750–1950*, edited by Maureen Daly Goggin and Beth Fowkes Tobin, 75–90. Aldershot: Ashgate.

Smetzer, M.A. 2014. "From Bolts to Bags: Transforming Cloth in 19th Century Tlingit Alaska." *Journal of Material Culture* 19 (1): 59–73. http://dx.doi.org/10.1177/1359183513508030.

Stoddard, Charles W. 1899. *Over the Rocky Mountains to Alaska*. St. Louis: B. Herder.

Teichmann, Emil. 1963. *A Journey to Alaska in the Year 1868: Being a Diary of the Late Emil Teichmann*. New York: Argosy-Antiquarian.

Union Pacific Railway Company. c. 1890. *Sights and Scenes in Oregon, Washington and Alaska for Tourists*. Chicago: Rand, McNally.

United States. 1893. *Report on Population and Resources of Alaska at the Eleventh Census: 1890*. Washington, DC: US Government Printing Office.

United States. 2016. Table 1. United States Resident Population by State: 1860–1920. US Censuses of Population and Housing. http://lwd.dol.state.nj.us/labor/lpa/census/1990/poptrd1.htm (accessed 15 September 2016).

Verplank, Ashley Kristen. 2009. "Form Follows Function: The Evolution of Tlingit Daggers." Master's thesis, University of Washington.

Willoughby, Barrett. 1930. *Sitka, Portal to Romance*. Boston: Houghton Mifflin.

Wright, Robin K. 1977. "Haida Argillite Pipes." Master's thesis, University of Washington.

Wyatt, Victoria. 1984. *Shapes of Their Thoughts: Reflections of Culture Contact in Northwest Coast Indian Art*. New Haven: Peabody Museum of Natural History, Yale University.

9 Experiments in Inuit Tourism: The Eastern Canadian Arctic

NELSON H.H. GRABURN

Tourism to the Eastern Canadian Arctic has been operating sporadically since the 1960s, with the attractive combination of hunting, fishing, and coming to see Inuit arts and crafts. This chapter explores two features. First, there is a continuity between traditional Inuit social visiting and some aspects of contemporary "mechanized" tourism, where one pole of growth is urbanized Inuit visiting other communities or natural features in their own vast territories; this "indigenous tourism" may be intra-ethnic as well as cross-cultural. Second, one important feature has been the variety of forms of cooperation between Inuit and non-Inuit, with the partners drawing on two sets of cultural capital in the "white" and Inuit worlds, operating both as private companies and as Inuit cooperatives. This chapter discusses different kinds of experiments in Inuit tourism, and queries the notion that cooperation between Inuit and *Qallunaat* ("English-speaking white people") is "selling out."

The James Bay Treaty (1975) and the creation of Nunavut (1999) gave Inuit control and made capital available through land claims, and tourism emerged as a major potential for economic development. In many Inuit villages, this possibility is only realized through the lucrative licensing of sport hunting of polar bears. Just one major area, Pangnirtung, Baffin Island, attracts more than a few hundred people a year to visit and "trek" in Auyuittuk National Park. Since 2000, cruise ships have become more numerous, but most passengers spend little time ashore and focus mainly on wildlife and Arctic sea and landscapes.

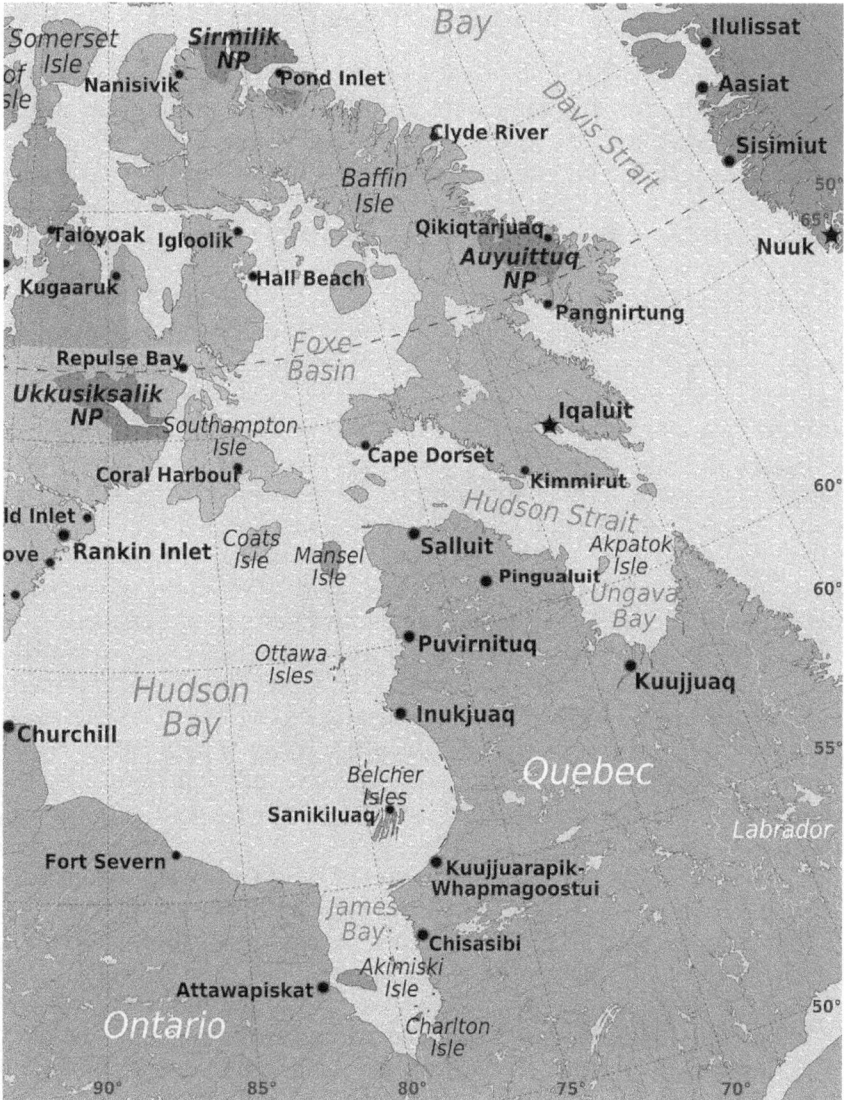

Figure 9.1 Map of the Eastern Canadian Arctic. Wikimedia Commons

The Historical Background: Inuit "Touring"

We may start by asking whether, in Inuit traditional life, there were kinds of tourism: this may help us understand the ethnographically observed and much changed contemporary Inuit behaviour that represents partial continuities from the past, and more important, whether there is a prior basis for the Inuit to comprehend and empathize with the "tourist behaviour" of *Qallunaat* (English-speaking white people) visitors, most specifically "white" people (see Bunten 2010).

It is often said that tourism is a product of "modern" societies; but in this case we must agree with Nash et al. (1981) that is possible to identify aspects of "leisure travel" – traditional hosting and visiting – among the Canadian Inuit. The term *pulaktuk*[1] means "he/she visits," usually a neighbour within the camp or village, but it can be applied to visiting people in other communities. Such behaviours were differentiated from *asivallaktuk,* "travels on the land looking for game and other resources," and, more purposefully, *maqaituk,* "leaves home to hunt" (and these days for other kinds of work). Given the differential distribution of resources, travel was undertaken to vary one's diet or to procure important materials (e.g., for thong ropes, made of walrus or bearded seal skins) or food when one's own area was depleted. Inuit visiting would always involve seeing relatives and friends and, for many, looking for girlfriends (or future wives if members of their own camps were close relatives) or temporary sex partners. Women rarely travelled without their male kin for either social or practical purposes.

More problematic is the consideration of Inuit views of (non-tourist) workers who used to arrive by ship but have increasingly arrived by plane in the past sixty years. To categorize these sailors and other temporary workers as tourists is ambiguous. However, from the Inuit point of view, without a deep understanding of the industrial system in which these people were employed and paid, they had a hard time distinguishing between "amateurs" and "professionals." They could clearly see that these visitors had plenty of free time, and sought to engage in "pleasure seeking" such as socializing, dancing, playing cards, and having sex (just as Inuit visitors would). Until the Inuit were enmeshed in the system themselves, they would have had little reason to distinguish between visitors and tourists, though they could clearly understand the stratification of officers and sailors (workers). In places such as Iqaluit, now the capital of Nunavut, the Canadian Inuit first came into contact with military forces, from World War II through the Cold War (Graburn 2006a).

The Contemporary World of Settled Inuit: New Forms of Visiting

The vast changes wrought on Inuit societies in the past century, first by fur traders and in some areas whalers, then by missionaries, and finally by the "urbanization" of the 1960s brought about by government policies of sedentarization, formal education, permanent housing, electrification and water supplies, and the proliferation of bureaucracies in the North (Graburn 1969), have not completely altered the structure of leisure and travel. However, visiting within one's own community and entertainments such as movies, bingo, hockey, watching TV, and the internet have become dominant with the decrease (and complete cessation for many) of hunting and living on the land. Visiting other communities has become less frequent since the hunting camps coalesced into villages in the 1960s (Damas 2002); travel is increasingly undertaken by plane rather than by dogsled, snowmobile, or boat. In the past three decades, as villages have grown, other reasons for visiting have emerged. These include episodic events such as music festivals; sports such as hockey matches and the Arctic Games; and seasonal and regional festivals such as at Christmas and Easter and Toonik Tyme in Iqaluit;[2] even serious events such as political meetings, such as Inuit Tapirisat (now Inuit Tapiriit), bring crowds together for the inevitable partying. Visits from smaller to larger villages and towns, for any of the reasons mentioned, involve not only visiting friends and relatives but more "urban" delights such as shopping and going to movies, restaurants, and bars. Motivation for travel may be enhanced or even primarily caused by the desire to leave "dry" communities (where liquor is banned or contraband) for "wet" ones with legal bars and liquor stores.

In the past two decades it has become more common for Inuit to travel "down south," visiting *Qallunaat* and urban Inuit friends, selling sculptures to stores or individuals, and shopping for items that are far cheaper in the South. Regularly employed Inuit, often themselves bureaucrats, have increasingly taken to vacationing in southern Canada or even in Florida and Hawaii. These same people are also beginning to become tourists in the North. We will now consider the development of different types of tourism in the Eastern Canadian Arctic.

Institutionalized Commercial Tourism

The earliest organized efforts to bring tourism to the Eastern Canadian Arctic[3] were made by Austin Airways and the Povirnituk Inuit Cooperative spearheaded by Father Steinmann and NSO Pat Furneaux and local Inuit, and on Baffin Island by the West Baffin Island Coop originally led by Jim Houston and the Putuguk family. Mr Austin always wanted to help the communities along the Hudson Bay and on Baffin Island. For instance, he transported fruits and vegetables for free from Timmins, Ontario, for all the stores, coops, and government employees along the route.[4]

At that time Jim Houston in Cape Dorset and Father Steinmann of Povirnituk were rivals in implementing development for "their" villages (Graburn 2000). Houston had promoted (commercial) art production, which achieved worldwide fame (Goetz 1977). Small numbers of outsiders visited Cape Dorset using the "puddle jumper" DC-3 or CANSO[5] flights from Timmins.[6] More famous was one of the first of the "high-end" tourists to the region, Arthur Houghton, the CEO of Steuben Glass, New York, who flew north with his family in his own rented CANSO in 1961. Houston treated them like personal guests during their three-week stay as they visited camps along the coast in the CANSO. Rather than directly benefitting the Inuit hosts, this event resulted in Houston's being offered a position as a head designer at Steuben Glass; he moved to New York.[7]

Father Steinmann fostered the creation of the Povirnituk (POV) Cooperative by forming a Sculptors' Guild for the improvement of quality and prices of Inuit carvings (Simard 1982). With a top Inuk artist, Charlie Arngnaituk, Steinmann travelled in the United States to drum up sales and promote tourism to Povirnituk via Austin Airways. The POV Coop expanded beyond arts and crafts to include a general store and credit union (Vallee 1968). With Austin Airways, they tried to start a more regular tourism, with government officer Pat Furneaux using welfare funds to employ Inuit to build a three-thousand-foot runway, thereby eliminating the two or three months of isolation during fall freeze-up and spring break-up. He also employed local Inuit to build stone houses for the tourists.

Inspired by the POV Coop, more coops were established by enthusiasts such as Paulasi Sivuak and ex-Hudson's Bay Company employee Peter Murdock (Balikci 1968). Steinmann's contacts with the Caisse Populaire Desjardins (credit unions) led to the formation of the

CoopFederation (*ilagiisak*) to buy wholesale goods for the coops and to market the Inuit productions, mainly arts and crafts, in the South. The ideological empowerment fostered through these coops helped to pave the way for the formation of the Northern Quebec Inuit Association, which negotiated with the Quebec government for the settlement of land claims in the James Bay Agreement (1975), the establishment of the politico-economic foundation Makivik Corporation and the Kativik School Board, and the emergence of *Takamiut Nipingit* (the voice of the Inuit of Northern Quebec), which demanded the Inuit be allowed to create their own radio and TV programs, leading to the establishment of the Inuit Broadcasting Corporation.[8]

Hunting and Fishing

Until the 1990s, hunting and fishing were main attractions for people contemplating tourism to the Canadian North. In the 1960s, sportsman Bobby May, married to Nancy, a local Inuit woman, ran a hunting lodge at Kangirqjualukjuak (George River), flying his own plane to ferry hunters to and from Fort Chimo (Kujjuak) and taking them from the lodge to hunting camps. Tourism was high end, in small numbers, and definitely seasonal. Bobby May raised the capital, and his bicultural children grew up advantaged compared to their peers and eventually took high positions in Canada. His son Johnny learned to fly and became celebrated as "the first Eskimo pilot." Later, Timun Alariaq and his Finnish wife Kristiina opened Huit Huit Tours in Cape Dorset. They offered dog sled trips to the floe edge in the winter and canoeing and ATV trips over the tundra in the summer, and access to the West Baffin Eskimo Coop's art studios. These operations can be considered in terms of intimate collaborations between Inuit and non-Inuit entrepreneurs working side by side to accommodate guests

One of the attractions of Puvirnituk tourism was fishing. The local cooperative hired Inuit to take the tourists, usually wealthy American men, up the local Povirnituk River and as far as Kovik, where they could fish till they dropped. Anything over the limit was given to the Inuit. The tourists were very generous to both Inuit and non-Inuit. Personal relationships were established by some tourists who wanted to support the Inuit and their cooperatives. Soon after a branch coop started in Kangirksuk (Payne Bay), the manager, Anaqatak, started another tourism experiment in imitation of Povirnituk. He set up a summer hunting and fishing camp on the Payne River. This was successful for a few years, even bringing in Italians (Betsy Anaqatak, personal communication, 26 October 2012). The relationships between the Inuit and the tourists were not entirely different from those between the local Inuit and the local white people, who would pay to go hunting or fishing by boat, going with the Inuit on their normal excursions – hunting seals, and occasionally walrus or beluga whales, or migrant birds, especially geese and murres, as well as fishing for Arctic char, lake trout, or delicacies such as mussels, clams, or bullhead.

Polar bear hunting is another matter. Polar bear populations are internationally regulated throughout the circumpolar regions; each country divides up the permitted number of kills by region. Commercial polar bear hunting began in the 1970s: a Canadian national quota of up to eight hundred bears may be killed every year (Wenzel 2008). Each subregion is given an annual quota, which is adjusted to maintain a healthy population. The Hunters & Trappers Association of each Inuit community decides what proportion they want to kill themselves versus how many licenses they will sell to non-Inuit hunters, and how to distribute the Inuit quota among themselves.[9] Since the 1980s, polar bear hunting has become a major source of income in the Northwest Territories (Freeman and Foote 2009). Not only did the hunter have to buy a license for ten thousand dollars and up – whether he killed a bear or not – and a complete set of fur winter clothes and boots, but had to pay for a guide and dog team (snowmobiles are not allowed) for a minimum number of days. If he got a bear, he paid for the flaying and flensing, transport back to the village, and the preparation of the skin, while the meat all went to the community. He also paid the expensive airfares and freight, using Air Inuit or First Air, both 100 per cent owned by the Makivik Corporation. The prices have risen steadily.[10] In 2008 the community of Resolute decided to sell sixteen of their community's quotas of thirty-five bears to outsiders, each paying US $20,000 for the thrill of taking part in a polar bear hunt. This annual income of $320,000 is a substantial proportion of total earned income. By 2012, the cost per hunter (and income to the village) had risen to $35,000.

Inuit often became friends with the hunters, who were enamoured of the Inuit lifestyle and generous to their hosts. Some hunters returned more than once. Since the US government has categorized the polar bear as threatened, Canadian Inuit are scared that some world regime will diminish their quotas. They are also afraid that all the "cuddly" publicity by environmental and animal rights activists will decrease the demand for hunting, and most specifically afraid of a possible ban on the import of skins by the prime sources of hunters, the United States and the European Union.

Inuit Arts and Crafts

The Inuit have long been symbols of Canadian "northernness." Government and private enterprise tried commercializing the relationship for nearly a century, searching for ways for the Inuit to produce souvenirs for and of Canada (Graburn 2004). Canadian artist James Houston was finally able to capitalize on Inuit arts and crafts in 1948–49 when the Canadian Guild of Crafts and the federal government cashed in on Houston's efforts and encouraged the production of Inuit arts and craft across the North (Graburn 1967). At first, Inuit products were exported by ship to southern Canada for retail sale, becoming what Aspelin (1977) called "indirect tourism." However, from the 1960s on, local whites (missionaries, government administrators, teachers, store managers and clerks, nurses, and so on) and visiting ships' and aircraft crews have also formed a sporadic market. They acted like tourists, buying souvenirs from the places they visited, asking about the artists and about depictions of Inuit and Arctic animals (see Graburn 1987; Horner 1993).

While Houston was posted to Cape Dorset he taught the Inuit printmaking, with the first public exhibition and sale of an annual print series in 1958. Father Steinmann also encouraged sculptors and got the Puvirnituk Coop to hire a visiting artist to teach printmaking in 1960 (Graburn 2000). Subsequently, the Puvirnituk Inuit carried on with annual print editions and some sporadic productions for local sale with no *Qallunaat* advisor. The government later established print shops in Holman Island, Baker Lake, Northwest Territories, and Pangnirtung, the latter of which also started what is now the oldest weaving studio in Canada. More recently, jewellery workshops have flourished in Iqaluit and elsewhere. But it is the continuity and fame of the sculptures and the print shops at Cape Dorset, Pangnirtung, Baker Lake, and Holman Island that continue to attract tourists (Milne, Ward, and Wenzel 1995).

When tourists arrived by plane or cruise ship (see below), the print shops were the main attraction – everybody wanted to see and photograph the artists drawing and the prints being made. Arts are deemed more "authentic" if the tourists sees them being made and buy them from the artist or at least in the place where they are made (Lee 1991; see also Douney and Marcuse, this volume). Most prints were destined to be exported, so small (unnumbered) series and mini-prints were often produced as local souvenirs. Outside the print market, most tourists buy sculptures made of soapstone, serpentine, or lighter and less breakable bone or ivory. Since the late 1960s, nothing made out of ivory or sea mammal parts, even archaeological whalebone, has been allowed into the United States, sharply diminishing the market.

In good weather, most Inuit men still carve stone outside, forming picturesque subjects for tourist's photographs, which in turn provides the Inuit with opportunities to "happen to have" a few lying around for sale. While most Inuit artists were and are happy to have admirers, some feel objectified by the cameras and the "tourist gaze" (Goo-Doyle and Mitchell 1992; see also Urry 1990). In the larger communities, Inuit may hang around hotel lobbies or restaurants to sell small crafts or jewellery such as ivory rings and bracelets to "captive" customers. This is not encouraged, especially when the establishment has their own crafts displays for sale.[11] However, as noted in other chapters in this volume, tourists seem to prefer to purchase arts and crafts directly from the makers themselves rather than a gift shop.

Other crafts, including Inuit clothing and boots and dressed dolls, are increasingly in demand. Inuit women have continued to develop new forms, adapting cloth materials instead of skins because they are easier to work with, are much lighter, and can be worn in warm weather or outside the North; they can feature attractive new designs and colours that can be washed (King, Paukszat, and Shorrie 2005). Mitts, scarves, crocheted or sewn hats, slippers, and miniature booties are cheaper, less fragile, and more easily packed than most sculptures (see Graburn 1976).

In the larger villages, "visitors centres" and in Pangnirtung, Iqaluit, and Povirnituk, "museums" have been established both for visitors and for the education of younger Inuit (Graburn 1998a). These *pulakvik* (places to visit) usually have displays or photos of "traditional" ??Inuit life, perhaps some local history, and exhibits of fauna and flora. In these contexts, "traditional" does not mean "pre-contact," which no living Inuit remember: Even the 1950s and 1960s are now displayed as "traditional," with exhibits including early-model snowmobiles, bolt action rifles, and so on. My early photos are now in demand in such places. "Tradition is a moveable feast," constantly being forgotten and remade.

The images of Inuit and the Arctic have changed since the 1980s as more and more Inuit visit or live in "the south" (Kishigami and Lee 2008); they can be seen creating and selling their arts without an expensive Arctic tourism location. Inuit are more often on television and in movies, and recently Inuit themselves have been making media. Films such as *Atanarjuat: The Fast Runner* bring fame to the North and expose many people in both North America and Europe to Arctic scenery. They serve as advertising, but some show traditional life (that no longer exists) or, in *Ullumi*, contemporary Inuit "urban" life, with drinking, spousal abuse, and suicidal youth, which tourists do *not* want to see.

The Inuit are aware of and try to manage their changing image. Inuit in the North and South have revived near-moribund performances, particularly drum dancing, singing (*pisiit*), women's *katajjait* (throat singing),[12] and lighting of seal oil lamps. All four have become "iconic" of "Inuit heritage" at political and intercultural performances in the South. Artists such as Tanya Taqaq have developed their own non-traditional musical repertoires. Such performances appear on public media and DVDs but would rarely be found in everyday life in the North, probably disappointing some tourists. Such staged shows are not a staple part of Eastern Arctic tourism, though they are available on some cruise ships and in places where large numbers of tourists arrive.

Trekking, Scenery, and Ecotourism

The Arctic landscape and its fauna have long fascinated Westerners. Explorers wrote well-illustrated books and gave lantern slide shows. Arctic animals have inhabited the Western imagination – walrus, polar bears, narwhals, lemmings, wolves, white foxes, wolverines, caribou (or reindeer), musk oxen, snowy owls, ermine, and the fur-clad Inuit were part of the same imaginary (see Thomas 2012).

White residents and visitors wanted to hunt or fish or wear fur clothing. They enjoy walking over the tundra or the winter snow and trying out Inuit dog teams, kayaks, umiaks and, recently, outboard canoes and snowmobiles. Inuit might walk miles for hunting or fishing or visiting but not for sheer pleasure. Only recently have some Inuit, especially photographers, become interested in landscape from the angle of the "gaze" (King and Lidchi 1998).

Relatively few places of outstanding landscapes are known by tourists. Some have been designated as national parks, Territorial Nunavut parks, or provincial Quebec parks. The most famous is Auyuittuk ("it never melts") Park, the glaciered mountains north of Pangnirtung. It garnered a few hundred tourists a year by the 1980s and over a thousand a year in recent years, benefitting Pangnirtung, where there are lodges/ hotels, an elders' room, and two *pulakviik* (visitor centres). Visitors fly in onto the airstrip in the centre of the town,[13] stay in lodges, and go by canoe, dog sled, or snowmobile up the fjord to Auyuittuk. There they can trek and camp: there is one permanent tourist hut. In the 1990s, Pangnirtung received at least two thousand dollars per tourist, including employment and purchases. Pangnirtung is the prime example of successful community-park tourist cooperation (Robins 2007, 87–94). Even though the national, territorial, and provincial governments have created numerous parks, there are few that attract many tourists. On Baffin Island, Katanillik Park near Kimmirut hosts adventurous whites and Inuit on their way overland from Iqaluit, and there is a large bird sanctuary on the west coast.

Nunavik (Nouveau Quebec) and Labrador also have parks to attract tourists.[14] Unique is Pingualuit (Chubb Crater), a huge round meteor crater south of Kangirksujuak. Planes land on nearby Lake Laflamme to take tourists to the rim. Perhaps contrary to expectations,[15] most recent visitors are Inuit exploring their landscape as tourists, a trend that may become significant in the Canadian Arctic. Pingualuit visitorship has risen from 50 to over 150 visitors in the first four years of the park's operation. More than 95 per cent of visitors come from Quebec and 75 per cent from Nunavik itself. These visitors come on group trips organized by agencies such as the Junior Rangers or school or health services. In 2012 the price of trips was reduced to encourage more visitors. The park currently employs several Kangiqsujuarmiut, including the park warden, two tour guides, a receptionist/interpreter at the museum, and several others part time.

Further east, Park Kuururjuaq straddles the Torngat Mountains on the boundary of Quebec and Labrador (Joliet and Blouin-Gourbilière 2012). This can be approached either from Kangirkjualukjuak (George River) or from Hopedale on the Labrador side. The 2011 brochure for a safari appealed with iconic animals and wild nature, spirituality, exotic northernness, and Inuit traditions – balanced by domestic luxury and leisure variety:

An *intimate safari* experience awaits on Labrador's *wild and stunningly beautiful* Northern coast. This *Inuit homeland* is also Canada's newest National Park, the Torngat Mountains. *Inuit legend* holds that in these mountains *everything* – the rock, the soil, and the air – *has a spirit – and we say, it's where you can find yours*. The Torngat Mountains have been home to Inuit and their predecessors for *thousands of years*. The *spectacular wilderness* of this National Park comprises 9,700 km² of the Northern Labrador Mountains *natural region*. The park extends from ... the provincial boundary with Quebec in the west, to *the iceberg-choked waters* of the Labrador Sea in the east. The mountain peaks ... *are dotted with remnant glaciers*. *Polar bears hunt* seals along the coast, and both the Torngat Mountains and George River *caribou herds cross paths* as they migrate to and from their calving grounds. Hosted by *Inuit expedition professionals* and scientists from Nunatsiavut [Labrador] and Parks Canada, this Safari gives you an *up-close look* into the life, culture and wilderness of this Northern world. Your base is a safari-style *standing tent camp complete with all the creature comforts. Designed after traditional Inuit camps*, your tents are insulated and have raised beds for ultimate warmth. Daily activities vary from hiking, archaeological site visits, *wildlife viewing of polar bears, foxes, and whales, fishing and kayaking*, and cultural activities including *soapstone carving, storytelling* and sampling *traditional foods*. (emphasis added)

Cruise Ship Tourism

Often called "expedition cruises" by tour operators, cruises in the Canadian Arctic generally carry one to two hundred passengers and may cover an area of several thousand nautical miles over the course of a seven-to-fourteen-day cruise. Similar to land-based ecotourism ventures, they focus on Arctic landscapes and fauna. Weather permitting, excursions of several hours take place onshore each day, with transfers from ship to shore completed using ten-to-fourteen-passenger inflatable Zodiac boats. Meals and accommodation are all provided onboard. In-residence lecturers and guides give talks about the natural and human history of the region, with the latter often focusing on the history of the "heroic age" of European exploration in the Arctic. One or two short visits to Inuit communities may be scheduled on the cruise, and a local guide may also travel onboard the ship, sharing information about local life and culture.

The popularity of the Canadian Arctic as a cruise ship destination steadily increased after the Northwest Passage was first traversed by a tourist ship in 1984 (Stonehouse & Snyder 2010, 32). This, and subsequent Northwest Passage cruises, have invited passengers to "follow in the footsteps" of "famed," "fabled," and "ill-fated" European expeditions. From 1990, the availability of Russian icebreakers and ice-strengthened vessels for commercial cruise operations expanded the geographic range of Arctic cruise ship tourism, extended the tourist season, and increased passenger capacity (Stonehouse and Snyder 2010, 34).

Cruise ship numbers have increased tenfold since 2000 as the Eastern Arctic has become better known and the summer sea ice has retreated due to climate change. Cruise ships extended their routes to explore areas previously unreachable (Tommasini 2012b). Cruise ships are controversial due to threats they pose to the environment and to quality of life. Some captains veer off course to close in on icebergs, spectacular scenery, and exotic fauna: John Hughes Clarke, director of the Ocean Mapping Group on the *Amundsen*, noted that cruise ships are deviating from safe shipping lanes towards "riskier areas ... where there is more dramatic topography or stunning wildlife." The 2010 grounding of the *Clipper Adventurer* therefore evoked little surprise (George 2010; Stewart and Dawson 2011). Fortunately no oil escaped and nearby ships rescued the passengers. However, such will not always be the case and many fear future disasters.

Though each ship carries a hundred or more tourists, this has not translated into vastly increased numbers of tourists in Inuit communities (Tommasini 2012a) because these ships generally visit communities for several hours only and do not require extensive tourism infrastructure, such as accommodation and food services. Early hopes were held out for high economic gains: it was expected that cruise ships to Pond Inlet, Cape Dorset, Kimmirut, and Pangnirtung would result in each visitor spending five thousand dollars on arts and crafts, food, and interpretation (Andra-Warner 2002). But for the most part, information in brochures and time allotted during voyages have focused more on northern scenery and geography than on Inuit people and culture. The promised sights include icebergs, mountains, cliffs, and historic places. There are pictures and descriptions of Arctic wildlife, including whale watching and bird roosts on cliffs.

The tour "Adventure Canada: Introducing the Northwest Passage 2012" started in Greenland, passing through UNESCO-listed fjords and iceberg-filled seas, before stopping in the village of Mittimatalik (Pond Inlet) in Baffin Island. There, the tourists are entertained by throat singing and Inuit games, before entering the Northwest Passage in the wake of Amundsen, touching on abandoned RCMP sites and the graves of the Franklin Expedition on Beechey Island (Craciun 2011). Passing through the Bellot Strait, home of whales and polar bears, they visited the Inuit community of Taloyoak, famous more for the nineteenth-century Ross expedition than for its present inhabitants, before going on to the Queen Maud Gulf Bird Sanctuary and finally to Kugluktuk, Nunavut. There is an avoidance of modern Inuit communities, which may not fit the "timeless model" of what the tourists expect (Antomarchi 2009; Kohler 2011; see also Salazar, this volume). Even though opportunities for tourists to go ashore have increased, the goal was mainly to examine the northern lands and wildlife. Humans were often present only in archaeological sites and historical features connected to famed explorers.

When tourists did go ashore to Inuit communities, it was usually to look at and buy village arts, which were often portrayed, inaccurately, as "traditional" (Graburn 1976, 2004). Occasionally the arrival of cruise tourists has raised anxieties: contemporary Inuit fear that *Qallunaat* may be silently condemning them for whaling and hunting wild animals. They may be ashamed to eat raw foods, which they have heard *Qallunaat* think is disgusting (Stewart and Draper 2006). They are loath to see these tourists poking into their lives, looking into their houses and tents (see Smith 1989). This partly explains the reported Inuit lack of enthusiasm for major tourism developments (Ruffin 2013). As cruise ship tourism has the potential for major impact on Inuit communities, we focus on the Makivik-owned "Cruise North," a joint venture with Adventure Canada, which attempted to ameliorate possible harm. Unlike most cruises, this one started in the Inuit community of Kujjuak and sailed through the Hudson Strait, stopping at the Inuit communities of Kangirksujuak and Cape Dorset.[16]

Cruise North

A 2011 Cruise North brochure reads:

> Welcome to Cruise North Expeditions' 2011 Arctic season. This is your chance to travel north in *comfort and safety*, while truly experiencing *the amazing scenery, animal life and culture* of one of the *wildest places* on earth – the far North. We are an *Inuit-owned* and operated business. Therefore environmental and economic well-being, *honest and accurate representation* of the Arctic, and local guiding are fundamental to our expeditions. For these commitments we have been placed among the Best Travel Companies on Earth by *National Geographic* ... Inuit are among the most resilient cultures in the world, and have been *passed down centuries of traditions, skills*

and knowledge. Aboard Cruise North, our Inuit guides share this invaluable knowledge with you, our guests. Our role is to *protect the past,* while preparing for the future. One way we do this is through our *on-board training program,* where Inuit youth are taught a wide variety of skills, like guiding, cultural interpretation, zodiac driving and ship navigation. We travel to islands where *enormous polar bears sit among ice floes* with *thick-billed murres in the thousands* flying overhead. We take you to *ancient hunting grounds and spiritual sites literally untouched for thousands of years. Inuit hosts treat us to cultural performances* in small coastal villages. While relaxing on deck, we glide alongside *immense icebergs,* view *quaint villages* and towering fiords that go on for miles. This is your true Arctic experience with Cruise North. We hope you can see it through Inuit eyes. Cruise North is a joint venture between a family-owned Canadian business and the Inuit. (emphasis added)

Elspeth Ready describes a recent visit of Cruise North to the small Hudson Strait community of Kangiqsujuaq:

In summer 2011, while participating in archaeological fieldwork with the Avataq Cultural Institute[17] in the region of Kangiqsujuaq, Quebec, I had the opportunity to participate in a cruise ship visit to the community. The cruise line was Cruise North, and I would estimate that there were at least 100 or so passengers on the trip. While it appeared to me that the majority of the cruise ship passengers were French-Canadian, there were also some Europeans aboard, including a well-known archaeologist from Britain ... The visit to the community was mainly coordinated by a Scottish expat who works at the community landholding office and who has lived in the Canadian Arctic since the 1960s. He noted that while the cruises are an economic benefit to the community, it is difficult to motivate local people to participate in the visits; however, Kangiqsujuaq generally has more success in doing so than other communities, and so it is visited somewhat more regularly. During the visit, the passengers were brought to the community gym, where they had an opportunity to taste local foods, see local handicrafts (unfortunately none were for sale, except a few earrings), to watch a seal skin being prepared, learn about Inuktitut syllabics, watch a demonstration of the high-kick game, and listen to some local youths throat-singing and drumming. (Elspeth Ready, personal communication, 18 December 2011)

Another Cruise North passenger, also an archaeologist, provided a tourist's point of view:

The expedition leaders had great respect for the local communities and for Inuit history and politics. We had an excellent lecture on the political genesis of Nunavut. When we visited the different communities we were encouraged to spend money among them, to talk to the local people, and to buy the things they were selling. It was emphasized that we were a significant source of income for the people in the communities we visited. The communities treated us to demonstrations of such things as throat singing and hide preparation. We were provided with opportunities to try local foods on the boat and in the villages – though few converts were made to the eating of whale blubber. It was hard for we visitors to say how much the people in the local communities were pleased to receive our visits but the cruise leaders made the effort to offer some compensation (other than our spending money). Members of the community were invited back to visit the ship, which one must hope was some recompense for the trouble they had gone to. The cruise leaders (Inuit and others) pulled no punches about hunting and how it was the basis of economic and social life. They also stressed the importance to the economy of Nunavut of the sale of skins of seals, polar bears and other Arctic animals. On the trips ashore the guides respected the wildlife. (Dale Serjeantson, personal communication, 17 April 2012)[18]

In 2012 a larger French cruise ship, Le Boréal, visited the community on 27 August. No plans were made for a community welcome, but a couple of dozen passengers wandered about visiting the coop and municipal offices. Cruise North planned for a number of Arctic "expeditions" in 2013, including one each to Kangirksujuak and Kujjuak (in Nunavik) and to Kimmirut, Iqaluit, Mittimatalik, and Kangirktugaapik (on Baffin Island), but most of Cruise North's voyages are typically much further north, involving Greenland and the Northwest Passage, with the emphasis on nature and archaeological and historical sites.

Inuit Tourism Futures

Native American sociologist Duane Champagne writes, "Native communities are greatly concerned about economic issues, but they do not wish to sacrifice culture, preferred institutional relations, and their internal social relations in favor of economic development"(2008, 58). Alaska Native anthropologist (and co-editor of this volume) Alexis Celeste Bunten (2010) expanded these ideas in the context of Native Alaskan and Maori tourism enterprises, which share the following components: rituals of hospitality, collective leadership, stewardship of land/natural resources, cultural perpetuation, and building under-standing through education. The Canadian Inuit have not yet encoun-tered institutionalized tourism to the degree that Northwest Coast First Nations or Maori have, hosting tourists for over a century. These Inuit lacked hierarchical and enduring social structures. Leadership was always situational and flexible, with disagreements leading to group division, migration, and new alliances. Leadership in contemporary tourism is of three kinds: individual and family entrepreneurship, including married couples; local community initiatives, such as the Hunters and Trappers Associations or community groups with mixed membership; and Native corporate enterprises such as Makivik with business-like ideologies. The latter case is reflected in a statement made by the general manager of business and culture for the Maori corpora-tion, Wakatu Inc.: "Not commercializing our culture, but culturalizing our commerce!" (cited in Bunten 2010). Inuit entrepreneurial individu-als and groups are involved in a number of commercial enterprises, with and without subsidy, resulting in both success and failure. Given the variety of types and scales of leadership, we could not expect uni-form patterns of development.

Indeed, Inuit cultural values influence and are influenced by the pres-ence of tourism. Stewardship of the land and respect for fauna continue to be strongly emphasized even among those who rarely hunt and trap.[19] Such expressions are both a statement of Indigenous identity and attrac-tive slogans to tourists interested in exploring nature. This ethnic value is passed on to the younger generations in the very act of working as tour guides, making them more aware of the land's ecological and moral val-ues than if they were unreflexively pursuing a traditional lifestyle. Inuit have become so worried about the loss of their culture and language that it is frequently discussed both at home and in schools and community and government meetings (Graburn 1998b, 2006b). But the advent of tourists "puts Inuit on the spot." Individuals and communities feel they have to perform or be shamed. In this way, tourism and the modern media have reinforced aspects of "externalized" culture such as clothing, arts and crafts, drum dancing and singing, lamp lighting and country food.[20]

Building understanding through education applies in the informal processes of tourism. Guides and demonstrators are not didactic but expect attention. Mutual experience of sledding, boating, hunting, and fishing leads to discussion and learning. The stops at historical and prehistoric sites increase mutual understanding but are probably more important in the long run for the Inuit than the visitors. Most importantly, close contact between tourists and hosts in these small-scale operations breaks down the shyness and anxiety that are so common cross-culturally.[21]

Tourism has been seen as a livelihood and a form of economic development for as long as Inuit have been sedentarizing with government programs, moving them away from hunting and trapping over the past fifty years. Tourism fits well with *pre*-Fordist occupations: it doesn't necessarily require a lot of schooling, is compatible with the production of commercial "export" arts (begun in the 1950s as a substitute for falling pelt prices), and little other wage labour is available. Early initiatives were led by strong willed *Qallunaat* who were already working hard on many fronts. These people were able to override rules and pull strings to get things done, but *none* of them did it for their own monetary profit. Only since the land claims settlement has government policy included tourism, but these plans go little beyond the already imagined or established private or local institutions. The Quebec government's proposed Plan Nord, promulgated in 2011, is a stronger initiative in favour of vast mineral, hydropower, and other developments north of the forty-ninth parallel, in Inuit and Cree lands.

The case of Pingualuit Crater Park brings up another overlooked tourism future: tourism within the North by Northern residents, especially Inuit. At a tourism planning session in Kimmirut in 2000, it was suggested that this "country" village should attempt to attract the relatively wealthy employed "urban" people from the nearby Nunavut capital, Iqaluit; Kimmirut has beautiful scenery and available lodgings, and the Iqalumiut have since then visited either by First Air or by snowmobile through the new Kattanilik Park. This is a kind of "domestic tourism" within the region; visitors form the distant *Qallunaat* outside parallel "international" tourism. So the Inuit are continuing to visit other communities much as they used to, using new forms of transport; they may pay to stay in a lodge and they may experience "the scenery" as well as continuing visiting friends and relatives.

Climate change must be taken into consideration. At first climate change actually increased the array of animals/fish available in many seasons, but it increased the risks of travelling on weakened ice. Increasing numbers of cruise ships have adjusted their trips northwards, away from most Inuit villages, following the retreating fauna (walrus, polar bears, seals) that go with ever diminishing ice. Inuit life is rapidly evolving away from the traditional stereotypes still offered in tourist publicity. "Everyday Inuit" will cease to be tourist attractions, and only a small proportion of Inuit will be actively engaged in the tourism industry, as hosts, guides, cooks, entertainers, and demonstrators. It would be wise to train young Inuit as navigators, ship's crews, and airline pilots and crews as well as businesspeople and administrators.

This short history of tourism in the Inuit Eastern Arctic shows the breakdown of former colonial roles and hierarchies. Entrepreneurial organizations (families and companies) have Inuit and whites in managerial roles and, contrary to the original expectations, a large proportion of the clients may well be Inuit.

NOTES

1 It also means "one who visits" – Inuit verbal and nominal expressions are very close.
2 Toonik Tyme is a popular secular spring festival in Iqaluit, invented in 1965 to attract tourists but eagerly enjoyed by local inhabitants. "That's the aim of Toonik Tyme, to provide as many activities as possible for everyone in Iqaluit to enjoy," said its board president, Janet Brewster (Toonik Tyme Society 2015). It includes traditional (dog sled) and modern (snowmobile) races, hockey, soccer, dances, music, eating, and drinking.
3 Aside from steamships up the Labrador coast visiting the Grenfell missions (Harvey Lemelin, personal communication, 30 August 2011).
4 The government paid for five dollars worth of fruits and vegetables per employee per month.
5 The CANSO, also known as the Catalina or PBY, was an amphibious flying boat with a three-thousand-mile range. It could land on the sea or land, but Austin Airways removed the engines and used them in DC-3s in winter.
6 It would be rare for a DC-3 or a CANSO to fly north from Timmins to Cape Dorset in one day, stopping at Great Whale River, Inukjuak, Povirnituk, and Salluit on the way. Passengers might be disembarked in any village and told, "Come back at 7 a.m. tomorrow."
7 At the same time, his marriage to Alma Houston broke up. He and son John Houston continued to foster Inuit art and coops. He also makes movies and TV programs about the Inuit.
8 Soon after the James Bay Treaty, Makivik formed Air Inuit, which bought up Austin Airways. The Coop was at first a rival to Makivik; in fact the people of Povirnituk and Ivujivik refused to ratify the James Bay Agreement. This undercut the Coop, and many Inuit turned against Father Steinmann, who then retired.

9 Ways of allotting the quota include first-come-first-served until the quota is used up; one per hunter until the quota is used up; subquotas by subregion or camp; or distribution by lottery – when this last was tried, the hunters were flabbergasted that some *women* won, which no one thought of: and the women claimed their rights!

10 Inuit who kill the bears themselves then sell the skins mostly to the monopolistic Fur Harvesters auction house of North Bay, Ontario. Canada is the only major country for unrestricted export of polar bear pelts, and the buyers know that this may only be possible for another year or two (Köhler 2012).

11 Although tourists may be buying directly from the artist, this is a low-prestige form of collecting. The pieces are often hurriedly made, for "target marketing" (to buy food, drink, or cigarettes or to gamble); there is no documentary assurance (e.g., the Canadian government's Igloo Tag, usually attached by the first institutional buyer). There is no guarantee that the piece was made by the artist that the seller claims; the seller is often a child or relative of the artist, or even someone who stole it or won it by gambling.

12 Throat-singing *katajjait*, performed by two women standing mouth to mouth, was remembered by fewer than ten Inuit by the 1960s but has been relearned and performed in most communities and in the broadcast media. Drum dancing was lost in the eastern Arctic, but reintroduced from west Hudson Bay.

13 Gravel air strips close to the community restrict the types of aircraft that can land. Nunavut plans to upgrade airstrips to enhance tourism.

14 New parks are planned: Tursujuaq on Hudson's Bay, and Leaf Bay and Ulittaniujalik on Ungava Bay.

15 Information from Stanford graduate student of anthropology Elspeth Ready, who researched the Takamiut in 2011, 2012, and 2013–15. See also Ruffin (2013).

16 In 2012 Makivik merged Cruise North with the larger Canadian company Adventure Canada.

17 Based in Montreal and Inukjuak, Avataq is the cultural institute of the seven thousand Inuit in Nunavik (Northern Quebec). It sponsors archaeology, cultural property preservation, and the perpetuation of Inuit traditional knowledge.

18 Serjeantson also wrote: "I had always wanted to visit the Arctic ... I was interested in the environment, the wildlife, the archaeology and the culture of the people. Art was relatively low on my list – but in the event that too was very interesting."

19 Very few Inuit live off the land. Many have jobs or receive welfare, which
    is of little interest to tourists. Active hunters and artists are more attractive
    to tourists.
20 This reflexive externalizing of cultural features is discussed by a number of
    contributors to Stern and Stevenson 2006.
21 The Canadian Federal Department of Heritage tried to foster inter-ethnic
    tourism, especially with First Nations, as a means of breaking down
    barriers and increasing social equality. It was rarely successful, and
    research revealed that the media and educational systems made most
    mainstream Canadians feel intensely guilty about the treatment of First
    Nations.

REFERENCES

Andra-Warner, Elle. 2002. "Nunavut Tourism: Creating a Buzz to Lure
    Tourists." *Nunatsiaq News,* 26 April.
Antomarchi, Veronique. 2009. "Tourisme, identité et developpement en milieu
    Inuit: Le cas de Puvirnituq au Nunavik." *Téoros* 28 (1): 52–60. http://dx.doi.
    org/10.7202/1024836ar.
Aspelin, Paul. 1977. "The Anthropological Analysis of Tourism: Indirect
    Tourism and Political Economy in the Case of the Mamainde of Mato
    Grosso, Brazil." *Annals of Tourism Research* 4 (3): 135–60. http://dx.doi.
    org/10.1016/0160-7383(77)90005-6.
Balikci, Asen. 1968. "Two Attempts at Community Organization among the
    Eastern Hudson Bay Eskimos." In *Eskimo of the Canadian Arctic,* edited
    by Victor F. Valentine and Frank Vallee, 160–72. Toronto: McClelland and
    Stewart.
Bunten, Alexis C. 2010. "More Like Ourselves: Indigenous Capitalism
    through Tourism." *American Indian Quarterly* 34 (3): 285–311. http://dx.doi.
    org/10.5250/amerindiquar.34.3.285.
Champagne, Duane. 2008. "Social Change and Cultural Continuity among
    Native Nations." *Social Forces* 87 (2): 1153–4.
Craciun, Adriana. 2011. "Writing the Disaster: Franklin and Frankenstein."
    Nineteenth-Century Literature 65: 433–80.
Damas, David. 2002. *Arctic Migrants/Arctic Villagers: The Transformation of
    Inuit Settlements in the Central Arctic.* Montreal/Kingston: McGill-Queens
    University Press.
Freeman, Milton M.R., and Lee Foote, eds. 2009. *Inuit, Polar Bears and
    Sustainable Use.* Occasional publication no. 61. Edmonton: CCI Press.

Goetz, Helga. 1977. *The Inuit Print/L'estampe Inuit*. Ottawa: National Museum of Man.

Goo-Doyle, Oviluk, and Marybelle Mitchell. 1992. "The Artists Speak – Iyola Kingwatsiak: On Being Patronized." *Inuit Art Quarterly* 7 (2): 26–9.

George, Jane. 2010 "Expert: Clipper Ran into Known Hazard." *NunatsiakOnLine*, 4 September, p. 1.

Graburn, Nelson H.H. 1967. "The Eskimos and 'Airport Art.'" *Transaction* 4: 28–33.

Graburn, Nelson H.H. 1969. *Eskimos without Igloos: Social and Economic Development in Sugluk*. Boston: Little, Brown.

Graburn, Nelson H.H. 1976. "Eskimo Art: The Eastern Canadian Arctic." In *Ethnic and Tourist Arts: Cultural Expressions from the Fourth World*, edited by Nelson Graburn, 39–55. Berkeley: University of California Press.

Graburn, Nelson H.H. 1987. "Inuit Art and the Expression of Eskimo Identity." *American Review of Canadian Studies* 17 (1): 47–66. http://dx.doi.org/10.1080/02722018709480976.

Graburn, Nelson H.H. 1998a. "The Present as History: Photography and the Canadian Inuit: 1959–1996." In *Imaging the Arctic: The Native Photograph in Alaska, Canada and Greenland*, ed. Jonathan H.C. King and Henrietta Lidchi, 98–104, 147, 149, 155. London: British Museum.

Graburn, Nelson H.H. 1998b. "Weirs in the River of Time: The Development of Canadian Inuit Historical Consciousness." *Museum Anthropology* 22 (2): 54–66.

Graburn, Nelson H.H. 2000. "Canadian Inuit Art and Coops: Father Steinmann of Povirnituk." In "Missionaries and Natives Arts," edited by M. Lee and E. Schildkraut, special issue, *Museum Anthropology* 24 (1): 14–25,.

Graburn, Nelson H.H. 2004 "The Invention of Authentic Inuit Art." In "Beyond Art/Artifact/Tourist Art: Social Agency and the Cultural Value(s) of the Aestheticized Object," ed. Nelson H.H. Graburn and Aaron Glass, special issue, *Material Culture* 9 (2): 141–60.

Graburn, Nelson H.H. 2006a. "Canadian Anthropology and the Cold War." In *Historicizing Canadian Anthropology*, edited by Julia Harrison and Regna Darnell, 242–52. Vancouver: University of British Columbia Press.

Graburn, Nelson H.H. 2006b. "Culture as Narrative: Who Is Telling the Inuit Story?" In *Critical Inuit Studies*, edited by Pam Stern and Lisa Stevenson, 139–54. Lincoln: University of Nebraska Press.

Horner, Alice. 1993. "Tourist Arts without Tourists." *Annals of Tourism Research* 20 (1): 52–63. http://dx.doi.org/10.1016/0160-7383(93)90111-F.

Joliet, Fabienne, and Claire Blouin-Gourbillière. 2012. "La participation photographique des Inuit dans le developpement touristique du parc national Tursujuq (Nunavik)." *Études Inuit Studies* 36 (2): 99–123. http://dx.doi.org/10.7202/1015980ar.

King, Jonathan H.C., and Henrietta Lidchi, eds. 1998. *Imaging the Arctic: The Native Photograph in Alaska, Canada and Greenland*. London: British Museum.

King, Jonathan H.C., B. Paukszat and R. Shorrie (eds.). 2005. *Arctic Clothing of North America: Alaska, Greenland, Canada*. London: British Museum.

Kishigami, Nobuhiro, and Molly Lee, eds. 2008. "Inuit urbains/Urban Inuit." Special issue, *Etudes/Inuit/Studies* 32 (1).

Köhler, Nicholas. 2012. "We're Shooting Polar Bears?!?" *Maclean's* 125 (6): 22–6.

Kohler, Valerie. 2011. "Fossilisation d'un imaginaire touristique? Le cas du Grand Nord canadien face à sa mise en tourisme par le web." Paper presented at the conference "Tourist Imaginaries/Imaginaires touristiques," Berkeley, 18–10 February.

Lee, Molly. 1991. "Appropriating the Primitive: Turn-of-the-Century Collection and Display of Native Alaskan Art." *Arctic Anthropology* 28 (1): 6–15.

Milne, S., S. Ward, and G. Wenzel. 1995. "Linking Tourism and Art in Canada's Eastern Arctic: The Case of Cape Dorset." *Polar Record* 31 (176): 25–36. http://dx.doi.org/10.1017/S0032247400024839.

Nash, Dennison, Anne V. Akeroyd, John J. Bodine, Erik Cohen, Graham Dann, Dymphna Hermans, Jafar Jafari et al. 1981. "Tourism as an Anthropological Subject." *Current Anthropology* 22 (5): 461–81. http://dx.doi.org/10.1086/202722.

Robins, Mike. 2007. "Development of Tourism in Arctic Canada." In *Prospects for Polar Tourism*, edited by J.M. Snyder and B. Stonehouse, 84–101. Wallingford: CAB International. http://dx.doi.org/10.1079/9781845932473.0084.

Ruffin, Émilie. 2013. "Cultural Tourism in Nunavik." *IPinCH* (Intellectual Property Issues in Cultural Heritage Project). Newsletter. 5: 7–11.

Simard, Jean-Jacques. 1982. "Le production cooperative d'art et d'artisanat Inuit au Nouveau-Quebec." *Etudes/Inuit/Studies* 6 (2): 61–91.

Smith, Valene. 1989 [1977]. "Eskimo Tourism: Micro-models and Marginal Men." In *Hosts and Guests: The Anthropology of Tourism*, ed. Valene Smith, 55–82. Philadelphia: University of Pennsylvania Press.

Stern, Pam, and Lisa Stevenson, eds. 2006. *Critical Inuit Studies*. Lincoln: University of Nebraska Press.

Stewart, Emma J., and D. Draper. 2006. "Community Response to Tourism in the Canadian North." In *Climate Change: Linking Traditional Knowledge*, ed. R. Riewe and J. Oakes, 245–56.Winnipeg: University of Manitoba.

Stewart, J., and J. Dawson. 2011. "A Matter of Good Fortune? The Grounding of the Clipper Adventurer in the Northwest Passage, Arctic Canada." *Arctic* 64 (2): 1–5. http://dx.doi.org/10.14430/arctic4113.

Stonehouse, Bernard and John Snyder. 2010. *Polar Tourism: An Environmental Perspective*. No. 43 in *Aspects of Tourism*. Bristol: Channel View.

Thomas, Annie. 2012. "Ecotourisme au Nunavik: Manifestation de la postmodernité." *Études Inuit Studies* 36 (2): 79–97. http://dx.doi.org/10.7202/1015979ar.

Tommasini, Daniela, ed. 2012a. "Le tourisme dans l'Arctique/Tourism in the Arctic." Special issue, *Études Inuit Studies* 36 (2).

Tommasini, Daniela. 2012b. "Tourisme de croisière et communautés eloingnées au Groenland." *Études Inuit Studies* 36 (2): 125–46. http://dx.doi.org/10.7202/1015981ar.

Toonik Tyme Society. 2015. "Welcome to Toonik Tyme." http://tooniktyme.com.en/en. Accessed 1 April.

Urry, John. 1990. *The Tourist Gaze*. London: Sage.

Vallee, Frank G. 1968. "Notes on the Cooperative Movement and Community Organization in the Canadian Arctic." In *Eskimos of the Canadian Arctic*, ed. Victor Valentine and Frank Vallee, 218–27. Toronto: McClelland and Stewart.

Wenzel, George. 2008. *Sometimes Hunting Can Seem Like Business: Polar Bear Sport Hunting in Nunavut*. Occasional publication no. 59. Edmonton: CCI.

10 Beyond Neoliberalism and Nature: Territoriality, Relational Ontologies, and Hybridity in a Tourism Initiative in Alto Bío-Bío, Chile

MARCELA PALOMINO-SCHALSCHA

Neoliberalism has been described as "both a political economic and environmental debacle" (McCarthy and Prudham 2004, 276). Although it remains a complex and contested term, "neoliberalism" is usually understood as an ideology, a policy framework, and a form of governmentality referring to "new forms of political-economic governance premised on the extension of market relationships" (Larner 2000, 5). Neoliberalism has had diverse and uneven consequences, and over time has dramatically shaped the ways in which we relate to "nature." Based on the premise that the market is the best mechanism to allocate goods and services efficiently, neoliberal environmental governance and management have become highly technocratic, rationalist, and driven by economics. They promote discourses that produce a particular kind of nature, society, and political subjects (McCarthy and Prudham 2004), affecting numerous Indigenous peoples and their territories around the world.

Chile is known to be one of the first and most radical experiments in the application of neoliberalism since Pinochet's military regime in the 1970s (Klein 2007, 76; Larner 2003). It is also one of the Latin American countries that has made deeper neoliberal reforms with regard to the environment and resources (Liverman and Vilas 2006), reforms that have affected Indigenous peoples directly (Haughney 2007; Toledo 2006, 45; Yáñez 2008, 11). Alto Bío-Bío, part of Mapuche-Pewenche territory in the central-south Andes Mountains, has become one of the most emblematic sites of these tensions.

Examining an Indigenous tourism initiative conducted by four Pewenche communities in Alto Bío-Bío, this chapter explores the ways in which they are addressing and contesting the neoliberalization of nature. Bringing together academic work on neoliberal natures and relational ontologies, I argue that through Trekaleyin (their Pewenche tourism organization) the communities are defending their connections and rights to their territories, while reworking neoliberalism and its multiple possible impacts on nature. By engaging in tourism, they are making visible their ancestral occupation of their lands, but also enacting and putting forward Pewenche ontologies and particular ways of relating with non-humans. Thus, the trips that Trekaleyin conducts with tourists along ancient tracks in the mountains simultaneously constitute a physical and emotional journey through different times and meanings, a moment and place when they are reactivated and articulated. The organization is enabling the construction of multiple possible neoliberalisms and politics, loaded with ancestors, laughs, history, pain, and resistance.

Indigenous tourism is an interesting avenue to explore the effects and contestations of the neoliberalization of nature because, as other chapters in this book also demonstrate, it tends to articulate economic development, self-determination, and cultural awareness, and critical research has identified it as a crucial arena for cross-cultural interactions, where issues of policies, subjectivities, and representations are often addressed by Indigenous peoples (Bunten and Graburn 2009). Therefore, this chapter aims to contribute to more nuanced understandings of the workings of Indigenous tourism, and to the needed inclusion of Indigenous perspectives on how they articulate tourism with relations with non-humans (Wright et al. 2009). Recognising Indigenous communities' agency, this chapter adopts a post-humanist stance that also acknowledges the material and affective interlinkages between humans and non-humans (Lorimer 2009, 344). This chapter also responds to calls for the exploration of creative and unexpected counterhegemonic ways to relate neoliberalism and nature (Bakker 2010), and to embrace "ontological pluralism," including Indigenous ontologies in resource management (Howitt and Suchet-Pearson 2006). In order to do so, I first briefly introduce the location and tourism initiative involved in this research. I then refer to the neoliberal nature literature and explore the case of Chile and Alto Bío-Bío, to expand the notions of neoliberalism and nature. Finally, I explore how community members are reworking the neoliberalization of nature in their territories through tourism, bringing implications that go beyond the local and the Indigenous.

Chile, Alto Bío-Bío, and Pewenche Tourism

Chile is usually presented as one of the most successful countries in Latin America, combining high levels of economic growth and a peaceful return to democracy after the Pinochet dictatorship in 1990. However, the consolidation of neoliberalism in the last decades has had complex consequences. Along with alarming inequalities, poverty levels increased in 2009 for the first time since 1990 (Ministerio de Planificación 2010), and social conflict has been a constant. One of the most critical and active sectors questioning neoliberalism in Chile have been the Mapuche people and organizations. Representing the largest Indigenous group in Chile, the Mapuche are part of the one million Chileans (6.6 per cent of the country's population) that self-identify as Indigenous. Mapuche rights and demands have on many occasions clashed with private and state interests, and to deal with these conflicts the state has developed a dual and contradictory approach. On the one hand, it has implemented multicultural polices through development- and poverty-oriented solutions, neglecting the recognition of collective political, economic, and territorial rights. On the other, it has simultaneously embarked on the "criminalization" and repression of Mapuche social protest, involving human rights violations, the use of antiterrorist legislation, and even the death of Mapuche activists at the hands of police officers (Marimán and Aylwin 2008, 142; Richards 2010). This twofold strategy has led some to suggest that Chile is an "extreme example of the mixing of 'armed neoliberalism' and limited recognition policies reduced to a neo-indigenism or 'neoliberal multiculturalism'" (Assies 2006, 16).

In this context, Alto Bío-Bío has become an icon of Indigenous resistance. It is one of the few places in Chile with a high proportion of Indigenous people, as around 80 per cent of its 6,403 inhabitants self-identify as Pewenche (Ilustre Muncipalidad de Alto Bío Bío 2006), a subgroup of the Mapuche people whose name literally means "the people of the Pewén tree." Located in the central-south part of the Chilean Andes bordering Argentina, Alto Bío-Bío acquired national and international relevance during the mid-1990s due to conflicts over the construction of the Ralco hydroelectric dam by ENDESA, a then Spanish-controlled power company. Ralco fuelled the first Indigenous conflict of this scale in Chile, involving the affected communities and national and international Indigenous, environmental, and human rights organizations (Anguita 2004, 206). Among the Pewenche communities of the area, the construction of Ralco reactivated identity discourses and demands over lands and self-determination, to this day increasing the tension in their relations with the state.

But despite promises of "development" made during the construction of Ralco, or the state's multicultural administrative tools, indicators have proved otherwise, and in 2009 Alto Bío-Bío was declared the poorest municipality in Chile, with 49.1 per cent of its population living below the poverty line (Ministerio de Planificación 2010). This fact has not been ignored by the media, which often characterizes Alto Bío-Bío as a site of failure, powerlessness, and conflict. They talk about misunderstandings and unfulfilled commitments, such as the agreement not to flood the bodies buried in Quepuca cemetery during the construction of the dam, which has generated a struggle by part of the community to recover the now-submerged bodies, highlighting the contrast between communities and corporate and state views with regard to place, ancestors, and nature. But how can the communities face this striking "clash of ontologies" (De la Cadena 2009)? Many have argued that communities have been forced into despair and alienation. In this chapter I suggest that, although true in part, that has not been the only response. Interwoven with frustration and anger are also creative forms of resistance among the communities, which are often not fully acknowledged, usually because they are "unthinkable" –we lack the tools to understand and think about these efforts (Blaser and De la Cadena 2009). In this chapter, questioning ideas of neoliberalism and nature, I explore the ways in which Trekaleyin, as one among those "invisible" responses, is through tourism articulating and defending Pewenche ontologies and their relations to their territories in a neoliberal context.

Alto Bío-Bío comprises two main valleys, the Bío Bío, where the dam was built, and the Queuco, where this research was conducted. It is characterized by its attractive and diverse natural landscape. Community members practise seasonal transhumance, staying from May to November in the lowlands (or *invernadas.* in Spanish) where their permanent houses are, and moving to the highlands (*veranadas*) during summer to feed their cattle and gather forest products such as the Pewén nuts. Trekaleyin offers tourists ancient paths into their mountains.

A fully Pewenche-owned and -operated tourism initiative that started in 2004, Trekaleyin involves members, leaders, and activists from four of the five communities of the Queuco valley. As a tourism association that aims "to share and give value to activities we have traditionally carried out since times immemorial" and to promote the communities' development by conducting "an activity that is respectful of the traditions of our territory, and its cultural and natural heritage" (Trekaleyin 2010), Trekaleyin offers mainly horseback riding trips, camping, and accommodation services. For various reasons, including the desire of communities to maintain the ability to control and reflect on the development of tourism in their communities, tourism has remained small scale and continues to be a complementary economic activity, and is articulated with development, resistance, and self-determination.

Neoliberal Natures and Tourism in Chile and Alto Bío-Bío

The ways in which Alto Bío-Bío is constructed and understood by different actors are framed by competing discourses that have changed over time. Since the 1980s one of the most influential narratives both shaping and being transformed in Alto Bío-Bío has been that of neoliberalism. Identified as a distinct environmental project (McCarthy and Prudham 2004), neoliberalism conceptualizes nature as either a resource or a problem (Castree 2011, 290). Thus, the growing literature on "neoliberal natures" has explored how nature has been transformed and governed under neoliberalism and its impacts (Bakker 2010; Castree 2008). Heynen and Robbins suggest that there are four main broad relations involved in the neoliberalization of nature: governance or institutional changes; valuation or the pricing of natural elements; enclosure or the "capture of common resources and exclusion of the communities to which they are linked" (2005, 6); and privatization.

Literature on neoliberal nature has often conceptualized neoliberalism as a case of the "global penetrating the local," using Gibson-Graham's (2002, 27) terms, linking neoliberalism "with the 'upscaling' of regulation such that local, regional, and national differences are being subordinated to international and global similarities in how natural resources and other things are governed" (Castree 2008, 161). However, critical work has emphasized the ways in which differences in the political, historic, and geographical context, as well as in the biophysical characteristics of "nature," shape and distort neoliberal interventions in the ground (Castree 2008; McCarthy and Prudham 2004).

Neoliberal economic-driven, technocratic, and science-oriented approaches to nature have deeply influenced Chile (Budds 2009; Liverman and Vilas 2006). Based on Pinochet's legacy of a minimized state and an overemphasized market, market environmentalism and green capitalism have dramatically shaped Chilean environmental policies. Thus, property rights regimes have been introduced in several sectors, involving the enclosure and valuation of "resources," which has profited a minority and increased social inequality (Carruthers 2001). Alto Bío-Bío has been especially impacted by the privatization of water and mining resources, as well as of Indigenous land. The privatization of water started in 1981 with the creation of the Water Code during Pinochet's government. It created water rights for all flowing surface water and groundwater resources, which if available are granted perpetually for free, or can be purchased from current owners at market prices (Budds 2009). Water rights have become concentrated in the hands of a few, and ENDESA, the power company that built Ralco dam, controls 81 per cent of the total water rights for non-consumptive use in Chile (Gentes 2008, 18). ENDESA also owns most of Alto Bío-Bío's waters, including 80 per cent of the Bío-Bío River, and along with other companies, has plans to build several other dams in the area (Azócar et al. 2005).

The approval of the Mining Code in 1983 consolidated the neoliberal model of mining exploitation. It establishes the procedures to grant "areas of mining concession," which give the right to prospect and excavate any "open and uncultivated" land (with minor exceptions) apart from those already contemplated in another concession (Yáñez 2008). In Alto Bío-Bío mineral rights have been granted in an area of over thirteen thousand hectares, laying the ground for conflicts between communities and the owners of those concessions (Azócar et al. 2005).

For Chihuailaf (1999, 27) the term "privatization" (*privatización*) comes from "to deprive" (*privar*) or dispossess, which is what he says has been happening for Mapuche since the creation of the reservations through Títulos de Merced since the 1880s. Together with blatant usurpation, in Chile Indigenous lands first entered into the market through the division of Indigenous collective land titles via a series of legal reforms between 1927 and 1979. This process facilitated dispossession and, more symbolically, delegitimized Indigenous common property systems (Calbucura 1996). Of the eleven communities in Alto Bío-Bío only four, all of them in the Queuco valley, have communal property of their lands, being among the minority in this situation in the country (Aylwin 2002; Molina and Correa 1998). This was later modified with the passing of the Indigenous Law in 1993 during the first post-dictatorship government. Ironically, the state promoted another way to include Indigenous lands in the market, creating the Lands and

Waters Fund to buy privately owned lands in order to give them to Indigenous peoples. This has led to speculation and inflated prices in areas of heightened conflict (Toledo 2006, 101). Also, the law seeks to protect Indigenous land by stating that it cannot be sold or dispossessed unless under very special circumstances with the approval of CONADI, the state agency in charge of Indigenous matters. However, this exception was used in Alto Bío-Bío for the construction of the Ralco dam against the will of the then-national directors of CONADI – two of them dismissed due to their opposition – and most community members (Namuncura 1999, 26). In Alto Bío-Bío, demands for usurped lands have prevailed and ancestral demarcations are clearly remembered by community members. Land alienation, starting in the mid-nineteenth century, affected big portions of the *veranadas* and Pewén tree forests (Molina and Correa 1998), and currently over 50 per cent of them are either in the hands of private parties or in "ownership conflict" (Azócar et al. 2005).

Overall, Chile has developed a neoliberal project that has inspired discourses of the need for the "efficient" management of resources to incorporate them into the market economy, and despite its allegedly technical and neutral character, it has been shaped by strong ideological biases. In Alto Bío-Bío this project has been conducted through the understanding of Pewenche lands as empty and available, which, similar to many other Indigenous groups in the world, has deeply altered their relationship with their territories.

Tourism in general, and eco-tourism in particular, have been criticized for reinforcing neoliberalism along with Western ideas about nature as "wilderness" (or separated from humans) and of "Others" (mainly Indigenous) as exotic (West and Carrier 2004). Tourism, then, can be another path towards the "rational" use of Alto Bío-Bío's nature and their economic integration, involving discourses of development, sustainability, and environmental management. This is indeed one of the reasons why local government and other institutions support tourism in the area, and is a logic to which Trekaleyin also appeals. However, Trekaleyin is at the same time doing something different than merely complying with the influence of the market, the limited participation allowed in neoliberal terms and managerial approaches to "nature." Through tourism, members of Trekaleyin are bringing into neoliberal approaches to nature their particular ways and connections with place and more-than-human beings, dreams and longstanding political and territorial struggles, as will be shown in the following pages.

The way in which members of Trekaleyin articulate tourism with their "nature" contrasts sharply, for instance, with the decontextualized representations found in Alto Bío-Bío Museum. The museum, opened in 2006, is one of the few purposely built tourist attractions of Alto Bío-Bío. In it much importance is given to the Pewén tree and nuts, emphasizing the fact that the Pewenche are "the people from the Pewén tree," and the tree's spiritual and economic significance. There are pictures, objects, and tales that, although one could argue they reinforce Western notions of "the exotic" and "wilderness" (West and Carrier 2004), do communicate to some extent the meanings of the Pewén for community members. However, what is not mentioned and indeed is silenced in these exhibits are the struggles and threats the communities face with regard to these resources. For instance, overlooked in the museum is the fact that the gathering of the Pewén nuts has decreased, at least partly due to the dispossession of Pewén tree forests; also overlooked is the communities' ongoing struggles to regain those forests.

This fixed and decontextualized representation corresponds to what García Canclini (1999, 28) calls the "residual." For him, "residual" approaches consider elements that are deemed as "authentic" without addressing the many possible experiences and understandings of that past, and how they are embedded in their contemporary reproductions. Therefore, they result in static, apolitical, and isolated representations that overlook conflicts and contestations.

By contrast, community members involved in Trekaleyin engage quite differently with these elements of, connections to, and contestations surrounding the natural environment through tourism. To explore these issues tied in with the neoliberalization of "nature," I will turn to a branch of the literature on neoliberal nature that poses a call to move "beyond neoliberalism" and "beyond nature" (Bakker 2010).

Beyond Neoliberalism and Nature

The concept of neoliberalism has been questioned from many different stances. It has been argued that it is often presented as a hegemonic, monolithic, and inescapable project (Castree 2008; Heynen and Robbins 2005) when it is in fact characterized by variation and hybridity (Radcliffe 2007). This multiplicity has fuelled the proliferation of case studies on the neoliberalization of nature to explore the ways in which neoliberalism is shaped by particular contexts (Bakker 2005; Laurie and Marvin 1999; Mansfield 2004; Perreault 2005). But in her attempt to move "beyond neoliberalism," Bakker (2010) suggests that we also need to understand neoliberalism in broader terms and see it as both local and translocal, comprised of multiple dimensions including the political, economic, and ecological but also the cultural, psychological, emotional, and libidinal.

Bakker also advocates considering more carefully the notion of nature. She suggests that enlarging the narrow definition of "nature as resource" will yield more comprehensive accounts of neoliberalization that will allow us to address the multiple dimensions of the relationships between humans and non-humans. In order to do that, she turns to relational approaches (Bakker 2010). Comprising a broad body of literature (Braun 2002, 251; Ingold 2000, 14; Latour 1993, 6; Thrift 2008, 6; Whatmore 2002, 2), relational ontology approaches, despite their diversity and differences, share an interest in "denaturalizing" nature and questioning the modern ontological distinction between humans and non-humans (Castree 2011; Jones 2009, 295). Thus, they propose relational ontologies that incorporate non-humans as co-constitutive elements of the world and social and economic life (Braun 2002). This entails moving beyond anthropocentric politics and acknowledging the agency and political status of non-humans, involving rights and entitlements (Castree 2003; Escobar 1998).

Indigenous perspectives and voices have contributed prominently to debates within relational ontologies (Cajete 1994, 18; Descola 1997, 22; Little Bear 2000, 77; Steward-Harawira 2005, 32; Viveiros de Castro 2005, 36). Moreover, Johnson and Murton (2007, 127) suggest that by including and recognizing Indigenous ontologies, "we have the opportunity to re/write the colonial/neocolonial displacement of the indigenous voice," decolonizing constructions of nature that determine and marginalize Indigenous people, in a process that can benefit not only Indigenous peoples but all of us who are constrained by this divide.

In Latin America revaluing and acknowledging these ontologies made invisible by coloniality has become crucial and is at the root of most Indigenous movements (De la Cadena 2009). The adoption of neoliberalism in the area and the incursion of extractive projects in what have been considered "empty" or remote places has increased resistance and opened up "ontological disputes." Thus, Indigenous movements are crafting hybrid political conflicts "pluralizing" politics by enhancing Indigenous participation while also stressing the need to negotiate the role and rights of non-humans and different ontologies (De la Cadena 2009). Some examples of this "hybridization" of politics have been the declaration of the rights of nature in the new constitution of Ecuador, understanding it as the subject of rights (Gudynas, 2009), as well as Bolivia's call for acknowledgment of the rights of Mother Nature in international climate change debates (Prada 2010, 281).

Mapuche relational ontologies and their political consequences have been explored by Ramos (2009). She argues that they bring together people, ancestors, animals, objects, knowledges, dreams, mountains, rivers, stories, everyday practices, rituals, spirits, and songs. The relational co-constitution of these ontologies, in which the dead are still present, places maintain connections, rituals involve the dialogue of humans and non-humans, and dreams transport knowledge and strength, creates a framework that delineates the relations with multiple others and is inextricably linked to politics.

This is evident in many ways in Alto Bío-Bío. For instance, in 2008 I witnessed in the last day of a *Nguillatún*, an important spiritual ceremony, when a letter from a Pewenche political prisoner was read in public to be heard by the gods, making claims to his freedom and the communities' rights to land and encouraging people to continue fighting. Another example is the relations with Pewén trees and nuts. A sacred element for the Pewenche, the Pewén tree is also an important source of food. Like other elements, they have a *ngen* or "owner," and there are rules to interact with them that also regulate the gathering of the Pewén nuts (Herrmann 2005). However, the fact that the communities are struggling to regain control of half of these forests in Alto Bío-Bío has reduced their possibilities to gather Pewén nuts, bringing consequences beyond the economic, as Alberto, an elderly community member, comments:

> The collection of Pewén nuts is being lost and that I believe *Chau Dios* [god] is challenging us a little. Here, where we live, the trees no longer give every year, but every other year. But why? Because before we used to go to gather the Pewén nuts, it was an important food, but not anymore. That affects everything and the *Chau Dios* knows. (6 January 2009)

Alberto suggests the entanglement of land claims, livelihoods, and *Chau Dios* and her/his expectations. This constitutes what Escobar (1999) calls "hybrid natures," which blur the distinctions between the political/cultural and the "natural." Interestingly, Escobar mentions ecotourism as one of the ways in which this hybridity can be expressed to defend rights to territory, autonomy, and distinct views of development and economy. Thus, broadening our understandings of neoliberalism and the acknowledgment of these "hybrid natures" can allow us to identify viable "counter hegemonic forms of (re)production allied with alternative concepts of nature-society relations" (Bakker 2010, 728–9).

Tourism and Hybridity: The Experience of Trekaleyin

Their involvement in tourism has allowed the members of Trekaleyin to, as Bakker (2010, 729) has called it, enact a "creative engagement with processes of neoliberalization." This has shaped how they engage with tourism, which has become a continuation of their struggles over land and ontological difference, similarly to what Wright et al. (2009) identified in Bawaka cultural experiences in northern Australia. By explicitly addressing these struggles, Trekaleyin is enabling the inclusion of Pewenche knowledges and ontologies in spheres beyond "the cultural" such as the economy, political demands for autonomy, environmental management, and relations with "outsiders" such as tourists and institutions.

Using García Canclini's (1999, 28) words, in contrast with a "residual" and fixed representation of their relations with "nature" – as portrayed in Ralco Museum – members of Trekaleyin are addressing it in "emergent" terms. Emergent approaches, according to García Canclini, acknowledge new values, practices, and relations, influenced by certain groups' ways of understanding, inhabiting, and constructing a better life. Emergent approaches take into account current meanings, uses, and conflicts. In the case of Trekaleyin, this includes the changing, contested, and multidimensional connections they have with their surroundings, which involve multiple actors, emotions, stories, and values. Members of Trekalyn show these emergent ontologies through nature in several ways, such as the stories they share with tourists visiting their territories. In these stories, ancestors and present generations are intertwined, and the agency of non-humans and their territorial connections are addressed. For instance, Arnoldo, a community leader, told a group of tourists the story of the name of the Indian Stone, a sacred place in his community. He said that a long time ago, a Pewenche man was coming from Argentina to Chile in mid-April, a month known for its sudden changes in weather, when he encountered a snowstorm. He decided to take refuge and to "reside" in the Indian Stone, but he eventually passed away as the storm was too strong:

Our grandparents found the dead *peñi*.[1] They identified he was a Pewenche who was dead and said, "this is our territory," until here reaches our territory. So, as Pewenche this is our territory and it corresponds. That's why it's called Indian Stone, a holy stone that today we have to turn around three times. If you don't give three turns you fail. Suddenly you can get sick, break a bone, I don't know, you can fall from the horse or the truck can tip over ... Because here all of this is jealous, all of this has *newén*,[2] has power, when the *lonko*[3] asks for rain it just rains, they give him the strength. (28 November 2008)

Arnoldo refers to a time and a need, as today, to claim territorial limits and ownership, what "corresponds." The agency and *newén* of "natural" elements is acknowledged, which influences particular ways of being and appropriate conduct. That the mountains are "jealous" and you have to show respect to avoid dangers, that the *lonko* can ask for rain, and that because of the significance of the rock we must turn around it three times: all talk about the agency of more-than-human elements, which together with historical accounts and memories signify a connection, a right, a way of knowing and being on these territories.

These ways of being are also enacted before each trip when tourists are briefed about the existence of forces and *ngen*s in the mountains and forests. They are told the appropriate ways to behave to acknowledge them, and a *rogativa* (rogation)[4] is conducted before departing. Also, Pewenche ontologies are present in the ways in which things are done and decided in Trekaleyin. As on the occasion when a tourist guide decided to leave earlier than planned because he was told to do so in a dream, diverse and intertwined elements influence the everyday as well as long-term choices and activities. Among these long-term decisions, for example, Trekaleyin commissioned a study on tourism carrying capacity and "cultural-natural" zoning of a path in one community (Ramírez 2008). Although it has no legal recognition, the development of this study is motivated by the intention to demonstrate, through the use of technical (neoliberal) tools and terms, the existence and validity of the communities' "cultural-natural" knowledge, and to make it visible as a crucial element in tourism development and territorial management.

Efforts of Trekaleyin members to highlight elements of Pewenche ontologies have also inspired the publication of a Pewenche eco-cultural guide (Trekaleyin 2009) and a collection of Pewenche stories (Vita and Queupil 2007). These two works, distributed among communities and schools, are also incorporated in the visits of tourists and negotiations with institutions. With them, Trekaleyin "aim[s] to generate a space for the exchange of knowledge and learning, and to teach both future generations and visitors the important relationship and dependency that the Pewenche people have with nature" (Trekaleyin 2009, 2).

Issues of emotions and feelings, as well as of dispossession, colonization, and struggles are also included in conversations with visitors. For instance, Ramiro, a community leader, talking to a group of tourists, said:

> You see a little house in this *veranada* that is alone, no people or animals, but later this month the *peñis* will bring the animals and their family ... Because as Pewenche we don't have another alternative than to take care of our cattle ... There is no other resource here, so we are bound ... I feel so proud, so happy, because this *veranada* is ours now, that cost us too much. There were people here taking over our territory. This place, this tree was not ours. So today the *veranada* has a lot of meaning for us ... But we don't come here on holidays or for tourism. On the contrary, every day we have to go to look for the cattle to the mountains and that's a big sacrifice ... But we feel so proud, so happy that we feel free today. This is free, this is common, this is not plotted. What does plotted mean? That each one has their own *veranada* and "this is what I own." No. There are families here, animals can go around freely, and that's the most beautiful thing we have, that united we take care for the animals. (28 November 2008)

Ramiro talks about dispossession, long struggles for land, and all the suffering these struggles have "cost" them. He also suggests that these territories are not "empty" although visitors cannot see people or animals around, emphasizing ancestral and particular ways of occupying them. He suggests that raising cattle and gathering nuts are the only "resources" there, which – in a territory where water, underground minerals, forests, and geothermic assets are disputed and owned by outsiders – is a major and contentious statement. He also refers to emotions such as being happy and proud to have their land back, and the importance and beauty of common property, solidarity, and unity. By explaining the meaning of "plotted" land, he emphasizes how inappropriate and unacceptable the "enclosure" of these "commons" is, and how it is related to freedom.

He also explains that their life in the mountains is hard, contrasting Pewenche everyday life with the tourist experience, thus shattering the tourist imaginary of the Pewenche people as permanently "in harmony" with an always benign nature. Overall, we could say he is talking about culture and history. But if we look a bit deeper, we can see he is actually talking about entanglements of knowledges, histories, beings, memories, and relations that together shape Pewenche existence and their connections with their territories, as well as the politics of the ways they engage with tourism.

Mobilizing Indigenous Ontology

Members of Trekaleyin are hybridizing nature and neoliberalism. In contrast with the decontextualized, fixed, and "residual" (García Canclini 1999, 28) representation of the links between Pewenche people and their territory presented at Ralco Museum, members of Trekaleyin articulate them as "emergent," contested, and evolving. From this perspective, tourism for Trekaleyin has become an "entry point" to relate to political and territorial resistance, as well as to Pewenche relational ontologies.

Broadening our understandings of neoliberalism and nature can bring important theoretical and practical insights. It makes possible the acknowledgment of how, via Trekaleyin, the communities are developing counter-hegemonic and hybrid neoliberalizations of nature (Bakker 2010), through the transformation, appropriation, and subversion of neoliberalism, while also decolonizing modern divisions of humans and non-humans. As O'Malley has shown in her engagement with Aboriginal peoples' perspectives in Australia, these processes are crucial because "the existence of indigenous forms within the subjugating regime provides sites within rule for the operation of counter discourses and subordinated knowledges" (1996, 323).

Trekaleyin's use of the old paths creates the possibility to travel and get in contact with different temporalities, discourses, meanings, and uses. At an experiential level that is at the same time physical, affective, political, economic, and magical, it allows the interweaving of the connections of ancestors, memories, tourists, land rights, spiritual forces, and struggles by different actors that cohabit. Although their involvement in tourism is not unproblematic, community members have through that involvement increased their abilities to include, make visible, and actualize their relational ontology, thus changing the terms in which dialogues can take place and alternatives can be imagined.

Mapuche struggles have been deemed to be introverted, specific, and developing only "short" and nuclear solidarities, arguably one of the disempowering effects of neoliberalism and neoliberal subjectivities (Gómez 2010, 31). I believe otherwise, and suggest that Mapuche and other Indigenous peoples' struggles should concern us all. They prompt us to engage in conversations around coexistence, the decolonization of physical, legal, and mental boundaries, and the cultivation of the ability to question our relations among humans and with more-than-human beings. Along with the "Declaration of the Rights of Nature" (Gudynas 2009), or the calls made by the Bolivian government to account for the rights of *Pachamama* (Mother Earth) in international debates of climate change (Morales 2010), Trekaleyin constitutes another step by which Indigenous ontologies and knowledges (multiple and mixed), are hybridizing modern and Western knowledges and ways of being.

NOTES

1 *Peñi* means "brother" in Mapudungún, the Mapuche language.
2 "Force, strength" in Mapudungún.
3 *Lonko*, meaning "head," is the traditional leader of Mapuche communities.
4 A "rogation" is a Christian supplication consisting of the litany of the saints chanted on the three days before Ascension Day.

REFERENCES

Anguita, Aldison. 2004. "Chilean Economic Expansion and Mega-development Projects in Mapuche Territories." In *The Way Of Development: Indigenous Peoples, Life Projects and Globalization*, ed. Mario Blaser, Harvey Feit, and Glenn McRae, 204–10. London: Zed.

Assies, William. 2006. "Prólogo." In *El gobierno de Lagos, los pueblos indígenas y el "nuevo trato": Las paradojas de la democracia chilena*, edited by Nancy Yáñez and José Aylwin, 9–18. Temuco: Lom Editores.

Aylwin. José. 2002. "Tierra y territorio Mapuche: Un análisis desde una mirada histórico jurídica." In *Territorialidad Mapuche en el siglo XX. Temuco*, ed. Roberto Morales Urra. Concepción: Escaparate Ediciones.

Azócar, Gerardo, Rodrigo Sanhueza, Mauricio Aguayo, Hugo Romero, and María Muñoz. 2005. "Conflicts for Control of Mapuche-Pehuenche Land and Natural Resources in the Biobio Highlands, Chile." *Journal of Latin American Geography* 4 (2): 57–76. http://dx.doi.org/10.1353/lag.2005.0035.

Bakker, Karen. 2005. "Neoliberalizing Nature? Market Environmentalism in Water Supply in England and Wales." *Annals of the Association of American Geographers* 95 (3): 542–65. http://dx.doi.org/10.1111/j.1467-8306.2005.00474.x.

Bakker, Karen. 2010. "The Limits of 'Neoliberal Natures': Debating Green Neoliberalism." *Progress in Human Geography* 34 (6): 715–35. http://dx.doi.org/10.1177/0309132510376849.

Blaser, Mario, and Marisol De la Cadena. 2009. "Introducción." *Journal of the World Anthropology Network* 4: 3–9.

Braun, Bruce. 2002. *The Intemperate Rainforest: Nature, Culture and Power in Canada's West Coast*. Minneapolis: University of Minnesota Press.

Budds, Jessica. 2009. "Contested H2O: Science, Policy and Politics in Water Resources Management in Chile." *Geoforum* 40 (3): 418–30. http://dx.doi.org/10.1016/j.geoforum.2008.12.008.

Bunten, Alexis C., and Nelson H.H. Graburn. 2009. "Guest Editorial: Current Themes in Indigenous Tourism." *London Journal of Tourism, Sport and Creative Industries* 2: 2–11.

Cajete, Gregory. 1994. *Look to the Mountain: An Ecology of Indigenous Education*. Skyland: Kikakís.

Calbucura, Jorge. 1996. "El proceso legal de abolición de la propiedad colectiva: El caso Mapuche." In *Fronteras, etnias, culturas: América Latina siglos XVI–XX*, edited by Chiara Vangelista. Quito: Ediciones Abya Yala.

Canclini, García. Néstor. 1999. "Los usos sociales del patrimonio cultural." In *Patrimonio etnológico: Nuevas perspectivas de estudio*, ed. Encarnación Aguilar, 16–33. Granada: Instituto Andaluz del Patrimonio Histórico.

Carruthers, David. 2001. "Environmental Politics in Chile: Legacies of Dictatorship and Democracy." *Third World Quarterly* 22 (3): 343–58. http://dx.doi.org/10.1080/01436590120061642.

Castree, Noel. 2003. "Environmental Issues: Relational Ontologies and Hybrid Politics." *Progress in Human Geography* 27 (2): 203–11. http://dx.doi.org/10.1191/0309132503ph422pr.

Castree, Noel. 2008. "Neoliberalising Nature: Processes, Effects, and Evaluations." *Environment & Planning A* 40 (1): 153–73. http://dx.doi.org/10.1068/a39100.

Castree, Noel. 2011. "Nature and Society." In *The SAGE Handbook of Geographical Knowledge*, edited by John Agnew and David Livingstone, 287–300. London: SAGE. http://dx.doi.org/10.4135/9781446201091.n22.

Chihuailaf, Elicura. 1999. *Recado confidencial a los chilenos*. Santiago: LOM Ediciones.

De la Cadena, Marisol. 2009. "Política indígena: Un análisis más allá de 'la política.'" *Journal of the World Anthropology Network* 4: 139–71.

de Planificación, Ministerio. 2010. *Encuesta CASEN 2009*. Santiago: MIDEPLAN.

Descola, Philippe. 1997. *The Spears of Twilight: Life and Death in the Amazon Jungle*. London: Flamingo.

Escobar, Arturo. 1998. "Whose Knowledge, Whose Nature? Biodiversity, Conservation and the Political Ecology of Social Movements." *Journal of Political Ecology* 5: 53–82.

Escobar, Arturo. 1999. "After Nature: Steps to an Antiessentialist Political Ecology." *Current Anthropology* 40 (1): 1–30. http://dx.doi.org/10.1086/515799.

Gentes, Ingo. 2008. "Las aguas transadas: Hacia una evaluación del impacto social y ambiental del mercado de derechos de agua en Chile." In *La gestión de los recursos hídricos: Realidades y perspectivas*, 1–35. México D.F.: Instituto Mexicano de Tecnología del Agua (IMTA), Universidad de Guadalajara.

Gibson-Graham, J.K. 2002. "Beyond Global vs. Local: Economic Politics outside the Binary Frame." In *Geographies of Power: Placing Scale*, edited by Andrew Herod and Melissa Wright, 25–60. Oxford: Blackwell. http://dx.doi.org/10.1002/9780470773406.ch1.

Gómez, Juan C. 2010. *Política, democracia y ciudadanía en una sociedad neoliberal (Chile: 1990–2010)*. Santiago: Clacso Coediciones, Editorial Universidad ARCIS.

Gudynas, Eduardo. 2009. "La ecología política del giro biocéntrico en la nueva Constitución del Ecuador." *Revista de Estudios Sociales* 32: 34–47.

Haughney, Diane. 2007. "Neoliberal Policies, Logging Companies, and Mapuche Struggle for Autonomy in Chile." *Latin American and Caribbean Ethnic Studies* 2 (2): 141–60. http://dx.doi.org/10.1080/17442220701489555.

Herrmann, Thora Martina. 2005. "Knowledge, Values, Uses and Management of the Araucaria Araucana Forest by the Indigenous Mapuche Pewenche People: A Basis for Collaborative Natural Resource Management in Southern Chile." *Natural Resources Forum* 29 (2): 120–34. http://dx.doi.org/10.1111/j.1477-8947.2005.00121.x.

Heynen, Nik, and Paul Robbins. 2005. "The Neoliberalization of Nature: Governance, Privatization, Enclosure and Valuation." *Capitalism, Nature, Socialism* 16 (1): 5–8. http://dx.doi.org/10.1080/1045575052000335339.

Howitt, Richie, and Sandie Suchet-Pearson. 2006. "Rethinking the Building Blocks: Ontological Pluralism and the Idea of Management." *Geografiska Annaler. Series B, Human Geography* 88 (3): 323–35. http://dx.doi.org/10.1111/j.1468-0459.2006.00225.x.

Ilustre Muncipalidad de Alto Bío Bío. 2006. *Plan de desarrollo comunal del Alto Bío Bío*. AB Consultores Asociados.

Ingold, Tim. 2000. *The Perception of the Environment: Essays in Livelihood, Dwelling and Skill*. London: Routledge. http://dx.doi.org/10.4324/9780203466025.

Johnson, Jay, and Brian Murton. 2007. "Re/placing Native Science: Indigenous Voices in Contemporary Constructions of Nature." *Geographical Research* 45 (2): 121–9. http://dx.doi.org/10.1111/j.1745-5871.2007.00442.x.

Jones, Owain. 2009. "After Nature: Entangled Worlds." In *A Companion to Environmental Geography*, edited by Noel Castree, David Demerit, Diana Liverman, and Bruce Rhoads, 294–312. Oxford: Willey-Blackwell. http://dx.doi.org/10.1002/9781444305722.ch18.

Klein, Naomi. 2007. *The Shock Doctrine. The Rise of Disaster Capitalism*. New York: Metropolitan.

Larner, Wendy. 2000. "Neo-liberalism: Policy, Ideology, Governmentality." *Studies in Political Economy* 63 (1): 5–25. http://dx.doi.org/10.1080/19187033.2000.11675231.

Larner, Wendy. 2003. "Neoliberalism?" *Environment and Planning. D, Society & Space* 21 (5): 509–12. http://dx.doi.org/10.1068/d2105ed.

Latour, Bruno. 1993. *We Have Never Been Modern*. Cambridge: Harvard University Press.

Laurie, Nina, and S. Marvin. 1999. "Globalisation, Neoliberalism, and Negotiated Development in the Andes: Water Projects and Regional Identity in Cochabamba, Bolivia." *Environment & Planning A* 31 (8): 1401–15. http://dx.doi.org/10.1068/a311401.

Little Bear, Leroy. 2000. "Jagged Worldviews Colliding." In *Reclaiming Indigenous Voice and Vision*, edited by Marie Battiste, 77–85. Vancouver: UBC Press.

Liverman, Diana, and Silvina Vilas. 2006. "Neoliberalism and the Environment in Latin America." *Annual Review of Environment and Resources* 31 (1): 327–63. http://dx.doi.org/10.1146/annurev.energy.29.102403.140729.

Lorimer, Jamie. 2009. "Posthumanism/Posthumanistic Geographies." In *International Encyclopedia of Human Geography*, edited by Rob Kitchin and Nigel Thrift, 344–54. Amsterdam: Elsevier. http://dx.doi.org/10.1016/B978-008044910-4.00723-9.

Mansfield, Becky. 2004. "Neoliberalism in the Oceans: 'Rationalization,' Property Rights, and the Commons Question." *Geoforum* 35 (3): 313–26. http://dx.doi.org/10.1016/j.geoforum.2003.05.002.

Marimán, Pablo, and José Aylwin. 2008. "Las identidades territoriales Mapuche y el estado chileno: Conflicto interétnico en un contexto de globalización." In *Gobernar (en) la diversidad: Experiencias indígenas desde América Latina. Hacia la investigación de co-labor*, edited by Xochitl Leyva,

Aracely Burguete, and Shannon Speed, 111–50. México D.F.: Centro de Investigaciones y Estudios Superiores en Antropología Social, Facultad Latinoamericana de Ciencias Sociales.

McCarthy, James, and Scott Prudham. 2004. "Neoliberal Nature and the Nature of Neoliberalism." *Geoforum* 35 (3): 275–83. http://dx.doi.org/10.1016/j.geoforum.2003.07.003.

Molina, Raúl, and Correa, Martín. 1998. *Territorios y comunidades Pehuenches del Alto Bio-Bio*. Santiago: Corporación Nacional de Desarrollo Indígena (CONADI).

Morales, Evo. 2010. "Palabras del Presidente Evo Morales en la Cumbre de Cambio Climático de la Naciones Unidas, Copenhague." http://www.ecoportal.net/Temas_Especiales/Cambio_Climatico/palabras_del_presidente_evo_morales_en_la_cumbre_del_cambio_climatico. Last modified 1 January.

Namuncura, Domingo. 1999. *Ralco: ¿Represa o pobreza?* Santiago: LOM Ediciones.

O'Malley, Pat. 1996. "Indigenous Governance." *Economy and Society* 25 (3): 310–26. http://dx.doi.org/10.1080/03085149600000017.

Perreault, Thomas. 2005. "State Restructuring and the Scale Politics of Rural Water Governance in Bolivia." *Environment & Planning A* 37 (2): 263–84. http://dx.doi.org/10.1068/a36188.

Prada, Raúl. 2010. "Más allá del capitalismo y la modernidad." In *Descolonización en Bolivia: Cuatro ejes para comprender el cambio: Descolonización, estado plurinacional, economía plural y socialismo comunitario*, edited by Gonzalo Gonsálvez, 264–321. La Paz: Vicepresidencia del Estado, Fundación boliviana para la democracia multipartidaria.

Radcliffe, Sarah. 2007. "Latin American Indigenous Geographies of Fear: Living in the Shadow of Racism, Lack of Development, and Antiterror Measures." *Annals of the Association of American Geographers* 97 (2): 385–97. http://dx.doi.org/10.1111/j.1467-8306.2007.00544.x.

Ramírez, Pilar. 2008. "Capacidad de carga turística y zonificación cultural y natural del sendero Ptra Lafken, comunidad Pewenche de Cauñicú, Comuna de Alto Bío Bío, Región del Bío Bío". Diss., Universidad Católica de Temuco.

Ramos, Ana. 2009. "El nawel y el pillán: La relacionalidad, el conocimiento histórico y la política Mapuche." *Journal of the World Anthropology Network* 4: 57–79.

Richards, Patricia. 2010. "Of Indians and Terrorists: How the State and Local Elites Construct the Mapuche in Neoliberal Multicultural Chile."

Journal of Latin American Studies 42 (01): 59–90. http://dx.doi.org/10.1017/S0022216X10000052.

Steward-Harawira, Makere. 2005. *The New Imperial Order: Indigenous Responses to Globalization*. London: Zed.

Thrift, Nigel. 2008. *Non-representational Theory: Space, Politics, Affect*. London: Routledge.

Toledo, Víctor. 2006. *Pueblo Mapuche: Derechos colectivos y territorio: Desafío para la sustentabilidad democrática*. Santiago: LOM Ediciones.

Trekaleyin. 2009. *Guía ecocultural Pewenche, Alto Bío Bío, Valle del Queuco.*

Trekaleyin. 2010. "Trekaleyin: About Us." http://en.trekaleyin.com/.

Vita, Sandra, and Marcelino Queupil. 2007. *Pewencheiñ epeu: Los Cuentos del Pewenche, Cauñicú y Pitril, Valle del Queuco*. Concepción: Icaro impresiones.

Viveiros de Castro, Eduardo. 2005. "Perspectivism and Multinaturalism in Indigenous America." In *The Land Within: Indigenous Territory and the Perception of Environment*, edited by Alexandre Surrallés and Pedro García Hierro, 36–74. Skive: International Work Group for Indigenous Affairs.

West, Paige, and James Carrier. 2004. "Ecotourism and Authenticity: Getting Away from It All?" *Current Anthropology* 45 (4): 483–98. http://www.pngibr.org/publications/pdf/2004-WestCarrier.pdf.

Whatmore, Sarah. 2002. *Hybrid Geographies: Natures, Cultures, Spaces*. London: SAGE.

Wright, Sara, Sandie Suchet-Pearson, Kate Lloyd, Lak Lak Burarrwanga, and Djawa Burarrwanga. 2009. "'That Means the Fish Are Fat': Sharing Experiences of Animals through Indigenous-Owned Tourism." *Current Issues in Tourism* 12 (5–6): 505–27. http://dx.doi.org/10.1080/13683500903042907.

Yáñez, Nancy. 2008. *La gran minería y los derechos indígenas en el norte de Chile*. Santiago: LOM Ediciones.

Epilogue: Indigeneity, Researchers, and Tourism

NELSON H.H. GRABURN

Colleagues and reviewers of this project have suggested that I add a more personal chapter, by way of an epilogue, afterword, or conclusion. My work with Indigenous minority peoples in North America since 1959 and later in East Asia, combined with an upbringing in the bosom of an "ex-colonial" family in England, have left me with a very complex set of experiences and ideas about such peoples, partly reflected in my chapter 9 (this volume) on the Canadian Inuit. Indeed, as I have recounted (Graburn 2007), a close member of my extended family in England married a multilingual dark-complexioned "Native" from the Empire, and I spent most of my childhood Christmas and summer holidays staying with this childless couple after they retired to England, along with their immigrant nephews and nieces, leaving me with ambivalent feelings based on family behaviour and accusations. Less ambivalent was my joy at being told I was "like a Native" when it came to physical excellence, such as running, climbing trees, and seeing great distances. Some have guessed that is why I eventually became an anthropologist.

In this short chapter, I would like to consider the following topics:

1. the complexity of indigeneity as a concept;
2. tourism by, with, and to Indigenous peoples;
3. Indigenous researchers.

The Complexity of Indigeneity

We have covered a great deal of the literature on definitions, history, tourism to, and contemporary activities of Indigenous peoples in our introductory chapter, with detailed case studies in the ensuing chapters. From a personal point of view, I would suggest that the Western idea of indigeneity as used in the twentieth and twenty-first centuries is very much a product of settler colonialism, especially by Anglophone peoples, as constructed by their camp followers, the anthropologists. The European expansion to North and South America, to sub-Saharan Africa, to much of South Asia and to Australia and New Zealand provided the context for the emergence of the term, particularly because there was usually a distinct racial[1] difference between the newcomers and the local inhabitants, and most of the latter were non-literate and had locally based religions and cultural systems and non-industrial technological and agricultural systems. Whereas the colonials were Christian and spoke widely distributed European languages, most often colonized spoke more localized languages. Thus from settler colonies of Canada, the United States, Brazil, New Zealand, and Australia, we have for instance the stereotypic Iroquois, Ojibwa, Tupi, Yanomami, Maori and Tiwi or Arunta, and so on. And the arts and crafts of such people are often used as icons of identity for the new colonies/nations when they are trying to establish identities to differentiate themselves from other colonies with the same national settler origin or from the culturally dominant homeland (Graburn 1987). These "national symbols" are used in worlds' fairs, airline logos, and other forms of tourist imaginaries and advertising (Salazar and Graburn 2014). But at the UNICEF gift shop in Los Angeles, every country was represented by a parallel symbolic usage, a "minority": the United Kingdom by kilted Scots, the Netherlands by farms girls with wooden clogs, Russia by Evenki, the United States by "feathered Indians," India by "Tribals," and so on. This suggests an underlying unity of a nostalgic eternal recent past (e.g., "when my grandparents were growing up") between colonized indigenes, culturally recognizable minorities, and rural/pre-industrial ancestors. This, of course, stems from the nineteenth-century evolutionary model where "contemporary cultural difference = historical/evolutionary temporal distance."

Thus the situation of indigeneity is less clear in Europe (except for the Sami; see Graburn and Strong 1973, 11–32) and much of Asia, where most of the peoples have experienced the flows of larger communities and conquering powers, some of whom recorded history through literacy, for thousands of years. One reviewer of my *Ethnic and Tourist Arts* (1976) wondered why I had not included the Sami and the Basques and other Native Europeans. I was flattered and agreed that the term

"Fourth World" applied to many peoples who self-identified but no longer had a country of their own. However, even though *Wikipedia* classifies the Basques as "indigenous" with a unique language, they also pointed out: "Among the most notable Basque people are Juan Sebastian Elcano (led the first successful expedition to circumnavigate the globe after Ferdinand Magellan died mid-journey); Sancho III of Navarre; and Ignatius of Loyola and Francis Xavier, founders of the Society of Jesus. Don Diego de Garoqui Arriquibar (1735–98) was Spain's first ambassador to the United States" (https://en.wikipedia.org/wiki/Basques, accessed 18 September 2016; see also Urla 2012). Thus Basques were themselves long-time colonizers, bearers of Catholicism and the Spanish language, and powerful in the metropolitan world. We might find similar anomalies concerning the Bretons (Badone 1992, 2012; McDonald 1989) and especially the peoples of the Caucasus, such as the Alans (North Ossetians), who may in part also be ancestors of the Catalans (Goths and Alans) according to Sergei Arutiunov (personal communication, 1993) and others. However, Badone's work on the Bretons (1992) is an explicit comparison with Quebec, itself a settler colony inhabiting First Nations lands. Yet, because of the post-1851 situation of the francophone Quebecois, they have learned to emphasize *their own colonized status* (Handler 1988) and imagine and present themselves in some ways as "indigenous" compared with metropolitan anglophone Canada.

Even in the settler colonies, at the early stages there was not necessarily such a real or perceived power differential between the newcomers and the locals, for instance with the Tlingit and the Russians around Sitka, the British and the Algonkians at Jamestown, or the British and the Zulu at Rourkes Drift in what is now South Africa. Indeed, in any place where the local people continued to far outnumber the colonizers, even if settled, the concept of indigeneity is harder to apply, as in much of Africa, India, and Southeast Asia. Thus, in common parlance Indigenous peoples are usually seen as ethnic minorities especially when they are the focus of tourism, though it must be pointed out that by no means all minorities as tourist destinations are Indigenous (Diekmann and Smith 2015).

The situation of indigeneity in most of Asia is equally complex. In the nineteenth century the Russian part of Asia (mainly Siberia) generally conformed to settler colony patterns, on the rather extreme end of cruelty comparable to the colonizer-Indigenous relations in California and Australia; Japan's colonization of the Ainu was very similar

(Weiner 1997). For much of the twentieth century the minorities (mostly Indigenous) of the USSR were treated according to the social dictum "Nationalist in form; Socialist in content" (Levin and Potapov 1964). This formula, put in place by the first People's Commissar for Nationalities' Affairs, Joseph [Jughashvili] Stalin (himself a Georgian and therefore a "minority"), was based on Marxist political theory, following the materialist-based social evolutionary theory of American "anthropologist" Lewis Henry Morgan (1877).[2] The policy regarded all "nations" as having equal rights to their language, culture, and lands, but at the same time ranked them from the lowest "Savagery" through "Barbarism" to "Civilization." The task of the government of the USSR was to educate and guide those lower down the evolutionary scale to master the sociocultural and technical components of civilization so that they could take their place side by side with "civilized" Russians and others in leading their nations to equality within the socialist USSR. The main paths to this enlightenment were through education of promising young leaders at central institutions in St Petersburg and Moscow, and the provision of technically modern services, including electricity, health services, and especially scientific agricultural and veterinary services in rural areas, all governed through workers' councils (*soviets*). Thus, the modernization of Indigenous peoples was relatively rapid and ruthless (top down), allowing the educated to join the political elite while those in the hinterlands (these included Indigenous and other kinds of minorities, such as Jews with their homeland on the Chinese border) struggled with state-mandated occupations, and the ambivalence of home languages and local cultures versus Russianization (Krupnik 1992; Vakhtin 1992). Though exploited by the state, many remained severely dependent on state-supplied outside services.

For the question of Indigenous identity, the USSR and Russia (and the former Russian Empire) present many challenges, especially as enormous conquests, population movements, and religious adoptions have occurred in recent centuries. Though the Slavic Russians have been predominant politically and demographically in these centuries, they are surrounded (and have assimilated) many former powerful Turkic and Mongolic peoples (and empires), as well as Persian peoples. The Ukrainians, Georgians, Armenians, Kazakhs, Litvaks, Estonians, Latvians, Ukrainians, and Azerbaijanis are obviously capable of standing as their own modern nations. The Circassians and Adyghes are mainly in diaspora and are successful urbane minorities in other countries. The Caucasus, an area rich for many kinds of tourism in times of peace

(Graburn 2003), has long been a hospitable area in spite of great ethnic differentiation. Christian and minor Islamic religious tourism were
long known, and by the nineteenth century the more modern forms of
recreation attracted Russians and others to the Black Sea Riviera as well
as the mountains and valleys for their famous foods and wines.

The Caucasian peoples included the semi-tribal Chechen as well as
the Ingush, the Ossetians (Alans), and Tats, all of whom could be the
targets of ethnic tourism. Many of the larger ethnic groups, such as the
Bashkirs, Kalmyks, and Lezgin, are Muslim and would hardly consider themselves Indigenous even though they might qualify as Fourth
World. We have to look mainly to Siberia for those more typical ethnic Indigenous groups, some of whom have been subject to touristic
or at least media interest from outsiders. These include the northern
Yakuts (Sakha), the pastoralist Nenets, Evenki (Tungus), Chuckchi,
Inuit (Yupiit), Aleuts, the almost extinct Yukaghir, and the Finno-Ugric
Sami, Mari, and Karelians. Ethnic tourism to these peoples and their
territories is quite expensive and often takes place close to international
boundaries (with Finland, Norway, and China).

Ethnic tourism to minority Indigenous areas was not common
due both to vast distances and to urbanites' lack of interest. With the
breakdown of the Soviet Union in 1989, many Indigenous peoples
were appalled and terrified at the withdrawal of state services (Lappalainan 1990). This situation parallels many others around the world,
where conquered Indigenous peoples (Fourth World) are incorporated
into the socio-economic network of the surrounding nation and come
to depend on it for the provision of health care, schooling, housing,
and emergency supports, fear their withdrawal, and cannot imagine
a future independence. And many anthropologists/social scientists of
the USSR – some of Indigenous backgrounds faced with fixed salaries
with few benefits and possible withdrawal of state support – started
to organize summer research/tourist ventures (forms of adventure/
Indigenous tourism?) – along the Volga, through Chukotka or Siberia and so on – hoping to supplement their incomes by guiding their
wealthier Western colleagues.

After the 1949 revolution, China soon followed the Soviet policies.
The new Chinese nation, like the USSR, would be a pluralist nation of
many *minzu* (nationalities or ethnicities). Western-trained anthropologist Fei Xiaotong joined other experts and political authorities in organizing a nationwide *minzu shibie* (ethnic classification) exercise (Mullaney
2011; see also Chen 2008) in order to identify, classify, name, and assign

territory for all Chinese, 90 per cent of whom are seen as Han and speak *Putonghua* ("standard Mandarin language"), paralleling to a degree Russian in the USSR. Of more than four hundred named minorities groups, the group mapped and accepted thirty-nine *shaoshu minzu* (small nationalities) in 1954, mainly on the basis of shared language and history, geographical contiguity, cultural similarities, and pre-existing majority beliefs. With further research, they had designated a total of fifty-three by the 1964 census, and finally fifty-five by 1979. But for our purposes, which of them are "indigenous"? We can count out those whose majority population resides outside China, such as Russians, Koreans, and Mongols;[3] other problems include the status of the Man (Manchu = *Man-zu*), who not only are former rulers of China, but were reluctantly listed as they had allied with the Japanese in the Pacific War. But the agricultural Jingpo (Jinghpaw) and the pastoral Evenki (Tungus), mainly found in Myanmar and Russia respectively, could well qualify. The majority of the small peoples, stereotypically Indigenous, of the southwest such as Miao, Dong, Buyi, Yi, Sani, Hani, Tujia, Yao, She, and Wa, are targets of ethnic tourism (Graburn 2015, 2016), and they self-consciously see themselves as trying to presenting a saleable image and a distinctive off-site imaginary (Salazar and Graburn 2014). Other minorities present problems as "indigenous": the Bai were once a powerful, elite, literate military group who were pushed into mountainous Yunnan; the Uighur are Turkic Muslim who were once rulers of a khanate the size of China; the Hui are "Muslim Han" Chinese, urbane, literate traders and intellectuals; and the Tibetans, while an attractive and distinctive people – many of them still agricultural or pastoral – think of themselves as a *nation* with a distinct language, culture, and religion, typical of Indigenous Fourth World peoples (Graburn 1976, 1981). Other problems crop up, with some people – sometimes Han – assuming (other) minority *minzu* identity for touristic purposes; others believe their subgroup was misclassified; and yet others are *not* included as minority (such as Sherpa, Macanese, or Hakka). In some cases, the father, mother, or predecessor may, for some reason, have missed being classified as minority *minzu* (they were away, politically out of favour, or didn't see the purpose), and their descendants are forever cut off from their ancestral identity and even their ethnic communities. We may compare this memory of such losses, incurred within living memory (approximately 1954–64), to the common claims of many American and Canadian "whites" who nostalgically claim some Native American/ First Nations Indigenous ancestry, which might be called the Cherokee or Pocahontas syndrome, based on vague family folklore going back way beyond living memory.

Following the Russian socialist model, the Chinese government has attempted to "raise [minorities] up the evolutionary path," providing them with universal education, technical help such as electricity, work on infrastructural projects, governmental guidance, and access through roads. These minority *minzu* are treated specially in at least two ways: since 1978 they have not been restricted by the one-child policy, as have Han peoples, as long as they stay in their assigned areas, and their proportion of the population has risen noticeably. Even more important are their educational opportunities: they have placement quotas or lower admission requirements for many schools and colleges. In fact, there is a national system of *Minda*,[4] "peoples' universities," with the head one in Beijing, which admit and cater to official minorities. These institutions stress topics appropriate for minorities, such as development and applied anthropology, as well as encouraging their languages, cultural performances, and traditional artifacts, and may have the best anthropology departments and museums in China. As we shall see below, this has enabled a large number of minorities to become professors and professionals researching and developing ethnic tourism. This is not to say that these *minzu* are prevented from attending the best national universities for which they qualify: I know individuals from the urbane Bai-zu to the poorest backwoods Hani-zu who have excelled in classical Chinese formations at Beida, the highly prestigious Beijing National University.

This opening up of the remote and rural regions has conversely enabled the promotion of ethnic tourism as a form of poverty alleviation and national inclusion, though the strategies of development vary from "reinventing rural tradition" (in Guizhou) to training performers for extravaganzas (in Yunnan) to encouraging rustic commerce through *nong jia le* (peasant family happiness; see Chio 2014) in the form of small hotels and restaurants in Guangxi. The majority Han Chinese, who have long been fascinated with these nearby exotic cultures, see these minorities much in terms of their superficial differences from Han Chinese, with the "assimilated" Hui and Tujia as too close to be interesting (except for Muslim architecture) and the Tibetans and Uighur as very visible and awe inspiring, though possibly threatening in their different ways. Thus the more "backward" and accommodating – Schein (2000) suggests feminized – village peoples are most typically presented for ethnic tourism.

Indigenous Tourisms

The emphases of this book are the de-colonization of Indigenous peoples and their empowerment through self-knowledge, self-government, and control over the ethnic tourism that is directed their way. But let us step back for a moment and consider the many possibilities under this label. First, I agree with Dennison Nash et al. (1981) that nearly all peoples, including Indigenous and "pre-indigenous" (before colonization), enjoy mobilities that are worth considering as a kind of tourism. As I mentioned in chapter 9, the Canadian Inuit, before they were "settled" into villages with permanent houses, travelled as an annual cycle; they visited each other both in adjacent tents or igloos or between camps (tourism). They also went hunting, usually in male groups. While hunting was the basis of subsistence and was in deadly earnest, it also engendered the kind of camaraderie and enjoyment of the landscape characteristic of contemporary game hunters and perhaps parallel to those undertaking team sports and play (Huizinga 1949). I suggest that much of this hardy travel is very comparable to certain types of tourism today. In fact, I would agree with Ingold (2000) and others that in pre-industrial societies *there was no distinct opposition between leisure and work*; as I have shown elsewhere (1983), under all touristic circumstances only a certain part of the behaviour and experience contains that "magic" of tourism, whereas the rest approximates more routine everyday life. Similarly, we know that in the majority of pilgrimage experience, levity, companionship, and types of consumption leaven the religious experience (Graburn 1977a).

Considering the nature of their travel, Indigenous people developed both patterns of hospitality and patterns of playing the guest. Indeed, Inuit and others have words and concepts very close to "host" and "guest," which involved values of care, welcome, generosity, and sharing that not only saved lives under difficult circumstances but were subject to strong feelings of balanced reciprocity (Graburn 1977b; Sahlins 1972), and often involved sexual hospitality (Burch 1975) if a male visitor arrived without his wife (also known among Arab and Hebrew peoples). Recall that Sahlins (1968) once claimed that the Aboriginal hunters and foragers were the original affluent society, having lots of leisure time after relatively few hours of work. There are worldwide recorded accounts of such host-guest tourism-like relationships with both instrumental and emotional motivations and consequences.

There are many descriptions of Indigenous hospitality in accounts by explorers, traders, and anthropologists. Here we begin to bridge the gap between "truly indigenous" tourism and Indigenous hospitality in colonial situations as mentioned in chapter 1. The nature of the relationship might depend on the fact that the "outsider" was a visitor or is accompanying travelling local people; or the outsider was a representative of the colonizers, and whether he (and it was usually a he) was sympathetic or an instrument of the external power. The visiting relationships between pre-colonial Indigenous groups varied immensely, from fear of and (near) warfare between the Canadian Inuit and the Algonkian (Naskapi, Cree) and Dene peoples to their south (Graburn and Strong 1973) to, for instance, ritual exchange and material barter and the renewal of old friendships among the Trobriand Islanders and their neighbours in the Kula Ring (Malinowski 1922). We should be clear, however, that inter-Indigenous meetings and Indigenous-colonial meetings were, like the Kula exchanges, nearly always a complex mixture of sociability (tourism), boundary maintenance (political), and trade.

Indigenous Researchers

As Bunten has explained in the preface to this volume, we authors did our best to engage Indigenous researchers in our project, contacting them and inviting them to meetings in Alaska, California, New Zealand, and France. We can probably be faulted for our relatively narrow focus on the English-speaking world and our inability to sustain the motivations or directions that would have led those few Indigenous researchers we convened to contribute to this general academic volume. Most of these colleagues were already engaged in struggles in their own territories and would prioritize tackling the more immediate problems of their own communities and extended families over taking the extra time to contribute to the academic world of comparative "global" volumes. In spite of the paucity of educational opportunities and the present ghosts of colonialism in North America, some Indigenous peoples, Native Americans, First Nations, and Inuit peoples have become academics, including anthropologists, and have made great contributions. But we should not blame them for attending more to their own people or similarly colonized peoples than to the "colonizers" and the dominant academic world.

A number have reached the heights of their profession: Alfonso Ortiz[5] (Tewa Pueblo; University of New Mexico) divided his professional efforts between the deep ethnography of his own Tewa peoples and more expansive works about Native Americans, including editing two volumes of the *Handbook of American Indians*; JoAllyn Archambault (Sioux; Smithsonian) studied among the Navajo for her PhD and went on to write and organize exhibitions about Native Americans; the late Bea Medicine (Lakota; Cal State Northridge), like Ortiz, divided her career between writing about the Sioux and more generally about Native Americans, including the predicament of Plains Indian women like herself. She also published a volume entitled *Learning to Be an Anthropologist and Remaining "Native"* (Medicine and Jacobs 2001), tackling the problems of loyalty, stereotyping, and professional attachment that Ortiz had mentioned. As Medicine explains, there is tremendous pressure on young Indigenous academics both on behalf of their homes communities and networks and from academia itself. For instance, Heather Igloliorte (Nunatsiavimiut [Labrador Inuit]; Concordia University, Montreal) has survived and thrived under pressure as a leading Indigenous art historian, while artist-anthropologist Wendy Rose (Hopi-Miwok; Califormia State Fresno/Fresno City College) served for years as co-ordinator of American Indian Studies but has pursued a very active career as poet and artist. It is significant that other young anthropologists who identify as Native American but also have a parent from "white" America and have lived mostly in non-Native communities, such as Alexis Bunten (Bristol Bay Aleut/Yupik) and Robin DeLugan (Choctaw; UC Merced) have a more cosmopolitan professional view but at the same time go to great lengths to help and advocate for Indigenous communities with whom they identify or study (Alaska Natives [Bunten 2015] and the Indigenous survivors of the 1934 *Matanza* and the recent civil wars in El Salvador [DeLugan 2012]). And both of these scholars have made contributions to the study of tourism and heritage.

Like Medicine, Kirin Narayan (1993) tackled the problem of the "Native anthropologist" and shared Bunten's and DeLugan's dilemma of having an American "majority" mother in the United States; but her father was Indian and in the majority where she was brought up (with a "minority" mother). She came to Berkeley for her PhD and joined the profession she was ambivalent about being the "Native anthropologist" within. While having immediate access to some communities in India, she also explains the complexities of Indian society within which no one has total access, and of the multiple identity that she and others like her suffer yet take advantage of in the field, at home, and in "world anthropology" as a profession. In her case she may claim to be "Native" but not Indigenous, reminding us, as discussed above, that indigeneity as an autochthonous conquered "tribal" identity is problematic in most of East and South Asia, even in India where certain non-Hindu lower-caste people are called "Tribals."

In our consideration of (ex-)socialist "colonial empires" of Russia (USSR) and China above, we saw that these fundamentally progressive political systems attempted to train and educate the leaders of all Indigenous and other minority national groups. But Russia never used tourism as a major development tool, and China focused on tourism for the less developed areas (peoples) of the west and southwest, and developed an affirmative educational system for all official minorities. This has resulted in a high proportion of tourism researcher professionals – both theoretical and applied – who have a minority background. From my earliest encounters with tourism researchers in China, I was aware of this, especially in my work with Zhang Xiaoping (Bai; Yunnan University) and Yang Hui (Naxi; Yunnan University). These scholars not only focused their research – and made films – on minorities in their own region under the impact of tourism but, like some of the American scholars mentioned above, pursued the subject to the national level, attempting generalizations about ethnic tourism in China and examining the different approaches of Western and Chinese researchers (Tan, Cheung, and Yang 2001; Yang and Tan 2011; Zhang 2005). One can note the parallel with many Native American anthropological researchers (some of them listed above), but the sheer numbers are impressive. From my own knowledge, and consulting with friends in Yunnan, Xiamen, and at the National Minorities University, Beijing,[6] I have a list of at least thirty minority researchers, many of whom I know personally. They are from all over the country and represent urbanites such as Hui (five), Tujia (three), Manchu (two), and Korean, but also members of small, often rural groups such as Buyi (three), Yi (two), Li, Gelao, Dong, Miao (two), and Zhuang, as well as prominent scholars from the more distinctive Tibetans and Uighur.

Kanaaneh (1997) has tackled this question head on. Western(-trained) anthropologists, by definition, are enculturated as universalists, cosmopolitans, dedicated to "their community," which is humanity, all of which is in itself an elitist and self-centred point of view. I remember being challenged by someone who asked, "Why are you here teaching and writing books? You are an anthropologist; you should be out there applying your anthropology, helping people in their homes and villages." (I had spent a number of years living with Canadian Inuit in their homes and villages since 1959.) To which I facetiously replied, "Yes, I could be out somewhere giving medical aid, organizing village co-ops or helping in one-room schools, but I think I am doing more good in applying my anthropology by teaching four to five hundred of the future leaders of California every year."[7] This statement may have revealed my identity with or commitment to the people of California, but in my mind it was also intended to convey the idea that the leaders of California would be responsible for personal behaviour and socio-political policies that might affect Indigenous peoples, as well as the multicultural population of California and the United States and inevitably much of the rest of the world.

This does not mean that anthropologists have no commitment to the Indigenous or other communities where they have lived or studied, and some have more than others. Many have dedicated much of their lives and professional efforts to people or communities; for instance, Fred Eggan served as a witness for the Pueblo against the Navajo in a land dispute, Nancy Scheper-Hughes has often advocated for and visited the poverty-stricken communities of north-eastern Brazil, and Elizabeth Colson, who started field research work in Rhodesia in 1946, retired from UC Berkeley in 1994 and left Berkeley in 2005 to return to live in what is now Zambia, nearby the Gwembe Tonga and other peoples she had known over the previous sixty years. She continued to correspond with the Western anthropological world and was obviously not Indigenous; yet she was a long-term engaged member in the community and was honoured with a traditional Tonga funeral when she died in 2016.

Conclusion

Of the nine cases of Indigenous tourism discussed in this volume, six are situated in what are still settler colonial nations – three of them Anglo (Australia, Alaska, Canada) and three of them Latino (Costa Rica, Panama, Chile). The other three are cases of Indigenous minority peoples found in ex-colonies, now independent nations (Tanzania, Botswana, Mali) ruled by other non-European peoples. But in all cases, they conform to the model of peoples who are struggling to gain more control over their self-presentation to outsiders, especially tourists. They are facing a situation not of their own making where the world system of cultural – in this case ethnic cultural – tourism has powerful predetermined expectations based on global rather than local imaginaries. Key mediators in this process – the guides, advertisers, and image makers – are usually outsiders or educated insiders, who though sympathetic have to "sell" the image.

Yet in many of these cases, progress has been made; stereotypes have been modified and local voices heard. Some Indigenous minorities even have the power to control when and under which conditions tourists may gaze, and they may control tourist photography and maintain parts of their communities as off-limits. In the three Anglo-settler colonies, as well as in China, Russia, and Chile, members of Indigenous peoples have gained access to higher education and other specialized skills; they are writers, film and television producers, and politicians and have been able to rewrite or at least steer the direction of their identities, while bearing in mind tourist expectations. And in these circumstances, they too have been able to become tourists – Native Alaskan and Canadian Inuit visiting southern cities and even beach resorts in Hawaii and Florida, prosperous Chinese minority *minzu* visiting Beijing and Shanghai not as migrants desperate for work but as tourists investigating the places from which the majority Han tourists who visit their villages come (Chio 2014). Indeed, in much of today's world, many ethnic minorities are admired for their alterity, even if there are romantic and nostalgic bases for these positive judgments. They may be admired icons of their nations, as are the Maasai in East Africa, the Inuit in Canada, or the Sami in Finland; very often their professional performances are admired and emulated by members of the majority, and their artistic productions may be bought, collected, exhibited, and feted as among the most sublime of human creations. Perhaps the world is changing from the once dominant evolutionary model, in which most Indigenous peoples were subject to a mental construction that Rosaldo (1989) has called "imperialist nostalgia," a feeling of loss and regret for having destroyed peoples and cultures (and natural areas) that we now admire in retrospect or that we as tourists hope will be preserved from the long-expected fate of disappearance. Ethnic and Indigenous tourisms can be exploitative and stereotyping, but a new admixture of admiration (and guilt), education, and empowerment can bring more equitable relations and the hope for more stable multicultural national entities.

NOTES

1 The concept of biological race is said to have emerged from colonial conquests, especially as justification for the import of cheap labour known as slavery. Ethnocentrism and xenophobia have probably been universal, but their implications of hereditary traits and inferiority were used to justify servitude and permanent lack of freedom.

2 Morgan led a life closely intertwined with contemporary nineteenth-century Iroquois, a prominent Indigenous group. He was raised on former Iroquois lands in New York, formed a society (the New Confederacy) for the preservation of "doomed" Iroquois culture and language, and became a friend and educational sponsor of Ely Parker of Iroquois aristocracy. Morgan, a capitalist trained as a lawyer, successfully defended the Iroquois from commercial land grabs. Later he fell out with Parker, who had risen to the rank of brigadier and became a citizen during the Civil War, when he was appointed Commissioner of Indian Affairs, a position that Morgan had long sought.

3 And possibly Dai (Thai), Kazakhs, and Kirgiz.

4 Standard abbreviation for *Minzu dajie*, that is, nationality/ethnic peoples' universities.

5 A fellow student advisee of Fred Eggan at the University of Chicago; in this section I am only telling the stories of those who I knew well or over a long time: Archambault, Narayan, Rose, and Delugan were doctoral students at UC Berkeley, where Alexis Bunten was a postdoctoral fellow and a long-time collaborator; Bea Medicine was a colleague with fellow interests in Indigenous arts, film making, and European "Indian Players"; and Igloliorte, like her mentor Ruth Philips, is a colleague in the research, publication, and exhibition of Canadian Indigenous arts.

6 I thank Dr Zhang Ying (Minzu University of China, Beijing), Dr Ge Rongling (Xiamen University), and Dr Jin Lu (Ningbo University) for their information.

7 Perhaps my most important "applied" contribution was accidental, when I received a phone call in my Berkeley office from a lawyer who was a negotiator for land claims between the Canadian Inuit and the Canadian government. He said, "You're the only person that ever wrote that the Inuit traditionally used shrimp. If you can prove this and if you've got evidence, then they will have exclusive rights to all crustaceans in the Arctic for commercial exploitation from this treaty forward." They took my evidence, and based on it the Inuit could now have a claim to a six-million-dollar shrimp industry and other possible harvests.

REFERENCES

Badone, Ellen. 1992. "The Construction of National Identity in Brittany and Quebec." *American Ethnologist* 19 (4): 806–17. http://dx.doi.org/10.1525/ae.1992.19.4.02a00100.

Badone, Ellen. 2012. "La Bretagne depuis trente ans: Le regard d'une ethnologue canadienne." *Ethnologie Francaise* 42 (4): 635–45. http://dx.doi.org/10.3917/ethn.124.0635.

Bunten, Alexis. 2015. *So How Long Have You Been Native? Life as an Alaska Native Tour Guide.* Lincoln: University of Nebraska Press.

Burch, Ernest S., Jr. 1975. *Eskimo Kinsmen: Changing Family Relationships in Northwest Alaska.* New York: West.

Chen, J. 2008. "Nation, Ethnicity, and Cultural Strategies: Three Waves of Ethnic Representation in Post-1949 China." PhD diss., Rutgers University.

Chio, Jenny. 2014. *A Landscape of Travel: The Work of Tourism in Rural Ethnic China.* Seattle: University of Washington Press.

DeLugan, Robin. 2012. *Reimagining National Belonging; Post-Civil Way El Salvador in a Global Context.* Tucson: University of Arizona Press.

Diekmann, Anya, and Melanie Smith, eds. 2015. *Ethnic and Minority Communities as Tourist Attractions.* Bristol: Multilingual Matters.

Graburn, Nelson, and B. Stephen Strong. 1973. *Circumpolar Peoples: An Anthropological Perspective.* Pacific Palisades: Goodyear.

Graburn, Nelson, ed. 1976. *Ethnic and Tourist Arts: Cultural Expressions from the Fourth World.* Berkeley: University of California Press.

Graburn, Nelson. 1977a. "Tourism: The Sacred Journey." In *Hosts and Guests: The Anthropology of Tourism,* edited by Valene Smith, 17–32. Philadelphia: University of Pennsylvania Press.

Graburn, Nelson. 1977b. "Exchange and Transfer: A Case Study on Canadian Eskimo." In *The Origins of the Economy: A Comparative Study of Distribution in Primitive and Peasant Economies,* edited by Fred Pryor, 69–101, 410–18. New York: Academic.

Graburn, Nelson. 1981. "1, 2, 3, 4 ... Anthropology and the Fourth World." *Culture (Québec)* 1 (1): 66–70.

Graburn, Nelson. 1987. "Natives and Nationalism: The Appropriation of Symbols for Canadian National Identity." Address to annual meeting of the Western Association of Sociology and Anthropology, Boise, Idaho, 14 February.

Graburn, Nelson 2003. "Tourism and Tradition: Culture as Resource or Commodity, with Respect to the Caucasus." Paper given at the International Institute of Peoples of the Caucasus (IIPC), assisted by Department of

Caucasian Studies at the Institute of Ethnology and Anthropology, 25 November.

Graburn, Nelson. 2007. "Tourism through the Looking Glass." In *Tourism Study: Anthropological and Sociological Beginnings*, edited by Dennison Nash, 93–107. London: Pergamon.

Graburn, Nelson. 2015. "Ethnic Tourism in Rural China: Cultural or Economic Development." In *Ethnic and Minority Communities as Tourist Attractions*, edited by Anya Diekmann and Melanie Smith, 176–86. Bristol: Multilingual Matters.

Graburn, Nelson. 2016. "Strategies for Ethnic Tourism Development in China." 第36 卷第5 期中南民族大学学报(人文社会科学版) (*Journal of South-Central University for Nationalities* [Humanities and Social Sciences]) 36 (5): 39–47.

Graburn, Nelson, and B. Stephen Strong. 1973. *Circumpolar Peoples: An Anthropological Perspective*. Pacific Palisades: Goodyear.

Handler, Richard. 1988. *Nationalism and the Politics of Culture in Quebec*. Seattle: University of Washington Press.

Huizinga, Johan. 1949. *Homo Ludens: A Study of the Play Element in Culture*. London: Routledge and Kegan Paul.

Ingold, Tim. 2000. *The Perception of Environment: Essays on Livelihood, Dwelling and Skill*. London: Routledge. http://dx.doi.org/10.4324/9780203466025.

Kanaaneh, Moslih. 1997. "The 'Anthropologicality' of Indigenous Anthropology." *Dialectical Anthropology* 22 (1): 1–21. http://dx.doi.org/10.1023/A:1006815109475.

Krupnik, Igor. 1992. "One Nation – One Language: Ideology and Results of Soviet Policies in Siberia." In *Language and Educational Policy in the North*, edited by Nelson Graburn and Roy Iutzi-Mitchell, 191–202. Berkeley: IAS.

Lappalainan, Heimo. 1990. Nomads of the Taiga. Video. Helsinki: Illume Oy.

Levin, Maksim, and Leonid Potapov, eds. 1964. *The Peoples of Siberia*. Chicago: University of Chicago Press. (English edition edited by Stephen Dunn)

Malinowski, Bronisław. 1922. *Argonauts of the Western Pacific: An Account of Native Enterprise and Adventure in the Archipelagos of Melanesian New Guinea*. London: Routledge & Kegan Paul.

McDonald, Maryon. 1989. *We Are Not French! Language, Culture and Identity in Brittany*. London: Routledge.

Medicine, Bea, and Sue-Ellen Jacobs, eds.. 2001. *Learning to Be an Anthropologist and Remaining "Native": Selected Writings*. Champaign: University of Illinois Press.

Morgan, Lewis Henry. 1877. *Ancient Society; or, Researches in the Lines of Human Progress from Savagery, through Barbarism to Civilization*. New York: Henry Holt.

Mullaney, Thomas. 2011. *Coming to Terms with the Nation: Ethnic Classification in Modern China*. Berkeley: University of California Press.

Narayan, Kirin. 1993. "How Native Is a 'Native' Anthropologist?" *American Anthropologist* 95 (3): 671–86. http://dx.doi.org/10.1525/aa.1993.95.3.02a00070.

Nash, Dennison, Anne V. Akeroyd, John J. Bodine, Erik Cohen, Graham Dann, Symphna Hermans, Jafar Jafari, et al. 1981. "Tourism, an Anthropological Subject." *Current Anthropology* 22 (5): 461–81. http://dx.doi.org/10.1086/202722.

Rosaldo, Renato. 1989. "Imperialist Nostalgia." *Representations (Berkeley, Calif.)* 26 (1): 107–22. http://dx.doi.org/10.1525/rep.1989.26.1.99p0282w.

Sahlins, Marshall. 1968. "Notes on the Original Affluent Society." In *Man the Hunter*, edited by Richard B. Lee and Irving DeVore. New York: Aldine.

Sahlins, M. 1972. *Stone Age Economics*. Chicago: Aldine-Atherton.

Salazar, Nash, and Nelson Graburn, eds. 2014. *Tourism Imaginaries: Anthropological Approaches*. London: Berghahn. http://dx.doi.org/10.1007/978-3-319-01669-6_267-1.

Schein, Louisa. 2000. *Minority Rules: The Miao and the Feminine in China's Cultural Politics*. Durham: Duke University Press.

Tan, C.B., S. Cheung, and H. Yang, eds. 2001. *Tourism, Anthropology and China*. Bangkok: White Lotus. (published in Chinese as *Lüyou, renleixue yu Zhongguo shehui* [旅游,人类学与中国社会]. Kunming: Yunnan Daxue chubanshe.)

Urla, Jacqueline. 2012. *Reclaiming Basque: Language, Nation, and Cultural Activism*. Reno: University of Nevada Press.

Vakhtin, Nikolai. 1992. "The Linguistic System and Educational Policies in Chukotka." In *Language and Educational Policy in the North*, edited by Nelson Graburn and Roy Iutzi-Mitchell, 203–19. Berkeley: IAS.

Weiner, Michael, ed. 1997. *Japan's Minorities: The Illusion of Homogeneity*. London: Routledge.

Yang, H., and C.B. Tan, eds. 2011. 旅游,民族和文化多样性 [*Tourism, Ethnic and Cultural Diversity*]. Kunming: Yunnan University Press. (in Chinese)

Zhang, X., ed. 2005. *Anthropological Perspectives on Ethnic Tourism*. Yunnan: Minzu University Press. (in Chinese)

Index

Page numbers in **boldface** *refer to figures and tables.*

Aboriginal, 2–3, 10–11, 19, 31–6, 38–43, 46–8, 49n1, 49n6, 49n8, 49n14, 49n17, 49n19, 235, 249. *See also* Indigenous
acculturation, 169, 188, 190n4
advertising, 10, 16, 42, 60, 64, 189, 207, 243. *See also* brochure; marketing
Africa, 14, 56–7, 59–60, 67, 123–4, 126–8, 143n1, 134n4, 141, 155, 243–4; East Africa, 67, 69, 142, 254 (*see also* Arusha; Tanzania); southern Africa, 117, 118, 120, 132 (*see also* Botswana); West Africa, 69n7, 140, 142, 144, 160n11 (*see also* Mali)
agency, 16, 45, 74, 84, 117, 123, 125, 129, 131–4, 158, 190n4, 223, 230, 232–3
Ainu, 5, 9, 22n7, 244
airlines: Air Inuit, 204, 216n8; Austin Airways, 202, 216n8
Alaska, 9, 10, 16, 22n3, 50n14, 165–72, 176, 179–80, **181**, 182–4, 186–9, 190n7, 190n8, 190n12, 191n18, 192n21, 213, 250–1, 253–4
alternative tourism. *See under* tourism

Alto Bío Bío, 18, 222–9, 231
animism, 140
anthropologist, 3, 17, 23n11, 40, 69n2, 106, 112n9, 120, 123, 134n3, 164, 168–9, 213, 242–3, 245–6, 250–3; "Native anthropologists," 251
anthropology, 2, 178, 217n15, 252–3; applied, 248; of tourism, 100
Appadurai, Arjun, 22n4, 49n4, 89, 99, 170
appropriation, 2, 8, 10, 235
art: folk arts, 4; history, 2; as icons of identity, 243. *See also* artists; material culture; tourist art
artists, 16, 82, 86, 148, 165, 166–72, 174, 176, 179–80, 183–9, 190n6, 191n19, 205–7, 218n19
Arusha, **58**, 60, 63, 66–7, 70n8
Asia, 242–8, 252. *See also* China; Japan; Southeast Asia
Australia, 2, 8, 10–11, 19, 23n9, 23n11, 31, 35–6, 39–42, 45, 47, 49n1, 50n14, 51n21, 124, 232, 235, 243–4, 253. *See also* Tjapukai Aboriginal Cultural Park

authenticity, 9, 39, 41–2, 44, 50n12, 87, 91, 100–1, 105, 141–51, 153, 155, 168–9, 179–80, 183–4, 190n3, 191n20; commodification of, 140, 142, 151, 158–9; defining, 142, 144; experiential, 10; imagined, 39; and staging, 11, 43
autochthony, 123–5, 132; autochthonous, 3, 122, 252. See also Indigenous
autonomy, 74, 83, 231
Avataq, 212, 217n17

backstage, 44
Baffin Island, 198–221
Basques, 243–4
blacksmith, 149, 151–6, 158
border zones, 2. See also under cultural
Borges, Jorge Luis, 73, 77, 81, 87–8, 90, 91n4
Botswana, 13–14, 19, 117–18, 119, 120–34, 135n7, 253. See also Central Kalahari Game Reserve
boycott, 118, 129–31, 135n7
Bretons, 244
brochure, 81, 90, 134n2, 172, 208, 210–11. See also advertising; guidebook; tourist
Bruner, Edward, 3, 33, 46, 57–9, 61, 67–8
Bunten, Alexis, 3, 7, 10–11, 15, 33, 36–7, 45–7, 74, 100–1, 109, 126–7, 141, 158, 170, 190n3, 200, 213, 214, 223, 250–1, 255n5
bushmen, 121, 131, 134n2. See also San

California, 244, 250, 253
Canada, 8–9, 17, 23n9, 23n12, 178, 189n2, 191n12, 201, 203, 205,

208–11, 217n10, 217n16, 243, 244, 253–4. See also Eastern Canadian Arctic; Nunavut
Cape Dorset, 202–3, 205, 210–11, 216n6
capitalism: green, 227; late, 2, 18
Central Kalahari Game Reserve, 118, 127. See also Botswana
Chile, 18, 222–8, 232, 253, 254. See also Alto Bío Bío
China, 7, 9, 23n13, 246–8, 252, 254; Chinese minority peoples (minzu), 246–8; Chinook, 165
Chorotega, 12, 19, 73–9, 81–91; annual festival, 83, 89; Indigenous Territory, 73, 75, 76, 82–3, 85–90, 91n4
Christian, 146; missionaries, 146, 188, 236, 243, 246
climate change, 210, 215–16, 231
colonialism, 4, 6, 16, 40, 50n13, 57, 59, 63, 88, 142, 144, 166, 168, 171, 184–5, 188–9, 190n4, 192n21, 216, 230, 242, 250, 252–3; in Africa, 62, 124; British, 62; European, 134n3; French, 140; imagery, 11; in North America, 250; settler colonialism, 20, 40, 46, 243, 253. See also decolonization; ex-colonial; postcolonialism; precolonialism
commodification, 22n3, 117, 159, 21; of authenticity, 140, 141–2, 151, 153, 158; of heritage, 21, 141; self-commodification, 10, 126. See also authenticity; heritage
commoditization, 83; commoditized persona, 37
Community Based Natural Resource Management (CBNRM), 126, 128, 132–3

community-based tourism. *See under* tourism

conquistadors, 73, 76

conservation: Ngorongoro Conservation Area Authority, 65, 69n4; policies, 121; "spirit of," 77; of wildlife, 121, 131; World Conservation Union, 5

consumption, 2, 8, 33, 249; consumerism, 12

cosmogony, 142, 148

Costa Rica, 2, 8, 12, 19, 73–7, 82–5, 90, 253

corn, 84; festival of, 82, 87, 89, 92n9

crafts, 9, 16, 22n5, 22n7, 33, 127, 150, 169, 203, 205–6, 210, 212, 214, 243; craftspeople, 3, 160n7. *See also* material culture; tourist art

crest designs, 175, 187

cruise ships, 104, 198, 207, 210; community visits, 212–13; Cruise North, 211–13, 217n16; cultural tourism (*see under* tourism); safety, 210

"cultural tourism formula," 3, 22n5, 33, 36, 38

culture, 3; brokers, 34; contact zone, 46; model culture, 41

cultural: capital, 13, 17; intercultural border zones, 2, 46; loss, 35, 214; maintenance, 81; productions, 111; revitalization, 93n11, 106; strategies, 141

currency, 61, 151, 167, 171

decolonization, 120, 236

Delugan, Robin, 7–8, 251, 255n5

development, 1, 12, 16, 17, 19, 35, 46, 64, 67, 112, 125–6, 148, 214, 224–6, 228, 232, 248, 252; community,

47–8; economic, 14, 23n9, 36, 146, 149, 198, 213, 215, 223; ethnodevelopment, 6; national, 13, 145; postcolonial development initiatives, 57; tourism, 15, 67–8, 81, 90, 103–4, 118, 130, 143, 211, 233

diaspora, 245

difference, 2, 8, 10, 19, 21n3, 42, 45, 47, 61, 64, 66, 118, 125, 226, 243; capitalizing on difference, 2, 21n3, 36; cultural, 99, 109, 110, 243; ethnic, 134; marketing of, 18; ontological, 43, 232

discourse, 13, 34, 37, 45, 68, 74, 90–1, 93n11, 99–100, 104, 124, 126, 142n15, 144, 148, 222, 226, 228, 235; of alterity, 48; of authenticity, 39; of difference, 2; dominant, 17, 20, 36, 41; hegemonic, 10; historical, 84, 85; of identity, 225; of indigeneity, 12, 22, 125, 131; national, 134; political, 133; social science, 73, 82, 88

Disney, 41; Disneyland, 42; Disneyfication, 54

display, 8, 41, 44, 50n14, 74, 83–4, 142, 144, 146, 150–1, 168, 171, 191n17, 206; cultural, 10, 49n6, 145, 159; self, 141, 153; village, 149. *See also* museum

Djabugay, 32–3, 35, 39, 43, 49n1, 49n6, 50n17, 51n20. *See also* Aboriginal

Dogon, 14–15, 140–6, 148–156, 158–9, 160n8. See also *Hogon*

double-bind, 34, 39, 43, 46, 50n12

dreamtime, 31, 33, 40

Eastern Canadian Arctic, 198, 199,
    201–17
economy, 6, 108, 117, 132, 166, 170–1,
    190n8, 213, 232; cash economy,
    12, 16, 126, 134, 170, 188; colonial,
    166, 168, 185; global, 15, 20, 37;
    land-based, 48; local, 100, 141;
    market, 228; national, 121, 125,
    145; of performance, 67; political,
    126; post-capitalist, 36; pre-Fordist
    occupations, 215; in pre-industrial
    societies, 243, 249; and semi-
    subsistence, 13, 140; tourism,
    16, 102, 141, 165, 192n26. *See also*
    development
eco-tourism. *See under* tourism
encounters, 18, 56, 63, 129, 252;
    colonial, 1; cross-cultural, 10, 57,
    127, 166; Indigenous, 10; tourism,
    99, 117, 125–6, 132, 134
ethnic: groups, 3, 14, 57, 60, 66, 69n7,
    100, 117–18, 123, 125, 133, 134n2,
    146, 246 (*see also* Indigenous;
    minority); pride, 85; tourism (*see*
    under tourism)
ethnocide, 45
ethnography, 34
exclusion, 1, 5–6, 75, 92n7, 226
ex-colonial, 242
exhibition, 38, 65, 143, 205, 251;
    Great Exhibition, 9; museum, 42;
    World Fair, 9
exoticization, 101; self-exoticization,
    45

fieldwork, 35, 57, 65, 75, 101, 109,
    142n15, 159n1; ethnography, 34
films, 120, 207
First Nations, 3, 214, 218n21, 244,
    247, 250. *See also* Indigenous

fishing, 172, 190n6, 198, 203–4, 207,
    209, 214
floral work, 186
Fourth World, 3, 5, 23n9, 169, 244,
    246–7. *See also* Indigenous

gaze, 160, 207; host gaze, 51n18;
    tourist gaze, 7, 12, 34, 37, 40, 44,
    48, 51n18, 206, 254; twentieth-
    century gaze, 186; Western gaze,
    32, 36, 159
globalization, 90
Graburn, Nelson, 3–4, 7–8, 10, 17,
    21n1, 23n13, 36–7, 40, 59, 68, 74,
    100, 131, 169, 201–2, 205–6, 211,
    214, 223, 242–3, 246–7, 249–50
Greenland, 210, 213
Griaule, Marcel, 142–3, 148
guidebook, tourist, 143, 172, 174

Haida, 165, 167, 171–2, 174, 179,
    187, 191n17. *See also* Native:
    Native American
heritage, 18, 21, 22n3, 22n4, 22n5,
    33, 38–9, 41, 46, 48, 49n4, 69n3, 75,
    82, 87, 91–2, 142, 144–6, 151, 159,
    183, 207, 218n21, 225; cultural, 117,
    126, 128, 133, 142–3, 148, 159, 226;
    Indigenous, 76–7; intangible, 133;
    material, 153; national, 5; world,
    5, 14, 127, 140. *See also* tourism;
    UNESCO
Hogon, 153, 154, 155–6, 157, 158,
    160n12
hospitality, 146, 213, 249–50
host, 2–3, 7, 10–12, 14–18, 20–1, 22n5,
    32–50, 100–1, 110, 166, 202, 208,
    212, 215–16, 249; motivations, 19.
    See also gaze
Huit Huit Tours, 203

hunting, 13, 58, 60, 69n6, 102, 121, 127, 131, 143, 198, 201, 203–4, 207, 211–15, 249; Bobby May Hunting Lodge, 203; polar bear hunting, 198, 204, 209
hybridity, 169, 222, 229, 231–2

identity: class, 7; cultural, 3, 62, 64, 93, 103, 110, 143, 145; ethnic, 4–5; gendered, 7; global, 4; Indigenous, 3–7, 64, 68, 74; material, 140, 150, 159; and politics, 2, 5; racialized, 7; self-designation, 6; strategic public, 74. See also movements
ideologies, 20, 45, 60, 133, 214; dominant, 16, 18, 20, 41; hegemonic, 16; Western, 7
image, 12, 40, 57, 59, 62, 68, 69n1, 73, 77, 90, 143, 172, 184, 187, 206–7, 247; colonial, 11, 63, 67; embodied, 153; exoticized, 58; historical, 190n4; image makers, 254; media-based, 87, 89; "mythical image," 56; of noble savage, 57–8; nomadic, 64; public, 74; romanticized, 81; self-image, 128; stereotypical, 56, 73, 81, 85, 92n9, 128
imagery, 57, 79, 81, 84, 86, 93, 181–2, 185; Indigenous, 8, 76, 88, 90; local, 83; nature-based, 86; stereotypical, 73
imaginaries, 11, 18, 35, 37–8, 40, 42, 44–5, 47–8, 64–6, 68, 120, 125, 132, 207, 235; of domination, 44; double-bind, 50n11; of "Indigenous Other," 10–12, 31, 34–5, 43; local, 46, 254; popular, 74, 91n3; stereotypical, 128; tourist, 11,

37, 39, 41, 44, 46, 50n13, 110, 243; Western, 40
imperialist nostalgia, 40, 254
indigeneity, 2–8, 10, 12, 14, 18, 20, 34, 50n10, 58, 73–4, 76–7, 79, 84, 86, 88–90, 92n9, 101, 105, 107, 110, 118, 122–6, 131–3, 242–5, 247, 252
Indigenous: definition, 4, 5; development, 141; guide, 35; hosts, 7, 11, 16, 19–20, 37, 40–4, 101, 110, 166; status, 5, 7, 15; studies, 2; territory, 73, 76–7, 79, 81–90. See also Aboriginal; autochthonous; ethnic: groups; First Nations; Fourth World; identity; minorities; movements; Native; United Nations
Indigenous researchers: Inuit, 251; Native American, First Nations, 251
Indigenous tourism, 2, 3, 6, 8, 11, 12, 17–19, 21n1, 35, 40–1, 44–8, 56–7; Indigenous-operated tourism, 1, 22; Indigenous-owned tourism, 1, 36, 43
indirect tourism. See under tourism
intergenerational trauma, 20
intersectionality, 7
Inuit, 9, 17, 198, 200–3, 204–16, 216n1, 216n7, 216n8, 217n10, 217n12, 217n17, 218n19, 242, 246, 249–51, 253–4, 255n7; arts and crafts, 198, 202, 205–7, 217n11; Canadian, 249, 252–3, 255n7; festivals, 202, 216n2; heritage, 207, 218; Inuit Broadcasting Association, 203; local Inuit tourism, 215–16; music, 201, 207, 210, 212, 213, 214, 216n2, 217n12; Quebec Inuit Association, 203

Iroquois, 23n11, 243, 255n2
Islam, 140, 146; Islamic, 246

James Bay Treaty, 198, 216n8
Japan, 5, 9, 22n7, 244, 247
jewellery, 58, 61, 63, 121, 127, 151,
    174, 186, 205–6; bracelets, 107, 165,
    171, 174–6, 179, 186–7, 191n16

Kirshenblatt-Gimblett, Barbara,
    22n4, 41–2, 49n4, 58–9, 61, 67

Labrador, 208–9
land claims, 198, 231
landscapes, 21, 44, 140, 198, 207, 209
Latin America, 4, 124, 222, 224, 230.
    See also Chile; Costa Rica; Panama
leisure, 249
Levi–Strauss, Claude, 8

Maasai, 7, 11–12, 19, 56–70, 123, 254
MacCannell, Dean, 9, 46
magic, 11, 156; magical quality, 31,
    43, 153–4, 158, 160n12, 235; magic
    space, 32–3
majority claiming minority identity,
    247
Mali, 23n9, 140, 145–8, 153, 159n1,
    253
manifest destiny, 40
Maori, 22n5, 50n14, 213–14, 243
Mapuche, 18, 222, 224, 227,
    231, 235–6, 236n1, 236n3; and
    marginalization, 35, 64, 68, 75, 90,
    118, 120, 123–5,
marketing, 16, 23n9, 44, 49n8, 59,
    110, 117, 144, 166–7, 170
material culture, 15, 16, 32, 140, 145,
    149, 153, 159, 190n3; approach,
    141; mask, 9, 145, 148, 152, 155–6,

158, 160n13, 182; model totem
    poles, 176, 179; pendants, 79, **154**,
    155, **156**; producers of, 141, 151;
    textiles, 140, 145; totem poles, 9,
    173, 182, 187. *See also* crafts; tourist
    art
media, 7, 10, 59, 73–4, 86–7, 89–90,
    92n5, 93n11, 117, 120, 125, 131,
    133–4, 143–6, 207, 214, 217n12,
    218n21, 225, 246; local, 125,
    132; mass, 38; mediascapes, 89;
    multimedia, 19, 33; popular, 10,
    14; social media, 85. *See also* films;
    television
Medicine, Bea, 251, 255n5
mestizaje, 3
mestizo, 4, 9, 77, 79
mining, 117, 125–6, 130, 167, 179,
    190n8, 227
minorities, 3, 9, 121–2, 126, 243–5,
    247–8, 252, 254; ethnic minority
    education, 248; minority status,
    99. *See also* Indigenous
mobility, 11, 68, 133; (im)mobility, 56;
    labour-related, 63; mobilities, 249;
    social, 57, 62
model culture, 41
modernity, 7, 9, 104–5, 148. *See also*
    postmodernity
modernization, 59–60, 68–9, 245
Morgan, Lewis Henry, 23n11, 255n2,
    257
movements, 62, 83, 102–3, 245;
    identity, 10, 68; Indigenous, 12, 56,
    66–7, 75, 83, 118, 230; intellectual,
    2; knowledge, 15, 163; literal, 2;
    physical, 2; political, 12, 97; social,
    2, 12–13, 48, 142; tourist, 63, 74
multiculturalism, 6, 14, 18, 99, 224–5,
    253–4

museum, 2, 8, 32–3, 38, 4, 65, 142–3,
149–51, 153, 178, 180, 181, 182,
183–4, 185, 186, 187, 188, 189n1,
191n13, 206, 208, 229, 232, 235;
collection, 175, 176; collectors,
169; displays, 143; exhibitions, 42;
global museum, 3, 33; Inuit, 206–7;
local, 149; "museumizing," 22n4,
49n4; national, 75, 145, 153, 183,
191n13

Narayan, Kirin, 251, 255n5
narratives, 17, 57, 100, 128; colonial,
40; of conquest, 40, 46; cultural, 67;
Indigenous, 84; meta-narratives, 7;
national, 99
Native, 3, 8–9, 16–17, 22n5, 23n11,
33, 46, 50n14, 79, 123, 165–8,
170–2, 175–6, 179–80, 183–9, 189n1,
190n8, 191n19, 192n24, 213–14,
242–3, 247, 252, 254; host, 22n5;
Native American, 81, 168, 250–2.
See also Indigenous
nature, 4, 8–11, 19, 60, 62, 79, 86, 105,
117–18, 126–7, 130–1, 133, 208,
213–14, 222, 225, 228–36; "close
to nature," 11, 31, 77; neoliberal
natures, 223, 226, 229
nature-based tourism. See under
tourism
neoliberalism, 18, 222, 224–33, 235–
6; "armed neoliberalism," 224;
"neoliberal multiculturalism,"
224; neoliberal natures, 223, 226,
229
NGOs, 117, 120, 122–4, 126–8, 131–3,
134n2
nineteenth century, 56, 60, 165–8,
171–2, 186, 188, 189n2, 190n7,
190n11, 191n20, 211, 228, 243–4,

246; evolutionary model, 243. See
also Victorian
nomadism, 56, 59, 62, 64, 68, 69n7,
126, 131, 134n3
nong jia le (peasant tourist
restaurants), 248
North America, 35, 59, 81, 179, 187,
207, 242, 250. See also Canada;
United States
nostalgia (imperialist), 40, 254
Nunavik (Quebec), 198–221, 213,
217n17
Nunavut, 17, 198, 201, 207, 211, 213,
215, 217n13. See also Baffin Island;
Cape Dorset

ontologies, 17, 158, 222, 225, 232–3,
235; Indigenous, 34, 40, 223, 230,
236; ontological difference,
232; ontological pluralism, 223;
relational ontologies, 223, 230–1,
235; Western, 43
oral histories, 83–4, 88, 90, 167
Other/the Other, 7, 11–12, 20, 36–41,
43, 46, 50n13, 57–8, 69n7, 105

Panama, 13, 99–100, 102–8, 110,
111n7, 253
Pangnirtung 198, 205–8
parks, 41, 207, 208–9, 217n14;
Auyuittuk 189, 207; cultural, 41;
game parks, 59, 61; Katannilik 208,
215; Kuururjuaq, 208–9; national,
63, 207; Pingualuit (Chubb Crater)
208, 215; Territorial Nunavut, 207;
tourism, 50n13, 207
pastoralism, 62, 118
performance, 22n5, 32–3, 40, 42–3,
45–6, 49n8, 73, 76, 81, 83–5, 87, 91,
106, 142, 144–5, 152–3, 169, 184,

188–9, 190n3, 207, 212, 248, 254;
culture, 84; dance, 38, 50n14, 86,
183; domestic spectacle, 153, 155,
159; economy of, 67; mise-en-
scène, 143, 149, 152, 153; of "the
Other," 11, 46; potential of, 84,
87; staged, 192n22; and tourism,
61, 73, 101; of tradition, 43;
transformative nature of, 74, 84, 91
Pewenché, 18, 222–5, 228–9, 231–5
play, 249
pleasure (seeking), 200, 207
postcards, 177, 179, 184
postcolonialism, 57, 122, 124
postmodernity, 10. *See also*
modernity
potlatch, 166, 171, 188, 189n2,
190n10
Povirnituk, 202, 203, 206, 216n8
power, 4–5, 7, 13, 16–18, 20, 23n11,
24n24, 37, 40, 45–8, 50n17, 51n18,
56, 62, 84, 108, 123–4, 128, 141,
153–6, 158, 186, 243–4, 250, 254;
objects of, 153, 160
precolonialism, 19, 41
preservation: cultural, 217n17;
ecological, 47; strategies of, 146
printing: printmaking, 205; print
market, 206; print series, 205; print
shop, 205
privatization, 226–7
public-private partnerships, 117

Qallunaat ("English-speaking white
people"), 198, 200–1, 205, 211, 215
Quebec. *See* Nunavik
Quebecois, 244

Ready, Elspeth, 212, 217n15
relocation, 6, 130

representation: cultural, 46, 51n18,
57–8, 99–100, 111; Indigenous,
2, 20, 74; political, 5, 103;
representational self-awareness,
99, 108, 110; self-, 74, 93n11, 101;
touristic, 20, 42
resistance, 12, 17, 45, 56, 134, 223,
224, 226, 230, 235; covert, 11, 15,
45; creative forms of, 225
rights: animal, 204; communities',
6, 231; cultural, 120;
differential, 7, 14; human, 5,
7, 117–18, 120, 124–5, 129–30,
132–3, 224; Indigenous, 1, 4–5,
13–15, 21n2, 22n7, 67–8, 107,
118, 122, 124–5, 129–32, 134;
land, 5, 21, 108, 235; minority,
122; political, 13; property,
117, 227; territorial, 23n11, 123,
223–4; water, 227
Russia/Soviet Union, 167, 209,
243–8, 252, 254; Indigenous
peoples, 245–6

safari tourism. *See under* tourism
Salazar, Noel, 7, 11, 31, 37, 40, 45–6,
57–62, 64, 110, 243, 247
San: Khoisan, 14, 19, 134n2; San
people, 14, 117–18, 120–4, 126–30,
132–3, 134n2
self-awareness, 99–100, 108, 110–11,
143
self-determination, 5–6, 12, 16, 19,
35, 93, 108, 124, 223, 225
settlement, 36, 62, 64–6, 102–3, 127,
140, 170, 196, 218; Alaska Native
Land Claims, 189; land claims,
203, 215; resettlement, 127
social Darwinism, 60
Southeast Asia, 244

souvenirs, 9–10, 22n5, 33, 40, 58, 61, 63, 65, 165, 169–70, 176, 179–80, 183, 187, 190n3, 191n18, 205–6
sovereignty, 6, 83, 130; political, 21; tribal sovereignty, 7
stakeholder, 58, 60
stereotypes, 3, 37, 45, 46–7, 56–7, 64, 67–8, 73–4, 81, 86–8, 91, 106, 109–10, 128, 188, 215, 254
stewardship, of the land, 213–14
subjectivity, 84, 111, 117, 123; subjectivities, 134, 223, 236

Tanzania, 11, 56–7, **58**, 60, 62–4, 67, 69n1, 69n4, 252. *See also* Arusha
television, 58, 86–9, 143, 207, 254
Tjapukai Aboriginal Cultural Park, 31, 33–5, 43, 50n14, 51n19
Tlingit, 165–8, 170–2, 174, **175**, 179, 180–1, **182**, 183–4, 187–8, 189n2, 190n5, 190n7, 190n8, 190n10, 191n17, 192n22, 192n26, 192n27, 244
totemism, 8, 23n11
tour guide, 44–5, 60, 63, 65–6, 20, 214
tourism: alternative, 100, 105; community-based, 8, 126–7, 132; cultural, 2, 10, 13, 21n3, 22n5, 33, 36, 38–9, 41–6, 50n14, 74, 99, 101, 105, 110, 117–18, 121, 125–34, 135n5, 145–6, 166; "cultural tourism formula," 3, 22n5, 33, 36, 38; eco-tourism, 5, 13, 100, 105, 145, 207, 209, 231; ethnic, 7, 9, 218n21, 246–9, 252; guidebooks, 143, 172, 174; heritage, 73, 82, 90, 140, 142, 159; indirect, 8–9, 205; institutionalized-commercial, 202; market, 1, 3, 59, 110; nature-based, 117, 131, 133; rural, 82; safari,

58–61, 65–6, 127–8, **129**, 130, 208–9; studies, 2, 100. *See also* Indigenous tourism
tourism exchange, 100–1, 110–11
tourist: behaviour, 200; "ethical tourist," 130; expectations, 38–9, 74, 101, 184, 254. *See also* gaze
tourist art, 3, 4, 9, 63, 168–9, 243; baskets, 9, 165, 171–2, 184; daggers, 181–2; production of, 61; traders, 63. *See also* crafts; material culture
tradition, 4, 15–16, 18, 21, 33, 36, 41–2, 60, 65, 67–8, 74, 79, 82, 100–1, 111n5, 154, 158, 160n12, 176, 208
traditional, 6, 10, 12, 22n5, 23n13, 38, 43–4, 51n19, 58, 62–4, 76–7, 83–5, 92n6, 104, 106–7, 120–1, 127–8, 142, **147**, 151, 153, 166, 169, 185, 188, 198, 200, 206–7, 209, 211, 214–15, 216n2, 217n17, 236n3, 248; traditionalism, 56, 66; traditionalists, 144, 146, 148–9; traditionalization, 68
transnational Indigenous politics, 122
travel literature, 167
travelogue, 59, 165
treaty, 5, 6, 216, 255; James Bay Treaty, 198, 216. *See also* UN Treaty of Indigenous Rights
tribal, 3, 7, 9, 38, 88, 120–1, 129, 243, 246, 252. *See also* Indigenous
Tsimshian, 165, 171, 178, 181, 185

UNESCO, 6, 9, 14, 22n8, 143–4, 146, 210; Convention for the Safeguarding of Intangible Heritage, 133; World Heritage Site, 5, 140

UNICEF gift shop, 243
uniformity of prices, 174
United Kingdom, 243; England, 8, 242
United Nations (UN), 5, 21n1,
   50n10; Declaration on the Rights
   of Indigenous Peoples (2007),
   1, 4, 124–5, 132; Indigenous
   Peoples' Decades, 4; treaty
   of Indigenous rights, 5; UN
   Permanent Forum on Indigenous
   Issues, 4, 21n2; UN Working
   Group on Indigenous Peoples,
   67. *See also* UNESCO
United States, 6, 8–9, 23n9, 40,
   82, 165, 167, 189n2, 202, 243–4,
   253. *See also* Alaska; California;
   manifest destiny
urbanization, 7, 201
Urry, John, 81, 206

Victorian, 9, 16, 169, 172, 175, 184–6
visits (*pulaktuk*), 200, 201, 209,
   215n1

Western, 7, 9, 11–12, 14, 20, 22n5,
   32, 33, 36, 40, 43–4, 50n13, 57, 59,
   62–3, 86, 93, 104, 107, 110, 122,
   134n2, 142–5, 149, 153–4, 158–9,
   167, 170, 184, 207, 228–9, 236, 243,
   246, 252–3. *See also* consumption:
   consumerism; gaze; ideologies;
   imaginaries
"whiteness," 19–20, 23n16
wild, the, 56, 165, 208; wilderness,
   57, 67, 172, 182, 209; wildlife,
   59–62, 69n4, 117, 121, 126, 130–1,
   133, 135n5, 198, 210
World Bank, 6
World Fair, 9